YO-BEB-025

ANNAPOLIS
TODAY

J. M. HODGES LIBRARY
WHARTON COUNTY JUNIOR COLLEGE
WHARTON, TEXAS

ANNAPOLIS
TODAY

by KENDALL BANNING
revised by A. STUART PITT

19254

J. M. HODGES LIBRARY
WHARTON COUNTY JUNIOR COLLEGE
WHARTON, TEXAS

UNITED STATES NAVAL INSTITUTE · ANNAPOLIS, MD.

COPYRIGHT © 1938, 1939, 1942, 1945

by

KENDALL BANNING

Copyright © 1957, 1963

by

UNITED STATES NAVAL INSTITUTE
ANNAPOLIS, MARYLAND

Library of Congress Catalogue Card No. 63-11557

359.071
B22a
6th. ed.

19254

To
The Mothers
of the Brigade of Midshipmen

The Prayer
of a
Midshipman

•

Almighty Father, whose way is in the sea and whose paths are in the great waters, whose command is over all and whose love never faileth: Let me be aware of Thy presence and obedient to Thy will. Keep me true to my best self, guarding me against dishonesty in purpose and in deed, and helping me so to live that I can stand unashamed and unafraid before my shipmates, my loved ones, and Thee. Protect those in whose love I live. Give me the will to do the work of a man and to accept my share of responsibilities with a strong heart and a cheerful mind. Make me considerate of those intrusted to my leadership and faithful to the duties my country has intrusted to me. Let my uniform remind me daily of the traditions of the Service of which I am a part. If I am inclined to doubt, steady my faith; if I am tempted, make me strong to resist; if I should miss the mark, give me courage to try again. Guide me with the light of truth and keep before me the life of Him by whose example and help I trust to obtain the answer to my prayer, Jesus Christ our Lord. Amen.

William N. Thomas
Rear Admiral, (CHC) USN Ret.
Senior Chaplain to the Brigade of Midshipmen 1933–45

Acknowledgments

Grateful acknowledgments of the author are extended to Rear Admiral David Foote Sellers (retired), former Superintendent of the United States Naval Academy, and to Rear Admiral Wilson Brown, and Rear Admiral John R. Beardall, successors to Admiral Sellers as Superintendent, whose kind cooperation has made the preparation of this book possible. Special acknowledgments are also made for valuable aid in compiling the material, to Commander Marcy M. Dupré, Jr., whose care in checking the facts has added immeasurably to the accuracy of this work.

Thanks are also rendered to the following officers of the Administrative and Executive Departments (whose official rank has changed so rapidly as to make any current correction merely temporary) and of the Departments of Instruction for their aid:

Rear Admiral Milo F. Draemel, Commandant of Midshipmen; Captain Harry A. Baldridge (retired), Captain C. W. Crosse, Captain William W. Smith, Captain John F. Shafroth, Jr., Captain Ernest W. McKee, Captain Marion C. Robertson, Captain Edgar L. Woods, Captain Reynolds Hayden, Captain Daniel Hunt, Captain Manning H. Philbrick, Captain Thomas S. King, 2d, and to Captain Walter S. De Lany.

Also to Commander Richard L. Conolly, Commander Robert P. Luker, Commander Burton W. Chippendale, Commander Samuel P. Jenkins, Commander Charles T. Joy, Commander R. G. Tobin, Commander George B. Tyler, Commander Ralph U. Hyde, Commander C. E. Coney, Commander Benton W. Decker, Commander David O. Bowman, Commander Tucker C. Gibbs, Commander P. L. Woerner and to Chaplain William N. Thomas.

Also to Lieut. Commander C. H. Pike, Lieut. Commander Henry S. Neilson, Lieut. Commander Burton B. Biggs, Lieut. Commander Charles W. Humphreys, Lieut. Commander William P. Burford, Lieut. Commander Leonard A. Klauer, Lieut. Harold E. Parker, Capt. Robert O. Bare (Marine Corps),

Lieut. Rex S. Caldwell, Lieut. Carl G. Christie, Lieut. D. L. Martineau, Lieut. William R. Sima, Lieut. Vernon Dortch, 2d Lieut. John A. Saxten, Jr. (Marine Corps), Ensign Frank C. Jones, Ensign Alden J. Laborde, Ensign C. Snowden Arthur, Ensign Donald D. Snyder, Jr., Ensign Wilton G. Bourland, Ensign Condé Le R. Raguet, Ensign Frank C. Lynch, Jr., Ensign David K. Sloan, Jr., Ensign Elward F. Baldridge, Ensign William F. Jennings, Ensign R. V. Laney, Ensign Henry L. Harty, Jr., Ensign William H. Seed and Ensign Benjamin C. Jarvis; also to Gunner S. W. McGovern, Midshipmen W. C. Croft, John B. Nelson, Richard E. Leary, Robert P. Luker, Jr., and Robert Hailey.

In addition, thanks are extended to Professor Carroll S. Alden, Associate Professor Richard H. Duval, Assistant Professors Joseph W. Crosley and Allen B. Cook, Captain Morris D. Gilmore, Mr. Albert H. McCarthy, Mr. Charles Schlegel, Mr. Fred Avery, Dr. Edgar E. Miller, Mr. Louis H. Mang, Mr. John Schutz, Mr. Frank J. Sazama, Mr. Henry Ortland, Jr., Mr. Hamilton M. Webb, Mr. Walter Aamold, Mr. Basil Moore, Mr. Israel Katsef, Mr. John Flood, Mr. Harry A. Reichel, Mr. A. K. Snyder, Mr. V. G. Jones, Mr. George Hahn, Mr. Edward C. Heise and to Miss Grace Olivia Smith.

The Author

Preface to the Fifth Edition

Annapolis Today was first published by Kendall Banning in 1938 and revised by him in 1939 and 1942. After Mr. Banning's death in 1944, a further revision was prepared by Professor Louis H. Bolander, then Librarian of the Naval Academy, and published in 1945. In the present revision, occasioned by the numerous changes in Naval Academy life, routine, and study inevitable over a period of ten years, my aim has been to bring the book up to date without changing its general form or approach. I have endeavored to check all of the material in the book, altering, eliminating, and adding as necessary to make the book a true representation of Annapolis today. In some places this process has involved considerable rewriting. I have throughout enjoyed the special advantage, which not all revisers have, of making any changes I wanted; typographically, this is an entirely new book which has been completely reset. I have, however, preserved the original chapter plan.

For the opportunity to undertake this revision I am indebted to Mrs. Kendall Banning and Professor L. H. Bolander.

Chapter 13, "Midshipman Practice Cruises," is the work of Assistant Professor Don D. Thornbury, of the Naval Academy Faculty, who went on the midshipman practice cruise in the summer of 1954.

Many of the photographs in this edition were taken by Midshipman James W. Bibb, '57, and selected by him from his personal collection.

In the course of my revision I have pestered numerous people with innumerable questions. The most pleasant aspect of my work has been the fact that I have never received anything but kind, ready, detailed, and highly useful answers, and I am most grateful to all who have helped me.

I wish especially to record my sincerest thanks to the following:

Rear Admiral C. E. Coney, USN (ret.), Captain Wade DeWeese, USN (ret.), Captain M. D. Gilmore, USN (ret.),

Captain F. B. Smith, MC, USN, and Captain J. D. Zimmerman, CHC, USN;

Commander J. P. Coleman, USN, Commander J. G. Drew, USN, Commander M. M. Dupré III, USN, Commander A. G. Esch, USN, Commander J. D. Hazard, USN, Commander D. G. L. King, USN, Commander H. D. Stafford, SC, USN, Commander C. F. Vossler, USN, and Commander F. C. Wiseman, USN;

Lieutenant Commander R. N. Lyberg, USN, Lieutenant Commander J. W. Stribling, Jr., USN, Lieutenant F. M. Adams, USN, Lieutenant M. E. Corrick, USN, Lieutenant C. D. Grojean, USN, Ensign E. L. Turner, USN, Midshipman J. A. Woods, USN, and Musician First Class E. L. Hromadka, USN;

Senior Professor W. S. Shields, Professor D. C. Gilley, Professor R. E. Heise, Associate Professor Henry Ortland, Jr., Associate Professor H. O. Werner, and Assistant Professor R. M. Langdon;

Mrs. Grace Ortland, Miss Carol Logan, Mr. A. J. Droll, Mr. E. S. Duvall, Mr. G. B. Keester, Mr. W. H. McNew, Mr. J. A. Suit, Mr. H. W. Taylor, and Mr. D. R. Vansant, Jr.

To the anonymous or unspecified authors of all the official publications and midshipman periodicals on which I have relied heavily for factual information, I also express my gratitude.

A. S. P.

Preface to the Sixth Edition

Once again, *Annapolis Today* has been brought up to date. The text has been extensively revised, and two new chapters have been added. A fresh selection of photographs presents the modern Naval Academy's new look, and certain charts and diagrams have been added in the interests of clarity and completeness.

As in the past, the book owes much to many people, among whom the following have been particularly kind and helpful:

Rear Admiral W. F. Fitzgerald, Jr., USN (ret.), Captain Wade DeWeese, USN (ret.), Captain P. F. Wakeman, USN (ret.), Captain J. W. Kelly, CHC, USN;

Commander W. P. Carmichael, USN; Commander R. F. Gower, USN; Lieutenant Commander C. R. Jessup, USN; Lieutenant Commander J. E. Vinsel, USN; Lieutenant Commander E. A. Dewey, CEC, USN;

Lieutenant G. E. Biles, USN; Lieutenant G. D. McCarthy, USN; Lieutenant P. F. Malcewicz, SC, USN; Ensign C. R. Phoebus, USN; Midshipman David Cohen, USN;

Professor A. J. Rubino; Associate Professor C. W. Phillips; Mrs. Norma Lucas; Mrs. James G. Marshall; Mr. J. A. Brady; Mr. Paul S. Ehle; and Mr. W. E. Gantt.

Many thanks to these and all others who have helped.

A. S. P.

Contents

Illustrations

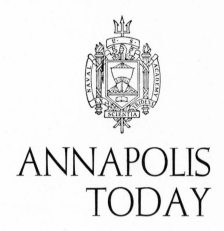

ANNAPOLIS
TODAY

Chapter 1

The New Plebe
Reports on Board

In the neighborhood of Number Three Gate, the main entrance to the Naval Academy, on a certain warm summer morning late in June, it is obvious that there is going to be something special about the day's proceedings in the Yard. Groups of neatly dressed young male civilians wait in the vicinity of the entrance, moving about just a little nervously, and occasionally mingling with other groups of people who are obviously mothers, fathers, well-wishers, and kid brothers and sisters. There is low-pitched, almost reverent conversation, some smiles and laughter, and an occasional rather sober wrinkling of the brow. The members of the Naval Academy guard force, the "jimmylegs," scurry about answering questions and helping to alleviate some of the general bewilderment. It is the first day of "Induction Week," and the important members of the crowd at the gate are waiting for their assigned time to report to Bancroft Hall and begin their careers as midshipmen and, eventually, officers in the United States Navy.

Each candidate clutches in his hand a precious document of three-fold value: it signifies that he has successfully met the challenge of the arduous mental and physical requirements of the Academy, that he has received his appointment, and that he is about to embark on his biggest adventure up to now, which will in most cases determine the course of his whole life.

This document is entitled: "Permit to report at U. S. Naval Academy for Admission as Midshipman." It has been preceded by many weeks, and more likely by many months, of planning, of correspondence, of personal interviews, of mental examinations of one kind or another, and by a very great deal of uncertainty. Even "nominations" for appointment do not grow on bushes nor are they thrust upon one unsought; they come as the reward of individual effort, of demonstrated capacity, and of political favor. But not until the postman delivers the long-anticipated document into his hands does the candidate know that the opportunity to become a midshipman is actually within reach.

The opening paragraph of a typical notification reads:

Dear Sir:

Having been nominated by Hon. . . . , United States Senator (or Representative, etc.) from . . . for appointment as midshipman at the U. S. Naval Academy, and having qualified scholastically . . . and physically, you are hereby authorized to report at . . . (8, 9, 10, or 11 A.M.) on . . . June 19 . . to the Superintendent, U. S. Naval Academy, Annapolis, Maryland, or his authorized representative, to be sworn in as a Midshipman, U. S. Navy.

Just where is Annapolis and how is the candidate to get to it? If he refers to *Reef Points*, that compendium of Naval Academy information known as the "Midshipman's Bible," he will find its location clearly and exactly specified thus:

The Latitude of Annapolis is 38-58-53 N.
The Longitude of Annapolis is 76-29-12 W.

While this information bears the earmarks of scientific accuracy and is expressed in suitably nautical terms, it may not always prove immediately helpful to the candidate; in that case he will likely resort to the practical expediency of applying at the local railroad or bus station. There he will learn that the approach to Annapolis lies through either Washington, D. C., or Baltimore, Maryland, and that it is about an hour's ride from each. Washington, Baltimore, and Annapolis, in other words, constitute the three points of an approximately equilateral triangle.

Cases are not unknown of penniless lads, bound for the Naval Academy, who have hitch-hiked their ways across the continent and who have found shelter in doorways; there are plenty of instances, too, in which those who have reached their goal "broke" have been identified by their more fortunate fellow-candidates and have been taken in tow and given a helping hand until they enter the Promised Land. There are triumph and heartache, comedy and tragedy, success and failure, packed into those uncertain first days; it is out of such elements that human drama is created.

It is ever a fateful day when a lad packs his bag, says farewell to the home folks, and sets out into the world to make his career. And it is a heterogeneous tribe of youngsters that wends its way from all corners of the country during that period when the incoming class of midshipmen is being mustered.

From every State in the Union they come: rich boys, poor boys, tall and short, from all walks of life. Sons of financiers and of farmers, of merchants and mariners, of teachers and tailors, of soldiers and scientists, of bakers and bankers they are. They constitute a genuine cross-section of American life. Some, fashionably attired and bearing expensive luggage, arrive in shiny automobiles driven by the family chauffeurs; others arrive humbly by bus, without coats or hats, carrying pathetically worn and makeshift bags tied together with bits of string. Over there is a handsome young chap wearing cordovan shoes and pleated slacks of conspicuous design held up by the latest mode of suspenders; he probably cuts a wide swath on Main Street of "Podunk" (the standard name given by midshipmen to the home town) and his attire loses none of its conspicuousness in Annapolis. Frequently a well-set-up young man shows up in the uniform of a sailor, of a marine, or of a soldier. But despite the wide variety of apparel and of caste, they have one outstanding quality in common: they are all good, healthy specimens of young manhood and as American as the American flag itself. As soon as they have been given the standard midshipman haircut and put into midshipman uniforms and given a few hours of instruction in military bearing and in walking, all the eccentricities of taste and the distinguishing earmarks of town and country, of east and west, and of social background will be obliterated; the transformation that takes place even within twenty-four hours is almost unbelievable. The process of molding the raw material into a midshipman begins the very first hour; it continues for four years—right up to the hour he graduates as an officer of the United States Navy.

When the hour arrives for the candidate to report, he follows the signs to Bancroft Hall to begin the process of his induction. Unless the visitor has seen Bancroft Hall before, or has at least seen a picture of it (most of them have seen neither), he is likely to be awed by its sheer size and splendor. It is the largest and the most expensive single dormitory in the United States (it cost about $24,000,000) and very likely in the entire world. Even the sweeping approach to it—over a hundred yards or so of terrace inlaid with slippery brown promenade tile—is in itself a bit breath-taking. Before the eyes of an approaching visitor rise two broad tiers of granite stairways, flanked by colonial French and Spanish cannon; at the top of the steps loom the three great bronze doors in their massive, ornate granite frames. The façade of Bancroft Hall, together with its approach, is probably unequaled in its magnificence by any structure of its kind anywhere. Yet, strangely enough, up to 1938, when plates were placed on both sides of the main doorway, the building bore no identifying label, possibly on the assumption that it was too huge and too famous to require a tag. The only clue the stranger could find to the identity of this enormous palace was to be found on a couple of small, portable metal signposts bearing pointed arrows and reading:

BANCROFT HALL—VISITORS' ENTRANCE

If Dad and Mother on their first visit should, by any chance, see one of these signposts inadvertently pointing to the bandstand, they might conclude that Junior has gone in for cramped quarters and fresh air in a Great Big Way.

The first thing the candidate does upon his arrival in the rotunda of Bancroft is to descend the ladder (You're in the Navy now—they aren't *stairs* any more!) to Smoke Hall, where he checks his baggage. Eventually all his civilian clothing and non-regulation equipment will have to be shipped home. He next goes down another ladder to the Mess Hall, where various officers and civilian members of the admissions staff are seated at tables waiting to begin the processing. The candidate presents his permit to report and has it time-stamped. His written oath of admission and his loyalty oath are checked over. At the last stop in the Mess Hall he is relieved of a check for $300, which he plunks down as the first installment of the $900 he owes the government for his initial outfit.

These details taken care of, he makes his way through a corridor to Sick Quarters, the midshipmen's dispensary, where he is given a physical once-over to insure that he has acquired no communicable diseases in the last few days. The dentists, too, have a go at him, chiefly to ascertain whether any last-minute dental work which the dentists at the formal physical examination found necessary has been accomplished. Except for such minor dental repairs, the candidate has long since passed his physical examination for admission to the Academy, either at the Academy itself or at one of the twenty or so service hospitals throughout the country, as well as Honolulu and the Canal Zone, authorized to conduct these physicals. These examinations are given early in May at the direction of the Bureau of Naval Personnel after the candidate has successfully qualified academically by the College Board examinations. In conjunction with his physical examination, the candidate must also pass the Physical Aptitude Examination to determine the "coordination, strength, and endurance of the body musculature." This consists of a formidable series of leg lifts, sit-ups, pull-ups, push-ups, squat jumps, duck walks, arm dips and arm hangs to determine not only whether the prospect can take it, but also if he has any latent orthopedic defects.

After the final physical review in Sick Quarters, the midshipman-to-be wends his way back to Bancroft Hall to the Steerage, normally the midshipmen's soda fountain, but converted at this point into a distribution center. Here he forms in another line and, when it comes his turn, he is assigned to one of the four plebe summer battalions (not the same as the regular battalions of the academic year). He also acquires a laundry number and is put into a specific company and squad. From here, he reports to his battalion area, where he checks in and gets an armful of literature: detailed instructions about the care of his room, the pamphlet "SpecInst" (*Special Instructions— Fourth Class Summer*), and that all-important and all-encompassing tome, *U. S. Naval Academy Regulations*.

Finally he makes his way to his company area, gets his room, and prepares for the thousand and one details to be accomplished during the remainder of Induction Week. Among his first duties will be to report to one of the barber shops and get an official USNA haircut. ("Midshipmen shall keep their hair closely trimmed. The haircut shall present an evenly graduated appearance and shall not exceed three inches on the top. Eccentric haircuts, sideburns, and mustaches are not permitted." *USNA Regulations*.) He must also this day obtain from the Midshipmen's Store his initial outfit of uniforms, bedding and books.

It has been quite a morning, but all things considered, affairs have gone smoothly. So-and-so may have packed his credentials in his luggage which hasn't arrived yet, and Such-and-such may have reported at ten instead of eleven, but in general there are no serious mixups. The supervising officials are ready for anything and can handle anything. Besides, first day for the plebe is nothing now compared with what it used to be when the entire formal physical was conducted *after* the candidate's arrival at the Academy.

Up to this point the entrant has been herded and hustled through his routine in a rapid-fire, systematic but perfunctory manner. Now approaches a moment that he will remember to the end of his days—the ceremonial in which he takes the oath of office and is sworn in as a midshipman in the United States Navy.

To avoid any possibility whatever that the entrant may fail to comprehend the deep significance of this step, he has been given the official form of this oath of office for his careful examination; at the same time he has been given a pamphlet in which this oath of office is interpreted in detail. The step he is about to take may well be the most important he will take in his lifetime; he must take it with a full understanding of its obligation and of its consequences. The oath reads:

I, _____, of the State of _____, aged _____ years, having been appointed a midshipman in the United States Navy, do solemnly swear (or affirm) that I will support and defend the Constitution of the United States against all enemies, foreign and domestic; that I will bear true allegiance to the same; that I take this obligation freely, without any mental reservation or purpose of evasion; and that I will well and faithfully discharge the duties of the office on which I am about to enter; So help me God.

Along the corridors, into the palatial grandeur of the rotunda the entrants stride. Here they line up, facing the great marble stairway to Memorial Hall and the most treasured of all the precious relics of the Naval Academy—the original dark blue flag on which are crudely lettered the immortal words of the dying Captain Lawrence, and which was hoisted by Commodore Perry as he engaged the enemy fleet at the Battle of Lake Erie:

DONT GIVE UP THE SHIP

There, under the banner that epitomizes the traditions and the spirit of the Navy, the entrants, erect and grave, raise their right hands and repeat word for word the oath of office, after the officer who swears them in. It is a moment marked by a solemnity as impressive as it is profound.

A momentary pause follows. Then the officer speaks:

Gentlemen, you are now officers of the United States Navy— if only in a qualified sense. I congratulate you, and welcome you into the service . . . Your duties are to prepare yourselves to become commissioned officers . . . You are entering with young men from every part of the country, and you will be judged by them according to your traits. They will not care whether you are rich or poor, whether you worked for your living or not; it's just the kind of man you are that counts . . . What you do from now on will reflect credit or discredit not alone upon yourselves but upon the naval service . . . When the work here seems hard; when the future looks dark; when you get homesick, come up here and take a look at that flag. Don't give up—ever!

What follows after the high-spot of the swearing-in ceremony is necessarily in the nature of an anticlimax.

The next stop is the stenciling machine, where the new arrival obtains the plate for marking his possessions with his name, initials and laundry number. During the plebe summer it is never difficult either to identify or to remember the name of any midshipman on the premises, inasmuch as his name is conspicuously emblazoned across the front of his white "works" blouse, H. J. THINGUMBUB.

After his name has been duly inscribed on his clothing and gear, under the appraising eyes of his Company Officer, the plebe is instructed in the arrangement of his locker in conformity with the printed diagram, which specifies precisely how and where every piece is to be folded, filed or hung.

From his preceptor he learns that when the upper classes get back in the fall and academic year begins, he must walk only down the centers of the corridors, turn square corners, and walk "braced," stiffly erect, with his head up, shoulders back, chest out, and with his fingers extended along the seams of his trousers.

"Fin out! Fin out!" he is cautioned, as he momentarily forgets to extend his fingers in the prescribed technique.

He is instructed how to "sound off" whenever he enters the room of an upperclassman or commissioned officer, by removing his cap, standing at attention on the door sill, and announcing:

"Midshipman Sniffleberg, Fourth class, Sir!"

That "Sir" is mighty important; never must he forget it. He is told about the daily routine, the posting of orders, the hours for the various formations from reveille in the morning until taps at night. He is shown the numbered table he shall occupy in the mess hall, and the seat assigned to him, and told just when and where and how he shall form in line to march to it and from it. Altogether he is overwhelmed with such a deluge of rules, regulations, musts and mustn'ts, that he falls into bed at last bewildered and dazed, his ears ringing with signal bells of which he knows not the meaning but which sound ominous and imperious.

Homesick? For the first few days he is kept too busy to think about much of anything except the task immediately at hand, which is usually performed on the run. Perhaps in a few days, when the excitement and the turmoil have subsided a bit and his numbed wits have had time to collect themselves, he may find an opportunity here and there to give a fleeting thought to mother back home and indulge in an intermittent attack of nostalgia, as the medicos call it.

"Nostalgia?" indignantly proclaimed an irate mother when

informed that Junior was suffering from an attack of it. "Well, all I can say is that he must have caught the disease at the Naval Academy; he certainly never had it at home!"

Induction Week lasts for five days, at the end of which time regularly scheduled drills begin in infantry, seamanship, orientation, physical education, and the handling of rifle, carbine and pistol. There are also various indoctrination programs conducted by the Executive, Mathematics, Physical Education, Weapons, Command, English, History and Government, Engineering, Foreign Languages, and Science Departments.

Before these drills begin, however, there are still innumerable things to be done in the four days which follow the excitement of First Day. The new plebe must absorb some elementary infantry instruction so that he will be able to get from one place to another in military formation. He must try out all his clothing to be sure it fits well and comfortably (especially his shoes, since sore feet account for more physical complaints during the early weeks than all other ailments combined). He must learn how to wear his uniform properly; the plebe's first naval uniform is White Working Dress "C" ("Charlie")—white working jumper, white working trousers, black shoes and socks, and the white hat with the blue trim on the brim. He gets his first experience standing watch. He learns how to make his bed and stow his gear. He must draw his rifle. He must get fingerprinted, photographed, blood-typed and measured for uniforms. And he must stencil, stencil, stencil, during every spare moment he can find, until all his clothing is properly marked with name and laundry number.

Just about all the shiny new plebes arrive and begin their new careers on First Day, but about a handful more straggle in at various times throughout the summer. The chief cause for delay is the filling of vacancies occasioned by the fact that some principal appointments, for one reason or another, do not accept their appointments, and their places must be filled from among the alternates. Sooner or later, however, the quota is filled, and by September the new plebe class, about 1250 strong, is ready to embark upon the four-year voyage that will make them officers in the military service of the United States.

Chapter 2

The First Year
of a Midshipman

Although Bancroft Hall is the largest single dormitory in the world, it has no walls, no floors and no stairways. This is one of the first astonishing bits of information imparted to the new plebe. Immediately upon his arrival his naval education is begun, and he goes definitely nautical. "Walls" and "floors" and "stairways" are lubberly words, he is warned, and have no place in the vocabulary of the sailor aboard ship. The newcomer must learn the language of the sea. Walls must henceforth be known as "bulkheads"; floors become "decks," and stairways become "ladders."

"Yes, sir!" is his unsophisticated acknowledgment whereupon he is again admonished.

"Say 'Aye, aye, sir'!" he is directed.

The lingo of Bancroft Hall is the lingo of the ship. A midshipman does not go away; he "shoves off." He is not told to stop, but to "knock it off." He is not warned to keep quiet but to "pipe down." When he is addressed by an officer or an upper classman he does not come to attention; he "braces up." Instead of being asked his name and class, he is directed to "sound off." He does not go to bed; he "turns in." He is not told to continue about his business with the term "as you were"; that is a phrase used by soldiers; he is directed to "carry on." He is given demerits not for having things lying around but for allowing articles "adrift." He is never flunked in a course; he is "bilged." He must even start all over again to learn the time of day and to reckon not in units of hours and minutes and the cumbersome P.M. and A.M. known to landsmen, but he must accustom himself to days of twenty-four hours that are num-

12

bered consecutively and logically from 1 to 24. The daily routine schedule of the midshipman's instruction does not begin at 7:45 A.M. and end at 4:30 P.M.; it is listed thus on the bulletin boards:

MORNING PERIODS

0735—Formation 1st period
0745—1st period begins
0840—1st period ends; formation 2nd period
0850—2nd period begins
0945—2nd period ends; formation 3rd period
1000—3rd period begins
1055—3rd period ends; formation 4th period
1105—4th period begins
1200—4th period ends

AFTERNOON PERIODS (except Saturday)

1305—Formation 5th period
1315—5th period begins
1405—5th period ends; formation 6th period
1420—6th period begins
1515—6th period ends; formation 7th period
1530—7th period begins
1625—7th period ends

The task of imparting this nautical education to the newcomer is not always as easy as it might be; lads from the farm belt as well as from smart spots whose lazy "uh-uhs" and whose drawling "oh, yeahs" are accepted by their contemporaries as American idioms find difficulty in snapping into a smart "Yes, sir!"

"Where are you from?" an upper classman asked of a new plebe.

"Chicago."

"Chicago, what?"

"Chicago, Illinois."

"Chicago, Illinois, what?"

"Why, United States, I guess."

Sensing that he was getting nowhere fast, the upper classman blurted out in exasperation, "Mister, do you ever say 'Sir'?"

"Yes."

"Yes, what?"

"Yes, I do."

The interrogator gave up.

During the first summer the newcomer is familiarized with the "plebe rates," meaning the privileges—or more particularly the lack of privileges—which are granted to him. There are certain definite things that he is required to do and others that are forbidden to him. The plebe is indoctrinated with the principle that "rank hath its privileges," and that the organization and the morale of the Navy are based upon a system of rates, customs and traditions which must be observed. "The privileges you do not have are the more appreciated when you do get them," he is told; he is likewise reminded that he will acquire all of them himself in time. Tasks that seem pointless to him, restrictions that are irksome, are all part of the system of training and of discipline; they all aim to inculcate the cardinal virtue of obedience; prompt obedience, willing obedience, cheerful obedience, the first law of the sailor as it is of the soldier. If the occasional recalcitrant plebe who has been a bit of a mama's boy at home, or who has been coddled by his teachers, or who has been accustomed to the free-and-easy ways of the modern youth, shows signs of resentment or a disposition to argue the matter, or to sulk, he is merely sticking his neck out and inviting the disaster that is sure to be meted out to him. If he is philosophical, he may find at least a crumb of comfort in the knowledge that all midshipmen who have preceded him have been subjected to the same course of sprouts, and that as he rises in the naval hierarchy he will impose the same system of training and of discipline upon his subordinates.

In addition to the plebe customs and regulations already noted, he learns that:

He must wear caps and hats squarely and well forward on the head.

He must never appear outside his room unless he is in complete uniform. (Exceptions: the first fifteen minutes after reveille, from the end of the evening study hour until taps, and emergencies.)

He must maintain a military brace at all times in Bancroft Hall.

He must march in the center of all corridors and square all corners smartly in Bancroft Hall. (The use of certain ladders and doors, reserved exclusively for upper classes, is prohibited.)

He must not drag any "young, unrelated, female guests" (except to June Week dances, when he is within hours of being a Youngster anyway).

He must keep his eyes "in the boat" (straight ahead) when seated at the table in the Mess Hall.

He must know the names of the commissioned officers of the watch, the midshipman officers of the watch, the menu for each meal, the movies in the Yard and in the Annapolis theatres, and all scheduled sports events and their scores.

He must know the number of days until leave, the Army-Navy football game, and graduation, and the name of the stewardsman at his table, as well as the names of all the midshipmen seated at his table.

He must never reply to a question, "I don't know, sir," if he doesn't know the answer, but always, "I'll find out, sir."

He must learn all the Navy songs and cheers.

He must never put his hands in his pockets.

He must proceed to and return from all formations at double time—meaning on the run.

He must not walk on Lovers' Lane or Youngster Cutoff, go into Smoke Park or sit in the First Class or Second Class benches. (If he doesn't like these restrictions, he knows where he can go.)

He must not turn in before taps or lie down on his bed during the daytime. (His bed must be left made up from breakfast time onward.)

While the newcomer is absorbing the rules and restrictions that apply only to plebes, he is also being educated in the routine that all midshipmen must observe.

His first shock comes—unless he has been brought up on the farm and is accustomed to early hours—when the electric signal gongs break out into a wild racket at reveille at 0600; translated into civilian talk, that means at 6:00 o'clock in the morning. His second shock comes when he is forced to the abrupt realization that this first bell means business right now and on the instant and no fooling; rolling over languidly in bed for another 40 winks is out, definitely; within 40 seconds, in fact, every door must be wide open and every room occupant must be standing in the doorway as the midshipman in charge of each room (the occupants alternate weekly in this duty) reports to the midshipman reveille inspectors as they double-time down the corridors, "All out, sir!"

Thirty minutes are allowed for bathing, shaving and dressing; then comes the breakfast formation. The companies line up on the terrace if weather permits, otherwise in the corridors of Bancroft Hall; the rolls are called, and off the companies march to the mess hall. The morning meal takes about 20 minutes; it is preceded by a short prayer by the Chaplain and followed by the return to quarters.

Right before breakfast comes the first "Sick Call"; a second sick call comes at 1800 in the afternoon. Midshipmen who are afflicted with any ailment from dandruff to the black plague or acute inertia report to the Sick Bay, where medical officers and attendants are always on duty and where more than a dozen beds are maintained for temporary use. During the academic year an average of 75 or 100 report daily for treatment for minor ills, mostly for colds. The case of every midshipman who reports is disposed of and listed at once and a daily sick report is made out and sent to each of the battalions. The patient is given medication or treatment and dismissed; he is put on "sick in room" status; he is kept in the Sick Bay for observation, or he is sent to the Naval Hospital; in any case, Mother may be assured that Junior is getting more prompt and more expert care than he would be likely to get at home.

If the patient's ailment is a sprain or a boil or a cut which requires bandaging and would mar his military appearance, or which would interfere with the movements of his body, he is placed on the "excused list"; this relieves him of the necessity of participating in drills. No midshipman, it may be noted, is permitted to keep any medicine in his room, unless specifically prescribed and issued by a medical or dental officer.

Instances do arise now and then when both medical officers and patients are faced with situations that call for a bit of *finesse*. When a doctor asked a midshipman who showed up hesitantly with a black eye and a bloody nose, how he had become injured, the patient, possibly mindful of the regulations against fighting, cautiously replied:

*M*idshipmen returning to
Bancroft Hall in the noon-meal
formation march off.

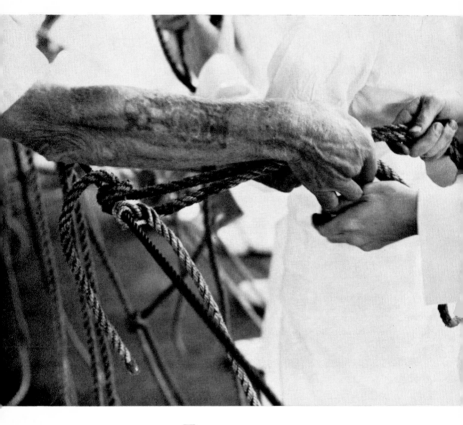

*L*earning the basic principles
of knotting lines from an old master
and a proper military bearing are
part of plebe summer.

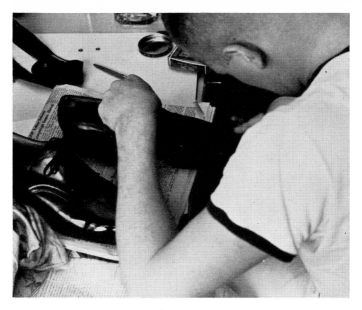

*P*lebes adapt to their new way of life in many ways—
from calling commands and getting basic instruction to
putting a spit shine on their shoes.

The "Ain't no more plebes" ceremony takes place immediately after graduation when the new youngsters scale the greased statue.

"Well, sir, I might have bumped into a post."

"So I thought," was the matter-of-fact response. "Come right in. The post is here too."

The morning recitation periods start at approximately 8:00 o'clock and end at approximately noon; during that time the rooms get the first of the several daily security inspections by the midshipmen mates of the deck as well as regulation inspections by the commissioned battalion and company officers. The hearty meal in the middle of the day is dinner, not lunch, following the ancient American custom. In the afternoon there are three recitation hours between about 1:00 o'clock and 4:00 o'clock.

Supper comes along at 7:00 o'clock, and is followed by a period of general relaxation and visiting-around. But at 8:15 o'clock the signal gongs send every man scurrying back to his own quarters for a two-hour study period, or to a lecture, movie, mass singing practice, or even a boxing exhibition. Tattoo is sounded at 9:55 o'clock, and at taps five minutes later every man must be in bed. To make sure that he is, a midshipman taps inspector enters every room, receives and verifies by personal observation the report "All turned in, sir!" and then turns out the overhead light and shuts the door. Midshipmen who need extra time to study may be granted the "late lights" privilege and thus burn the midnight oil—almost literally.

While the incoming class is being assembled and organized and welded into form, the plebes get the chance to size each other up. Those who are congenial arrange during this period to room together when the quarters are reassigned on a permanent basis at the beginning of the academic year in September; at that time the newcomers are distributed among the twenty-four companies of the brigade. The only proviso is that roommates must be taking the same language. Preferences are commonly shown for classmates who come from the same home town or from the same prep school; low-mark men, too, naturally like to team up with high-mark men, in order to benefit from their coaching.

There are five or six standard types of rooms, but the plebe does not have his choice of them; he is usually assigned to one of the less desirable "inboard" rooms, which face upon a court. The "outboard" rooms are usually assigned to the First and Second classmen.

The standard room accommodates two occupants. If it has a small bedroom adjoining, it accommodates three occupants. A few rooms have two small bedrooms adjoining; these suites are classed as four-man rooms. Most of the four-man rooms are occupied by First classmen, who are inclined to stick together in groups. Of necessity in late years some midshipmen have been housed five to a room. Nearly all of the rooms are equipped with showers; occupants of the rooms without showers use the nearest one available, thus (to paraphrase the old jest) "making the private baths available to the masses."

All summer long Mother and Father back home have been wondering how their boy is making out in his new life at the Academy and wishing they could come to see him and look over his new environment. Their wishes are fulfilled at the end of the summer term when the Academy entertains at Parents' Weekend and holds an Open House. Mom and Pop may come to Annapolis and see just how Junior lives and just what he does. They may have dinner with him one night in the mess hall. They may see in what kind of room he lives in Bancroft Hall. They may attend a forum in Mahan Hall where the Superintendent, the Commandant, and the Heads of Departments will describe for them the work of the Academy and willingly answer any questions they may have about their son's new school. They may attend a parade and beam proudly upon their favorite midshipman.

When Mother and Father visit the Naval Academy at any time other than Parents' Weekend, they will not be permitted to visit Junior's room, which is located off somewhere in the exclusively masculine confines of the dormitory sections of Bancroft Hall. But they will be welcomed to the typical room which is open to all visitors who want to see how the midshipmen live. This exhibition room is located right across from the reception room. It is completely equipped, even to textbooks, clothing and personal possessions, and the names of the occupants, Midshipman Joseph Gish and Midshipman W. T. Door, are carefully stenciled on their gear and written in their books.

Midshipmen Gish and Door are the two most widely known midshipmen at the Naval Academy, even if there are no such persons. They play much the same roles at Annapolis that Cadets Ducrot and Dumbguard play at West Point. Midshipman Gish derives his name from an extraordinarily dumb, clumsy and perhaps legendary sailor of some generations ago who emptied the slops to windward and tightened the wrong lines and turned the wrong valves and committed all the standard sailor crimes; whenever anything went amiss, the blame was always laid on Joe. His pal, Midshipman Door, derives his name from the familiar name plate, "Water Tight Door," that marks the entrance to watertight compartments of a ship.

The exhibition room of Midshipmen Gish and Door is so realistically furnished that, were it not for the sign at the entrance, one might think the occupants had just stepped out. The walls are bare, except that one chart or map is permitted. The desks in the center are scientifically lighted with fluorescent lights. The chairs are adjusted to the correct height. The room is heated, ventilated and lighted in accordance with the approved methods. The doors are unlocked, but officers of the watch, on their inspection tours, rap twice before entering, as a matter of courtesy. Until Midshipmen Gish and Door become First classmen, they will not be permitted to place portraits of their One-And-Onlies upon their desks; they must be content to tape them on the inside of their locker doors. Plebes who court the favor of upper classmen diplomatically display photographs of devastating charmers, known or unknown to said deponents. Should an upper classman be unimpressed with a plebe's choice of a girl friend, he may order his subordinate to "fall in love with a prettier girl and get her picture." Press photos of Hollywood lovelies are in brisk demand.

The lack of oriental splendor and the regulations which reduce opportunities for self-expression in Junior's room to practically nil, do not invariably meet with Mother's approval; indeed, the Spartan simplicity of undergraduate life in general sometimes leads to temperamental outbursts.

"The place is more like a jail than a school," an indignant mama once protested to the Admiral. "That barbed wire strung along the top of the surrounding walls makes the Yard look like a prison; it's an outrage!"

"Madam," the Admiral replied wearily, "that wire is not there to keep the midshipmen in. It's there to keep doting mothers out."

The location of the plebe's room depends chiefly upon the battalion to which he is assigned in the fall; and each battalion has its specified location in Bancroft Hall, even though to the stranger it may seem impossible to locate anything in the vast areas of this labyrinthine dormitory. With the aid of a map and a little judicious inspection, however, the visitor will discover that it consists essentially of eight wings, and they are so numbered for administrative purposes. As one approaches the main entrance to Bancroft Hall, the odd-numbered wings (first, third, fifth, and seventh) are on the left, or river side; and the even-numbered wings (second, fourth, sixth, and eighth) are on the right, toward Dahlgren Hall. The same system holds for the arrangement of the battalions: the First, Third, and Fifth Battalions are billeted on the left, and the Second, Fourth, and Sixth on the right. Obviously, since there are more wings than battalions, most battalions occupy one wing and part of another.

Old Grads returning to their former haunts in the Hall are in for a shock, and there may be some head-wagging. The seventh and eighth wings are brand new, and the others are renovated completely. The rooms are still severe and military, but the equipment and appointments are of the finest, and marble and chrome and tile gleam everywhere. Father will find things a lot more luxurious than when he was a midshipman.

The headquarters of each of the six battalions, where the commissioned officers and the midshipmen officers of the watch are on duty, are located on the ground floor, known in Navy parlance as the zero or terrace deck.

Every room in Bancroft Hall is designated by a number consisting of four numerals. Once the newcomer learns the system, each room is as easy to find as a room aboard ship. The first numeral indicates the wing of the building in which it is located; the second numeral indicates the deck it is on, and the two final numerals represent the room number. Thus room 3214, for illustration, is obviously located in the third wing (occupied by the Third Battalion), is on the second deck, and is room No. 14. The elevators in Bancroft Hall may be used only by officers and by civilian employees of Bancroft Hall.

Literally within a few hours from the time he is sworn in he is participating in the first of a series of drills that do not end until he graduates. At the same time he is given elementary instruction in military drill. No matter how extensive his experience may have been in the Navy, Army or military school, he starts his military work from scratch along with his fellows, on the assumption that he knows nothing about it, and he is put through the same mill. If he has had previous training and, more particularly, if he demonstrates his capacity, he may be picked out to help the duty officers to instruct his less experienced classmates.

After a few days of instruction a couple of squads are put together to form platoons, and finally the platoons are united to form a company. This proud accomplishment is celebrated with the introduction of the band. When all eight of the plebe companies have thus been formed, they parade as battalions. Joe Gish is really beginning to feel like a midshipman! By the time the fall drills of the brigade are resumed the plebes are sufficiently trained to take their places in their respective companies and carry on, even though they are relegated to inconspicuous places in the ranks. That is where every midshipman commander of the brigade started, isn't it?

The spirit of competition among the six battalions, which prevails during the entire four years of the course, finds its inception in the rivalry among the four plebe summer battalions. The battalion that wins the highest rating in the interbattalion competition earns an afternoon of town liberty. The acting officers and petty officers of the plebe companies do not actually win stripes that designate their temporary rank; they are merely being tried out in positions of responsibility, and in this way they get the chance to impress the duty officers with their aptitude—or ineptitude—for command.

Fourth classman Gish learns how many demerits are given for what—by the simple and logical method of being given the prescribed number for every infraction of a rule or regulation he commits.

The list of plebe delinquencies is a formidable one. Violations of the innumerable rules and regulations that govern the Naval Academy are numerous, inevitable and expected; needless to say, they involve no moral delinquency whatever. Only in those rare instances when actual turpitude is involved (known as "Class A offenses") do demerits mean anything more serious than an occasional violation of some small rule or other. It is a part of Midshipman Gish's job to familiarize himself with the rules and the penalties of infraction thereof, as printed in the *United States Naval Academy Regulations;* a copy of this volume is furnished to him upon his arrival. But that is an onerous and academic task and, besides, his time is otherwise engaged; in consequence, most of his instruction in discipline during his first summer is derived less from a book than from practical experience. When he is "put on report" for shutting the door of his room when all the occupants are absent, and he sees his name listed with other delinquents on the bulletin board and notes that he has been penalized five demerits for this infraction of the regulations, he is jolted into a realization that his door must not be kept closed when all the occupants of the room are absent and that the penalty for violating this rule is five demerits. It is all a part of the system of his education. But lest Midshipman Gish's countless minor infractions of rules and his accumulation of demerits during his plebe summer weigh against his conduct rating later, when he has passed through the valley of ignorance, the regulations considerately provide that:

> Unless specifically directed by the Superintendent in particular cases, the demerits received by any Fourth classman during the summer term will not be counted in computing his conduct multiple.

Thus the plebe's conduct slate is wiped clean and he starts afresh on the first day of September. Beginning on that date, however, every misstep becomes a matter of official record, and it stays there permanently to the end of his midshipman days.

Prolific sources of plebe demerits used to be found in the two-wheeled hose carts that were strategically stationed about the corridors of Bancroft Hall. These delightful vehicles held out so many fascinating possibilities as to prove irresistible, with the result that they were put into experimental service at informal plebe revels with unhappy consequences to the conduct records of all participants. Water fights, particularly in the earlier days when the hand of discipline bore less heavily upon the midship-men, have all but blasted the careers of many volunteer firemen who were out merely to enjoy a bit of good, clean fun while at the same time familiarizing themselves with the fire-fighting apparatus. Today the system of fire-fighting in Bancroft Hall has been organized and the regulations reduced to printed placards that are posted on all bulletin boards. Experience has shown that a fire alarm was the one infallible signal for sum-moning to a designated spot the entire and delighted under-graduate body, thus effectively blocking all traffic and giving the fire a chance. That is why rules had to be framed that seek rather to warn volunteers away than to summon them; in this respect they are unique. One rule reads:

> This bill is based on the premise of having as few midshipmen at the scene of the fire as is consistent with the requirements.

The Naval Academy is a hotbed of old traditions. The adage "Old traditions spring up overnight" is literally true. The setting for such phenomena is perfect. When an upper classman told a new and bewildered plebe, eager to do what he was told and ready to believe anything, that it was an old tradition that the plebes rise at dawn on May Day, garb themselves in running pants and full dress blouses and decorate the trees in Smoke Park with tissue paper, the plebe accepted the statement at its face value. So far as he knew, that had been the traditional ob-servance of May Day since Queen Mab was a little girl. The idea would not occur to him—why should it?—that this quaint conceit originated with an imaginative Youngster in quest of entertainment. As a matter of fact, this particular old tradition did actually materialize in some such casual way, to the vast enjoyment of all concerned. The spontaneity of the inceptions of these old traditions is matched only by the *Eilfertigkeit* (translated into English this would mean "instantaneousness" if there were such a word) of their obliteration. The Commandant merely issues an order to the effect that such-and-such a thing shall or shall not be done, and lo! the old tradition passes into history. When better old traditions are made, doubtless the Youngsters will make them and the plebes will solemnly ob-serve them.

Established customs, as distinguished from the more ephemeral "old traditions," impose a number of obligations upon the plebes; at the same time they extend a number of privileges. They permit the Fourth classman, for example, to leave the Yard on routine liberty on Saturday afternoons between dinnertime and supper formation; as he ascends in the academic scale these liberty hours are extended. They permit him to "carry on," meaning freedom from restrictions at mealtimes, until Sunday evening after every football victory; in case of victory over Army, he may be permitted to carry on right up to Christmas. On the other hand, custom demands that the plebes give the upper classmen the right to "trade in" their furniture for newer and more desirable pieces that may be found in a room assigned to a Fourth classman. They require the plebes to remain at "parade rest" while the upper classmen are relaxing "at ease." They demand that whenever a plebe appears in the corridors or even remains in his room he must be in uniform; not until he becomes an upper classman will he be permitted to indulge his sartorial whims in the much-decorated bathrobes that give the midshipmen their one chance to express themselves by attaching to this regulation article of clothing such devices as an admiral's epaulettes, athletic insignia, aviator's wings, swastikas, police brassards, advertisements and football scores. (Plebes *do* rate wearing official Naval Academy athletic awards on their bathrobes.)

Perhaps the most distinctive of the customs at the Naval Academy center about "my plebe."

Every Fourth classman is assigned to some First classman, who thereafter serves as the newcomer's guide, mentor and protector; whether he also becomes a friend depends upon individual circumstances. Most of them do.

As there are invariably more plebes than there are First classmen, several Fourth classmen may thus come under the wing of a single protector. The latter becomes known as "my First classman," just as the Fourth classman becomes known as "my plebe." The relationship between them is unique, approximating that of a somewhat aloof older brother with his kid brother, without the fraternal tie and possibly without any special affection between them.

The purpose of this new relationship is to give the plebe a friend at court; an older counselor who is experienced in the ways of the Naval Academy and who may guard his younger charge in a semi-official capacity from running foul of the rocks that beset his course. The plebe, on his part, pays in exchange for this guardianship in the form of certain obligations and services. He must report to his First classman five minutes before each meal just to check up and receive such last-minute words of advice as may be timely. Menial service is definitely frowned upon by the authorities; but just exactly where and how is the line to be drawn between menial service and a spirit of friendly helpfulness in reporting on a radio program, running an errand, dusting off a coat or giving a hand in making up the bed?

According to "tradition" a First classman never shook hands with a plebe; to do so would constitute a "spoon." Whenever a First classman shook hands with a plebe, he thereby raised him from his lowly estate and placed him upon a plane of social equality. The act was purely personal, and involved only the two midshipmen immediately concerned. By that gesture, the upper classman relinquished his traditional privilege of ordering the plebe about—except in his purely official capacity. So firmly implanted was this "tradition" supposed to be that even if a plebe's hand was grasped inadvertently, as was sometimes done in helping a lad clamber out of the swimming pool or in the joyous back-thumping and handshaking *melee* that followed a major football triumph—nevertheless the spoon was confirmed. Today this custom has little, if any, force, and class "rates" are kept pretty much on an objective basis. Besides, article 2102.1 of the *Naval Academy Regulations* states tersely:

"The act of shaking hands with upperclassmen does not necessarily constitute a cancellation of rates between classes."

During plebe summer the newcomer is introduced to the songs and cheers of the Naval Academy at the same time that he is introduced to the daily routine, military and boat drills and traditions and customs—which is at once.

One evening a week, for four weeks, is devoted to mass singing and cheering in Mahan Hall, to the lively accompaniment of a section of the Naval Academy Band. Here the new arrivals participate in one of the most unifying of all activities for an hour or so at a time. Under the direction of the Choirmaster the plebes are taught a group of Naval Academy and Navy songs, including the traditional Navy hymn, "Eternal Father, Strong to Save," and the Alma Mater, "Navy Blue and Gold." Cheer leaders selected from the new class, under the direction of one of the newly graduated ensigns, are also called upon to teach the other plebes the Navy yells.

During the summer the Choirmaster auditions all the singers in the plebe class. Those who have the best voices and can read music well are singled out for the Chapel Choir and the Catholic Choir; others may find their place in the Antiphonal Choir, which sings responsively from the rear of the Chapel during Protestant services, or in the Glee Club. During the summer, too, interest is stimulated among plebe instrumentalists in the opportunities for becoming members of the NA-10, which is the midshipman dance orchestra, the Midshipman Concert Band, and the Midshipman Drum and Bugle Corps.

When the academic year begins—about the first of September—and the midshipmen start to attend classes, the newcomer sheds his burden of plebe summer troubles and acquires a brand-new set of anxieties. Among these are his academic marks. His cumulative term average in every subject is computed periodically by the Machine Records Office, and the printed "Form A's" inform him of his status. But by Christmas time most plebes are happy and well adjusted, and ready for their first long holiday.

Christmastide is a happy festival and the celebration on the eve of the departure of the midshipmen is made memorable. Against the walls of Bancroft Hall, flanking the main entrance, Christmas trees are outlined in green electric lights, while over the main doorway a Yuletide wreath is similarly emblazoned in green and red. Two living fir trees that grow near the approach to the building are ablaze with globes.

Before dinner on the eve of the Brigade's departure for home on Christmas leave, members of the midshipmen's choir gather on the steps of the Chapel to sing some of the familiar old carols, with the band in accompaniment. As the singing pipes down, voices from the distant shadows take up the refrains as though in echo. Brief as the service is, it is staged with imagination and sentiment and a beauty that is unforgettable.

After the singing, there is a gala Christmas dinner with turkey and all the fixin's in the mess hall, and the Superintendent and the Commandant exchange warm greetings of the season with the Brigade.

"Merry Christmas!"

The training school for war, within the shadows of guns that have thundered in historic battle, pays its tribute to the Prince of Peace.

On the day Christmas leave is to begin, the excitement is all but uncontrollable, especially among the plebes, for whom this will be the first vacation since they became midshipmen seven months previously. The routine of classes is observed as on any other day, but there is a notable lack of concern for intellectual matters, and the midshipmen are present in the classroom in the physical sense only. The instructors normally yield gracefully (perhaps of necessity) to the pleas for a "free ride" and no quiz is given.

At last, after an eternity of anxious waiting, the bell ending the last class rings.

"Merry Christmas, sir!"

The midshipmen pour out of the buildings and back to Bancroft Hall to check out and get their luggage. The yard is full of the cars of families and friends waiting to transport their heroes home for two weeks of glorious leisure. Midshipmen homeward bound under their own steam emerge briskly from the gates and dash for buses and taxis.

It's here at last!

"Yea, furlough!"

Chapter 3

The Midshipmen Take to the Boats

The Navy is going plumb to hell. Ask any old sailorman and he will tell you so. Its downward course probably began when the husky oarsmen of the ancient rowing boats looked with disdain upon those new-fangled, labor-saving devices known as sails; its momentum was accelerated when the hardy sailors who risked their lives daily aloft in the rigging sneered at the crazy contraptions known as steamships, to say nothing of the strange, streamlined craft that came still later with the age of electricity. How could such fancy vessels fail to make seamen soft? Men accustomed to climb icy shrouds and cling perilously to yardarms disdained the weaklings comfortably esconced in the engine room, in the same spirit as the perspiring washwoman looked down, not without a touch of envy, upon her husband who had the soft job of working in a nice, cool sewer all day.

"Damned if I wouldn't get out of the Navy—if there was any other place to go," is the old sailorman's traditional complaint. But for the true sailorman there never is any other place to go; the Navy is his world.

From the moment the candidate enters the Yard, the Navy becomes his world. His attention is increasingly directed to the sea. Every effort is planned to make him sea-minded. The stage is deliberately and cunningly set for him. Boats meet his eye all along the sea wall; nautical terms displace civilian speech; time is told in ships' bells; naval guns and naval relics lie at every hand. And within a few hours from the time he is sworn in as a midshipman he is in a boat—in naval uniform.

The basic unit for drills in the Command Department—and

all other departments as well—during Plebe Summer is the squad, which consists of about seventeen men. The basic drills consist of instruction and practice in the handling of four types of boats, the YP boats, trim 26-foot sloops called "knock-abouts," the big 44-foot racing yawls, and the standard Navy motor launches; in the ancient nautical art of tying knots, called "Jackstay Drill"; and in signaling by flag hoist, semaphore flags, and "blinker" (flashing light). There is also instruction in "Rules of the Road," which are the seagoing traffic regulations, in the use and interpretation of charts, as the "maps" of the sea areas are called, and in the duties of a lookout. Each day during the periods assigned to Seamanship, most of these drills go on simultaneously, groups of from six to eight squads being assigned to each drill. Eventually, as the groups move from one drill to another day by day, all the new plebes go through all the drills in one sequence or another.

No longer included in the drill program are the pulling whaleboats, 12-oared rowboats propelled by muscle and beef alone without benefit of the refinements of sail or engine. The plebe's introduction to them took place under the boat shed on Dewey Basin, directly in front of Macdonough Hall—which originally was a mammoth boat house. The boats were suspended over the water; how to clamber up into them and then lower them into the water without spilling out the crews of plebes constituted one of the first lessons. Failure to heed the instructions brought its own obvious penalty. The plebe also learned how to pull an oar, steer a boat, get on and off a beach and row in formation as directed by signal flags.

These lessons were given by a picked group of present or former chief boatswain's mates, mostly former, including the redoubtable "Shorty" Metzger, who had been instructing midshipmen in elementary seamanship since 1916 and who had seen many a pupil return to the Academy as an admiral and the Superintendent. The crew of each boat consisted of fourteen men—twelve oarsmen, a coxswain and a signalman. This practical work was supplemented with a mimeographed instruction book, *Elementary Seamanship*, that had the answers to all the questions; it told how to rig the boat, how to pull the oars, and such details as how to ship the rudder and even how to put the plug into the hole in the bottom of the boat that keeps the bilge water drained off. Occasionally a plebe overlooked this item and the boat started to fill with water; when this happened, the standard inquiry was "Have you put in the plug?" The standard reply was "What plug?" That is how the plebe learns.

The biggest job was to teach the plebes how to use the oars, to demonstrate at the expense of their own energies the effect of the sea on the cutter's progress, how running on a reef interferes with mobility, and how fast they can get nowhere in the face of a head wind. For many years rowing was coached from the sea wall by an old tar who had a violent and profane aversion to the mishap known as catching a crab; when such occurred, he would (in the words of an old pupil) "swear longer and faster without taking a breath or repeating a word than any human being I ever heard." To start him going, a plebe would be directed to catch a crab, and to make it look accidental, at a point well within range of their master's voice. Invariably the old sailor would burst forth into a string of oaths that made the hair curl up into kinks, while the delighted crew would sit spellbound in goggle-eyed wonder and admiration.

The culmination of the summer's instruction in rowing boats was the Lysistrata Cup Race among eight boats, the best two from each summer battalion as determined by a series of elimination races. The course was from the old Severn River bridge to the vicinity of the Santee Pier, a good long pull in a heavy boat. The Lysistrata Cup was presented to the Naval Academy in 1910 by James Gordon Bennett, owner of the *New York Herald*, and was named after the donor's $625,000 yacht, which in turn was named after the play written in 411 B.C. by Aristophanes. In this event, as in many other tests and contests throughout the summer, the winners were awarded points that apply to the interbattalion competition.

The instruction in sailing boats begins at the moorings in Santee Basin with the knockabouts. These boats require a minimum crew of three and have a capacity of six for the old boats and eight for the new. Much is accomplished in a series of five drills. The plebes are taught the nomenclature of all the standing and running rigging and of all the orders and maneuvers essential in sailing a boat, how to "bend on" and make sail, how to sail, tack and wear, how to get the most out of sails and wind, what to do and what not to do afloat.

Plebes also receive summer instruction in the twelve much larger and more complicated sailing yachts, the big Luders yawls, which are also racing components of the Naval Academy Sailing Squadron. The principles are the same for handling both types, but the yawls have more complicated sails and rigging and the total sail area is much greater, so that the yawl man must be far more adept at his job than the knockabout handler. During both knockabout and yawl drills, every effort is made to qualify as many plebes as possible first as holders of a Primary Qualification, which will entitle them to take out knockabouts by themselves, and then as Yawl Handlers, qualified to serve as crew members in a yawl.

All the sailing boats must keep within a specified area on the Severn (except, of course, by the customary "special permission of the Commandant"), and that specified area is within sight of the special lookout on the barrack ship *APL* 31, from which signal flags are flown and orders transmitted either to the fleet in general or to individuals. A watch must be kept at all times by every boat on the barrack ship. Should the lookout observe any boat being improperly handled or violating any of the regulations, it may be recalled. Should a storm be brewing, a general order may be issued to reef sail and return to moorings; should an accident occur to any boat, aid is dispatched at once. Spills are uncommon, and so many precautions have been taken that the most serious consequences are usually confined to the explanations that the victims are called upon to make for their lubberly conduct.

On one occasion, when a knockabout had capsized and sunk, a launch was sent out to tow the submerged boat back to its mooring, where the commanding officer awaited the highly embarrassed and thoroughly soaked midshipman. In his eagerness to minimize the accident, he saluted and reported:

"No damage done, sir. Nothing has been lost. Everything is quite all right, sir!"

The boat was sunk; that was all.

Plebes must also know how to get around in a third type of boat, the power-operated vessel. The boat used for this instruction is the standard Navy 50-foot launch. To operate these, the midshipman stands high on the stern, tiller in one hand and bell rope in the other, ready to control the speed and direction of the boat by movements of the tiller and bell signals to the engineer. It is the first big nautical thrill for many a midshipman to have this boat of no small size completely in his charge for the first time.

The young aspirant must also acquire another fundamental and traditional skill in a sailor's life, knot-tying. This is accomplished at the jackstay, a long line rigged horizontally to which are attached at convenient intervals smaller lines in which the knots are tied. There is one long jackstay under the boat shed and another inside Luce Hall, for use during foul weather or by an overflow group of midshipmen.

These drills (any kind of instruction period other than a recitation in academic studies is known as a "drill") are really elementary lessons in tying knots, bends and hitches with ropes, after the manner of sailors from time immemorial. Within the period of three lessons each plebe must be able to tie twenty of them within a given number of seconds. He must be able, for example, to tie a figure-eight knot in six seconds, a bowline knot in ten seconds, and a bowline-on-a-bight in twenty seconds. In the final tests the plebes are lined up in groups and are started off on signal; as each man completes his task, he throws up his hands and his speed is clocked, just as is done in athletic contests.

Later, when the student is more experienced, he will learn some tricks that are not in the books.

"Let me borrow that new rope of yours for a couple of days," asked a neighbor of an old salt.

"Nope," was the reply. "I've got to use that rope today to tie up some sand."

"Aw, you can't tie up sand with a rope," protested the neighbor.

"Son," was the answer, "you can do almost anything with a rope when you don't want to lend it."

While a part of the plebe class is out in the boats and another part up in the rigging loft literally learning the ropes, a group is being given a series of drills in the more simple signal-flag

S ailing on Chesapeake Bay is great
sport and excellent training for future ship
captains. Professor Alden R. Hefler has helped
many midshipmen in his auxiliary capacity
as captain of the schooner Freedom.

codes. This starts with a knowledge of all of the different signal flags, with which the student must become as familiar as with his ABC's. He must know the 26 alphabet flags, the 10 numeral flags, the 10 numeral pennants, and the special flags and pennants. Instruction is given by means of a set of two miniature signal hoists set at far corners in the Field House; between them messages are exchanged with the use of the signal flags. No marks are given for these or for any other drills during plebe summer, nor are the students required to pass tests on the flag code; they will be sure to learn them in time by natural absorption.

They must also learn, in other drills, to identify letters and numbers sent in Morse Code by means of flashing lights. In competition they must transcribe 20 code groups of "blinker," flashed at the rate of three groups per minute. Wouldn't it be easier at sea just to talk to another ship over the radio? But in war radio silence must be maintained so that the enemy may not detect the ship's presence.

Another group of plebes, in the meantime, is beginning to learn something about charts, as the first simple steps toward the coming courses in navigation. What does a reef look like on the chart? How is a lighthouse indicated? What is a fathom curve? Where are the channels shown? How is the depth indicated? What is the character of the bottom? After the student has mastered such basic details, he is shown how to lay out simple courses, and is thus initiated into the mysteries of the chart room.

In case the midshipmen are driven to shelter by stormy weather, they can find plenty to do in Luce Hall, where there are movies, charts, exhibits and all manner of things arranged for just such an emergency.

Luce Hall is unique and merits a bit of attention on its own account. It is located near the sea wall just east of the gymnasium, Macdonough Hall. It is named in honor of Rear Admiral Stephen B. Luce, whose monumental book, *Seamanship*, written for the use of the midshipmen in 1862, was for years the most authoritative textbook on the subject in the world. It was hastily written immediately after the battle of Port Royal, in which Luce participated just before he was made the head of the Department of Seamanship at the Naval Academy. It underwent numerous alterations and revisions over a period of years. "Every youngster has grappled with it," states Park Benjamin,* "until its very words are crystallized into the brain structure of the Navy personnel."

Luce Hall was erected in 1920 at a cost of $672,000. Unlike most of the other academic buildings, it is constructed of granite; it is further distinguished by the fact that it is the only academic building on which are inscribed the subjects taught within its walls, "Seamanship and Navigation."

Up to the time that Luce Hall was projected, Congress had appropriated money for the construction of a building to be devoted to these subjects, and Macdonough Hall was the result. To all practical purposes it was a sort of glorified boat house, where instruction was given in the construction, use, and rigging of vessels. When that ancient relic, Fort Severn, which had been doing service as a gymnasium, was demolished in 1909 to make way for the east wing of Bancroft Hall, the brawn and muscle men transferred their activities to Macdonough Hall, which somehow developed into a gymnasium. Consequently Congress was again asked for funds for a hall to be devoted to seamanship and navigation. One wise old Solon with a long memory asked what had become of the building the Naval Academy already had, but which had apparently become lost in the shuffle.

"Be sure you don't mislay this new building," he warned. "Label it clearly so that it won't go astray again."

And that is why Luce Hall has emblazoned upon it, in great big letters, the words "Seamanship" and "Navigation." It probably will not get lost again.

More than any of the other academic buildings does Luce Hall reflect the glories of American naval history; it is, indeed, something of a museum on its own account; only the fact that it is used solely for instruction purposes dictates the necessity of excluding sightseers from it. At the right of the north entrance hangs, suitably enough, a life-sized portrait of Rear Admiral Luce, painted by A. M. Archambault; its label sum-

* In his book, *The United States Naval Academy.*

marizes his career: "Commandant of Midshipmen, 1865–1868; author of Luce's *Seamanship*; organizer of the Naval Apprentice System; founder of the Naval War College; president of the Naval Institute." The walls of the long central hallway are lined with brass name-plates of scores of vessels named after naval heroes, with biographical sketches of each.

Also on display in Luce Hall is a handsome bell taken from the German raider *Cormorant*, interned and seized at Guam on 6 April 1917. The bell is marked with the name "Hohenzollern," and the guess is that it had formerly adorned the Kaiser's private yacht of that name. Visitors may also see the elaborate stern ornaments of the old vessels *Franklin* and *Olympia*, the latter being, of course, Dewey's flagship at Manila Bay. At the north end of the ground deck is the original Tecumseh, the wooden figurehead of the old wooden line-of-battle ship *Delaware*, the bronze copy of which stands before the terrace of Bancroft Hall.

During Second and First class years, the sturdy and versatile Yard Patrol boats, or "YP's" as they are called, become the basic training vessel of the midshipmen. These stoutly built well-equipped boats are small enough (80 feet long) to be easily maneuverable in close waters, and yet large enough and detailed enough to contain the requisite training space and equipment. They simulate, as far as possible, the ships of the fleet, and are operated and manned in much the same manner: they are controlled by engine-order telegraph signals from the "bridge" to the engine room, they are propelled and maneuvered by twin screws, like many a larger ship, and they are fitted with the latest scientific gear for navigation purposes.

Aboard these ingenious little craft the midshipman can assimilate an amazing amount of practical seamanship. He learns how to get a ship alongside a dock and how to get her away from one safely and efficiently. In formations of divisions of four and squadrons of eight he practices tactical group maneuvers, such as simultaneous turns, column turns, screens and changes of position. He gains experience in all forms of navigating—coast piloting (navigating by bearings on objects on shore), radar piloting and maneuvering board plotting. He drills at signaling and emergency ship handling. During World

War II, in fact, when summer cruises were impossible because the ships of the fleet were not available for training purposes, the midshipmen of the war years got most of their training afloat aboard the YP's in Chesapeake Bay.

Of course, in normal times, the most direct and realistic work in seamanship and navigation comes during the summer practice cruises, on which the midshipman really becomes a sea-going man. Youngster cruise is his introduction to life aboard ship. He learns a ship's work by doing much of it himself and by standing watches. On First class cruise, he serves, in practice status, as a junior officer by assuming the duties and discharging the administrative responsibilities appropriate to that rank. He gets extended practice in celestial navigation, taking sights and determining the ship's position out where there are no light-houses or buoys to reassure him.

Thus when shiny new Ensign Gish reports to his first ship after graduating, he is no stranger aboard her; he has been there before. He has, as a midshipman, stood watch at a gun-turret battle station, been a member of a damage control party, served as a lookout, lifeboat crewman and burner tender, scrubbed a deck, fixed the ship's position, and conned her from the bridge. He is ready to fit into the ship's organization.

Chapter 4

Indoctrination
in the Mess Hall

The intensely personal extracurricular education of the plebes begins in the mess hall.

The course starts early in September; to be precise, on the day the upperclassmen get back to the Academy from summer leave. Up to that day, the plebes have seen no midshipmen other than themselves except for the Second classmen at various periods during second class aviation summer, but these latter have been quartered by themselves in separate wings of Bancroft and have not rated running the plebes. For nearly three months the new plebes have eaten and slept and drilled and gamboled unmolested and with a sense of simple-minded security, blurred only by an uneasy suspicion that maybe their life will be all different when the summer comes to an end.

It will be.

As the upper classes report in from leave, the hearts of the plebes skip a beat. Ominous rumors are recalled about the sudden and radical changes that are about to take place in the Naval Academy in general and in the mess hall in particular. They prove to be well founded.

The mess hall furnishes a gigantic area for the comedy and drama that is staged in it. It is perhaps the largest regular mess hall of any educational institution on the continent. Viewed from the balcony of Memorial Hall, it stretches out in the form of a colossal inverted T, with the crosspiece 623 feet long and the stem extending through Smoke Park to Cooper Road for some 300 feet. The impression of size on anyone standing inside the hall is enhanced by the fact that the two members of the T are relatively narrow (about 75 feet) and the arched, sound-proofed ceilings are comparatively low. When the brigade is disposing of a meal, the clatter of the dishes and the din of conversation are considerable, despite the sound-proofing. You cannot pour 3900 young men, who are bursting with animal spirits, into one room without noise. The original mess hall (the crosspiece) was enlarged and renovated in 1939, and the new wing (the stem) was completed in 1952. The resultant huge structure now has a capacity of nearly 4000. At present, the midshipmen sit at 160 "tables" (actually, 320 "half-tables") arranged in rows, one on either side of the central aisles, the long tables at right angles to the side walls, twelve men to a half-table. Each meal is served and consumed in about half an hour. This thrice-daily miracle of efficiency and expedition is a most impressive spectacle.

After falling in for meal formation, the midshipmen march by platoons to their assigned seating areas and, when the command is given, fall out and proceed to their seats (the plebes at double time) where they stand until the entire Brigade is in position. Each table is under the supervision of a midshipman in charge, who is responsible for good order and discipline.

Down the central aisles are four tables at which sit the commissioned and midshipman officers of the watch, and the brigade, regimental, and battalion staffs. When all are ready to be seated, the Six Striper bellows "Seats!"

The tribulations of the plebes begin at that instant, more particularly of the plebe who is burdened with a superiority complex or whose sense of social values has been a bit distorted by a fashionable prep school or by doting relatives.

The first lesson covers, in a rough sort of way, what might be designated as "the position of the plebe." No more may he lounge comfortably in his chair, converse at will and let his eyes wander; he must sit bolt upright, shoulders back, and, when instructed to do so, show the four top buttons of his blouse above the table top.

He must support himself gingerly on the edge of his chair; occupying at all times but a very small portion of its outermost edge. Failure to observe this simple rule brings a stern reminder and possible punishment. (For Sunday dinners and certain other special occasions he may be given the privilege of "carrying on," which in Navy lingo means that he may sit relaxed and at ease.)

He must keep his eyes gazing steadily before him—"keeping his eyes on the boat" is the regulation phrase—turning them only to look upon an upperclassman who may address him.

He must learn how to "eat a square meal" by raising his food perpendicularly from his plate until it is opposite his mouth, from which position it must be conveyed horizontally to its destination.

He must know how to perform the duty known as "rigging the red-eye." The business consists of prying the cap off the ketchup bottle, slitting the label up the side, and then reporting, "Red-eye rigged and ready for running, sir!" At the completion of this ceremony he bestows upon the bottle of ketchup the ceremonial sword salute—a table knife pinch-hitting for the sword.

At the command to "take a ride through the park" he must place a saucer upon his head and doff it to each one of his tablemates with the greeting "Good evening, Mr. ——" all round the table.

But all this covers merely the routine and purely physical aspects of his extracurricular training. There is a good deal more to it than that. He must master what is known as "Plebe Knowledge," a spate of miscellaneous information, such as "The USS *Kearsarge* (BB-5) was the only (American) battleship not named after a state," plus a series of weird answers to weird questions, such as "Who is Moaning Maggie? —No one. It is the fog horn at the edge of the San Pedro Harbor breakwater."

There have been for lo! these many years, certain stock replies that must be memorized and brought forth on request, to certain traditional questions. No plebe can enter the brotherhood of midshipmen fully until he has not only mastered these classics of sophomoric humor, but also—a more important point—demonstrated his eager willingness to acquiesce in the desires of his official superiors by reciting them. It is part of the system of discipline.

To the palpably reasonable query, "How long have you been in the Navy, mister?" the undeniably nautical but something less than reasonable answer demanded is:

"All me bloomin' life, sor! Me mother was a mermaid; me father was King Neptune. I was born on the crest of a wave and rocked in the cradle of the deep. Seaweed and barnacles are me clothes. Every tooth in me head is a marlinspike; the hair on me head is hemp. Every bone in me body is a spar and when I spits, I spits tar. I'm hard, I is, I am, I are, sir!"

In addition to this gem of Socratic pedagogics the Annapolis plebes share with their West Point brethren two other bits of classic dialogue. Here they are:

QUESTION. "What time is it?"

ANSWER. "Sir, I am deeply embarrassed and greatly humiliated that, due to unforeseen circumstances over which I have no control, the inner working and hidden mechanisms of my chronometer are in such inaccord with the great sidereal movement with which time is commonly reckoned, that I cannot with any degree of accuracy state the exact time, sir. But without fear of being very far off, I will state that it is _____ minutes, _____ seconds and _____ ticks past the _____ th hour."

QUESTION: "How is the cow?"

ANSWER: "She walks, she talks, she's full of chalk. The lacteal fluid extracted from the female of the bovine species is highly prolific to the nth degree."

During the football season every plebe must learn and be ready to sing the fight song of the next opponent on the schedule.

"What will be our dessert today, mister?" asks an upperclassman of Fourth Classman Door.

Mr. Door is supposed to know. The menus for the week are all duly posted, and it is part of Mr. Door's assignment to familiarize himself with them. And, of course, both Mr. Gish and Mr. Door are called upon to answer all questions concerning schedules for formations, sporting and social events, drills and other details of midshipman life. Thus are their powers of observation stimulated.

But it is in the distribution of nicknames that the widest opportunity is presented to indulge in imaginative fancies, modified only by certain standard names for certain standard types of plebes. That apparently slow-thinking young gentleman over there is designated as "Bucket," in accordance with the unwritten rule that applies to apparently slow-thinking young gentlemen. Across the table from him sits a chubby chap who shall thereafter be known as "Satchel." A tall plebe may be christened "Shorty"; a husky brute may be called "Tiny." All plebes named Rhodes are just naturally nicknamed "Dusty"; all Ingrams are called "Bill," in honor of the long line of famous Navy athletes of that name. And what could be more inevitable for a chap named Luker than to be burdened with "Filthy"? Names, proper and improper, are coined at the whim of the upperclassmen; perhaps they are suggested by nothing more profound than a physical peculiarity, by a news item or by a casual phrase uttered at the table. Four hapless plebes of some years back are still going through life under the names of the Apostles, Matthew, Mark, Luke and John.

As this course of instruction advances, Mr. Gish and Mr. Door are entrusted with a few kindergarten facts about the Naval Academy; nothing that taxes their intellects, of course, but brief items that may be classified under the "Interesting if true but what of it?" department. Such as:

> There are 489 panes of glass in the skylight in Memorial Hall.
> The height of the Chapel dome is 192 feet.
> The USS *Mercy*, ex-hospital ship, carried more guns than any other ship in the Navy. She was ballasted with them.
> The only two men who rate wearing their caps in Memorial Hall are Rear Admirals Sims and Evans. (The visitor to Memorial Hall will find out why.)

When such purely factual information is assimilated, the education of Messrs. Gish and Door is extended to include a few research assignments. They may be directed to dig up some facts about the former Superintendents of the Naval Academy after whom the roads and walks are named; to find out something of the careers of the men in honor of whom the Academy buildings are named and to whom memorials have been erected; to familiarize themselves with the details of the more important naval engagements of American history, with the organization of the Navy Department today, with the classifications of naval craft, the names and tonnage and armaments of our battleships; with the various types and functions of naval airplanes, as well as with a legion of other topics concerning which Messrs. Gish and Door reveal a lamentable but not unremedial ignorance.

Who was the first midshipman of record in the United States Navy?

What are the names of the seven masts of the one and only seven-masted ship?

What is the effective range of a 16-inch naval gun?

What is the tradition behind the three white stripes on the collar of a bluejacket?

What are the seven ropes in the Navy?

These are but typical of the thousand-and-one "professional" questions hurled at Mr. Gish. If he does not know the answers, he had better look them up and report back at the next meal— or else. Where can he find the answers? Well, that is all part of his training, too. He might try the library, or look in that compendium officially entitled *Reef Points* but popularly known as the "Plebe Bible"; he might even ask his First classman. He can't expect to go through life with a tutor to dig up information for him, can he? He is getting to be a big boy now, and it is time he began to think for himself.

The capacity to think is—or should be—the ultimate goal of any educational system. The trick of merely memorizing facts, figures and names certainly helps a lot at examination time, and it may win for its possessor the dubious designation of a "walking encyclopedia," but this peculiarity of mind is scarcely sufficient in itself to rank its possessor among the intellectuals. To train the plebes to think is a function that is not neglected in the extracurricular exercises in the mess hall, particularly to think up some kind of response, preferably a snappy one and if possible a correct one, to any question an upperclassman may be inspired to ask. Only two questions rate an "I don't know, sir," from the plebe. One is, "What is my name?" The other is, "What is in a cruise box?" No plebe rates knowing an upperclassman "by name."

The reason for a plebe's supposed not knowing what's in the box is this: Only the upper classes own cruise boxes, having received them just prior to departing on their Youngster cruise. Hence the ownership and use of a cruise box are known only to the upper classes. By the answer "I don't know," the plebe indicates another distinction between himself and the upper class.

Otherwise, "I don't know, sir" is an intolerable answer. The proper reply is "I'll find out, sir" and the ignorant one proceeds to do so.

To encourage the reading of newspapers and news magazines as well as to drive home the necessity for keeping up with current events, the plebe is also asked questions on the happenings in the world about him. "Who is the present ambassador to France?" "Where will the next meeting of foreign ministers be held?" "How many bills did the President veto this last session of Congress?"

Many of the questions directed at Fourth Classman Gish are sufficiently in lighter vein to test his ingenuity. If Mr. Gish demonstrates a merry wit, he may be rewarded by permission to "carry on" in comfort during the remainder of the meal. Should he snap back to the stock question "What are you famous for, mister?" some such reply as "For tightening up Luce Hall, sir," or "For pumping air into the wheels of progress, sir," he may provoke a laugh that has almost the value of legal tender.

Even a plebe's laughter is under control. Should he abandon himself to mirth, he may be told to wipe the smile off his face and dispose of it.

Contributions to the general entertainment of the table may be rewarded by a mere permission to carry on, up to a plebe pie-eating contest. This sporting event is held usually when the pie de jour is blueberry. The contestants start at a signal, and all pies must be consumed without benefit of hands or utensils; only the use of the bare face is permissible. The winner, who must prove his claim to the table championship by whistling upon the completion of his course, is rewarded with another piece of pie.

Of all mess hall shenanigans, the one most disconcerting to the uninitiated guest is likely to be the activities of the "Wild Man." A midshipman so designated makes his way to the seat of the guest and, with the cry of "Wild Man," proceeds to rumple the hair of the visitor and perhaps pour ketchup on it or commit other mad acts to the great consternation of the victim and the great delight of all others.

Incorrigibles may be disposed of for six weeks or more by

being dispatched on a "trip around the world" for corrective and (who knows?) perhaps cultural purposes too. This consists of making the rounds of all the tables in the mess hall, the skipper's stay at each port of call being determined by local conditions and the entertainment value of the traveler himself; it may range from one meal to several days.

Before the skipper raises anchor at his home port, he must provide himself with a log book. Armed with this volume, he sets forth into the unknown, finding such haven as he may at any table which has a temporary vacancy. The senior First classman at each table makes entries, dates and signs them, and thus gives him clearance. If the stranger reveals engaging traits of character or skill in the performance of his specialties, his visits may be prolonged.

From an actual log book of the days when the ceremony was more elaborate than it is now are extracted the following entries, starting with this typical "To Whom It May Concern" greeting:

> Know ye that, reposing special confidence and trust in the abilities of Midshipman John Q. Gulliver, I do hereby appoint him to take the good ship *Lollypop* around the world, from the 4th day of March. He is, therefore, carefully and diligently to discharge the duties of a skipper by doing and performing all manner of things thereunto belonging.

Just how the somewhat all-inclusive phrase "all manner of things" was variously interpreted may be gathered from a few specimen entries:

> The skipper put in here Sunday morning and had a hell of a time to anchor at this table. Teeth in good condition, as per statement under Vital Statistics. Can do good stoop falls with one arm. (*Table 81*)

Exhibitions of "good stoop falls with one arm" thereafter became a standard act by Midshipman Gulliver.

> Dropped anchor at 0649. Just a liberty party. Doesn't know what bell trousers are. Shoved off at 0710. A good cut to his jib, clean lines and sound. Departed for parts unknown. (*Table 57*)

The above entry marked the beginning of a long and troublesome search for knowledge about bell trousers.

The blowfish arrived ahead of schedule. Still doesn't know what bell trousers are. The best hog caller in these parts. Ordered to write for Junior G-Man badge; should have it by Tuesday. (*Table 67*)

Hog calling was thereafter included in the list of "all manner of things" so vaguely mentioned in the greeting.

Still doesn't know bell trousers, but he sure can do one-armed stoop falls and call hogs. Have him show how to break a bronco. (*Table 30*)

Demonstrations of bronco busting were duly added to Midshipman Gulliver's repertoire.

He's from Texas. So's my gal. He's okay. (*Table 94*)

Thus did the visiting stranger bask in the warmth of a romance from the Southland.

The skipper was properly christened; we had no champagne, so Clegg wiped his face with a cup of cocoa. Sings good western Indian yells, but still doesn't know bell trousers. (*Table 104*)

The list of "all manner of things" continued to expand.

Doesn't know Nelson's four great battles. Doesn't know bell trousers. Score, 10 questions, 0 answers. Left port on soundings, bound for sunnier climes, shoving off in the face of a terrific gale. (*Table 42*)

The rough sailing intimated in the above entry apparently had a sobering effect, as the next entry reads:

He seems to have learned considerable about bell trousers, but his best acts are still one-armed stoop falls, hog calling, Indian yells and bronco busting. Boy, how he can ride! (*Table 100*)

In the course of time Midshipman Gulliver completes his travels and reports back to his home table, possibly a chastened and certainly a more experienced man, and submits his precious log as evidence that he has accomplished his mission. Whatever characteristics may be attributed to the mess hall, monotony is hardly one of them. No single hall into which 3900 or so healthy midshipmen are poured three times a day is likely to subside into a dull and uneventful routine. When there is occasion to celebrate, the opportunity is seized avidly. At Christmas time the hall is hung with gay streamers, a lighted Christmas tree is set up in the Rotunda, the plebes decorate each table and the Naval Academy band dispenses music. Sunday evening meals are enlivened by "happy hours," when the plebes stage humorous skits for the edification of their superiors. At Sunday noon meal formation following a football victory, the brigade, on the command "Battalions, forward march!" chants, "One! Two! Three! . . ." on alternate left feet until the Navy score for the previous day has been reached. The last number is followed by a cheer.

If there is one occasion when the mess hall formation literally justifies its name, it is on Hundredth Night, which comes late in February.

This robust festival derives its name from the fact that it is celebrated exactly one hundred nights before graduation day. It is distinguished by an exchange of blouses and caps—together with the insignia of rank and intensely temporary prerogatives of office—between the First classmen and the plebes.

This traditional ceremony begins at supper formation in the corridors. As the warning bells pick up the signal and ring out through Bancroft Hall, the midshipmen pour forth from their quarters, the First classmen and the plebes hurriedly donning blouses that appear to be fitted variously by the tailor of the Seven Dwarfs and by Omar the Tent Maker.

"Put those shoulders back!" barks a strutting plebe in a three-striper's uniform as he contemplates a First classman, standing in line with hands dangling below his sleeves, and *wham!* powerful hands from the rear slap down upon his shoulders with a force that jolts him. The victim grins good humoredly.

"Put that hat on straight!" another First classman is ordered. Immediately willing hands reach out and pull it over his eyes and ears.

"You got out of it pretty easy, didn't you?" observed a returning veteran of the celebration.

"Oh, we'll give the plebes in our companies a chance at us some other night instead," was the sporting rejoinder. "After all, they have only one night a year to blow off steam!"

Chapter 5

The Mission of
the Naval Academy

The Naval Academy knows what it is doing. Beside the walk
leading to the main entrance of the Administration Building
is a bronze plaque affixed to a large block, once a capstone of
the old sea wall. Inscribed on this plaque for all to see is the
Mission of the United States Naval Academy:

> To develop midshipmen morally, mentally and physically and
> to imbue them with the highest ideals of duty, honor and loyalty
> in order to provide graduates who are dedicated to a career of
> Naval Service and have potential for future development in mind
> and character to assume the highest responsibilities of command,
> citizenship and government.

This mission is reproduced in various places throughout the
Academy, over the main stairway in Isherwood Hall for example, and repeated in *Reef Points* and other publications.

The roadway from the main entrance of the Naval Academy
runs straight as a die, topographically and symbolically, to
the sea.

From the moment the newcomer passes through the handsome bronze gates (erected as a memorial by the class of 1907
at a cost of $12,000), he is, figuratively, stepping upon a gang-
plank that leads him to the decks of the fighting vessels of
Uncle Sam's fleet.

Near Luce Hall he will see the masts of the knockabouts,
small sloops in which the midshipmen get "close to the water"
and learn the useful art of sailing. Just beyond gleam the white
hulls of the seagoing houseboats the *APL* 31 and the *APL* 32,
the barrack ships for the stewards. In the distance he may

glimpse, especially during the summer cruise season, aircraft carriers, battleships, cruisers or transports at anchor in the waters of Chesapeake Bay.

The clock in the tower of Mahan Hall strikes not the hours but the ship's bells—and it strikes them on a bell four feet in diameter, weighing 2500 pounds, that was cast, appropriately enough, from metal of the ships' bells on the battleships *Alabama*, *Indiana*, *Michigan*, and *Massachusetts*, all four of which were used for the midshipmen's practice cruise prior to the summer of 1922, when the bell was cast. Monuments surmounted by the figureheads of ancient frigates dot the greensward. Naval officers and midshipmen, the latter in garb ranging from the blue service uniform to the "white works" used in laboratory work, pass to and fro in the Yard. From the staff in front of the Administration Building flutters the American flag. Guns that once belched flame in epoch-making naval engagements are mounted at strategic points as trophies of war and mute memorials of bygone glories. The newcomer does not merely enter the Yard; he "comes aboard" the United States Naval Academy, which for the greater part of a hundred years has ranked first in the list of naval training schools of the world in size, length of course, and continuity and intensity of program.

To keep that roadway to the decks of the fighting vessels straight and unencumbered has been and still is the main objective of the Naval Academy.

How the courses of instruction were originally conceived and how they have fared since were once given graphic illustration that is not without dramatic aspects, in the modest Academic Board room in the Administration Building.

Against the wall once stood a small table-like cabinet; under its glass top was displayed the original *Journal of the Academic Board*, opened at the first entry on page one. This entry is dated October 4, 1845—six days before the institution was officially founded and five years before the "Naval School," as it was then called, acquired its present name. It is in the form of an order addressed to the members of the academic staff, who had been only recently ordered to report at Annapolis

*T*here is only one way to
wear the uniform—the right way.
Personnel inspection helps
to instill a sense of pride
in the uniform and what it represents.

*S*ummer cruises allow the midshipmen
to gain valuable fleet operating experience.

*A career in naval aviation
is the goal of many midshipmen.*

after serving as instructors at the moribund Naval Asylum School in Philadelphia.

The complete academic staff was then organized as follows: Commander Franklin Buchanan, Superintendent; Lieutenant James H. Ward, Executive Officer and instructor in gunnery and steam; Surgeon John A. Lockwood, instructor in chemistry; Chaplain George Jones, instructor in English; Professor Henry H. Lockwood, instructor in natural philosophy; Professor William Chauvenet, instructor in mathematics and navigation; Professor Arsene N. Girault, instructor in French, and Passed Midshipman S. Marcy, instructor in mathematics.

In the careful longhand of the newly appointed Superintendent himself this entry reads:

Naval School, Annapolis, Oct. 4, 1845.

Gentlemen:

You will convene as a Board and arrange the classes of Midshipmen attached to the Naval School, decide upon the hours of recitation, the number of hours necessary to be applied to study, and designate the hours and time required for the various lectures and submit for my approval the result of your deliberations.

The course of instruction will be comprised under the following heads—Mathematics, Natural Philosophy, Chemistry, Gunnery, the use of Steam, Geography, English Grammar, Arithmetic, History, the French and Spanish languages and such other branches desirable to the accomplishment of a Naval officer as your judgment may dictate. Lieut. Ward will act as President of the Board.

Very Respectfully,
Your obd't Serv't,
Frank'n Buchanan,
Superintendent.

This document is now in the Naval Academy Museum.

Within the room where this old document was once displayed stands the long table over which the Academic Board of today holds its sessions.

The Academic Board consists of five members: the Superintendent, the Commandant of Midshipmen, the Director of Naval Science, the Director of Social Sciences and Humanities, and the Director of Science and Engineering. The way in which the various branches of administration and instruction are coordinated is indicated in the following chart:

ACADEMIC ORGANIZATION OF THE U. S. NAVAL ACADEMY

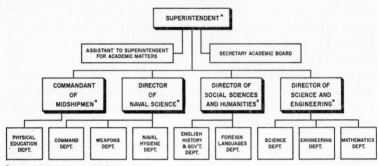

In view of the wholly revolutionary changes that have taken place during the past century, the consistency with which Buchanan's original conception of the objectives of the institution has been preserved is impressive, as is also the steadiness with which the courses of instruction necessary to attain them has been maintained.

Despite the introduction of such modern vessels of naval warfare as the aircraft carrier, the submarine and the landing craft, despite the substitution of diesel engines and atomic energy for coal and sail, and the invention of radio, radar and sonar, all unknown at the time Buchanan penned his first order, the main trend of the educational system has been steadfastly adhered to, sometimes in the face of the strongest pressure.

"Mathematics" is still being taught in the Mathematics Department; two and two still continue to add up to four, even though some of our more bewildered schoolchildren would induce us to believe otherwise.

"Gunnery" is still being taught in the Weapons Department, radically as the size and mechanisms of guns and the technique of naval gunfire have changed.

"French" and "Spanish" are still being spoken and both are still being taught in the Foreign Languages Department, to which has since been added Italian, Portuguese, Russian and German. (Japanese was also taught from 1942 to 1945.)

"English grammar" and "history" are still being taught in what is now known as the English, History and Government Department.

"Geography" doggedly maintains its character as the science of the earth's surface, unmindful of politics, and is still being taught in the English, History and Government Department and the Command Department.

"Natural philosophy" and "chemistry" are still included in the curriculum in the Science Department. And knowledge of "the use of steam" is still being imparted to the midshipmen by the more inclusive Engineering Department.

Only in the fields of physical training and hygiene has any important departure been made from the scope of the curriculum as it was conceived over a hundred years ago.

Responsibility for both the formulation and application of the Naval Academy's educational policies rests upon the shoulders of the Academic Board, headed by the Superintendent. He is assisted by the Commandant of Midshipmen, the Directors of the Divisions, and the Heads of the Academic Departments. Within each department there are committee chairmen who plan the actual courses, recommend textbooks, and supervise instruction.

Once every year there is appointed a Board of Visitors, who come to the Academy for a week for an inspection of the plant and the teaching methods and to consider the needs and problems that are put before them. As the concluding act of their deliberations they file a report setting forth their findings and recommendations with a view toward the constant improvement of the Naval Academy. The Board of Visitors is composed of the Chairman of the Committee on Armed Services of the Senate, or his designee; three other members of the Senate designated by the Vice President; the Chairman of the Committee on Armed Services of the House of Representatives, or his designee; four other members of the House of Representatives, designated by the Speaker; and six persons designated by the President, usually distinguished educators selected from among the presidents of leading universities.

In recent years the place of the Naval Academy in the educational system of the United States Navy as a whole has been very clearly and usefully defined. The Academy is the undergraduate "college" in the great "Navy University," which comprises many schools for advanced specialized study after the foundation of fundamentals has been laid. The curriculum of the Academy is designed to equip the midshipman with fundamental knowledge of the sciences, humanities, and naval subjects as a basis for the naval officer's future professional development and graduate work, which he will pursue in such "graduate schools" as the U. S. Naval Postgraduate School, the Naval War College, the Armed Forces Staff College, and the National War College. Just as the civilian student gets his general education at, say, Yale University and then, deciding to be a doctor, goes on to the Yale Medical School, so the midshipman lays the groundwork for his career at the Naval Academy and then goes on to advanced specialization.

The Naval Academy strives to strike an efficient balance between training and education through "a synthesis of theory and practice." It endeavors to build "solid foundations of professional thought, competence, and objectivity." It feels that education, however, must precede training as an indispensable prerequisite to it. The division of instructional time during the four-year course reflects this feeling: 50% of the time is devoted to scientific and engineering subjects, 22% to social-humanistic studies, and 28% to military and professional courses. The curricular emphasis indicated by these statistics is explained as follows:

It is highly important that a naval officer acquire the ability to think scientifically. This does not mean just a developed aptitude for chemistry, physics, or electronics. It means the ability to make the scientific approach, the capacity for casting a discerning eye upon data, the development of the instinct for breaking down problems into their elements in order to analyze them and effect their logical solutions. The Naval Academy provides a scientific-engineering background which places emphasis on basic principles, on awareness of relationships, the integration of knowledge, and logical thought founded upon facts. Familiarity with fundamental naval operational techniques and a broad knowledge of the potentialities and limitations of naval material are an essential part of the naval officer's factual background.

The naval officer must have the ability to recognize and analyze critically the national and international economic and social problems of our times. For example, foreign and domestic economic policies are determining considerations in naval activities. The naval officer must understand people. He must know how to exercise the responsibilities of command, how to cooperate and secure cooperation, and how to communicate ideas and ideals effectively. He must have the physical energy to accomplish his tasks.

Chapter 6

Academic
Training of Midshipmen

To the small boys of Annapolis the bronze figurehead of the old Indian chieftain Tecumseh, better known as the "God of 2.5," is a veritable Statue of the Profit. For it is they who collect the uncounted pennies that are cast in tribute by the midshipmen—more particularly by the "wooden" midshipmen, as the low-mark students are called, and who possibly for that very reason are more superstitious than their higher-ranking classmates—as they march past on their fateful way to the semi-annual examinations.

This custom of paying homage to the old warrior, accompanied by a left-hand salute, originated somewhere in the dim past when the original wooden figurehead stood a few paces from its present site, adjoining the building known during the period of its existence as the Lyceum. It has been surmised by competent surmisers that the wooden midshipmen found a kinship with this wooden Indian, and paid their compliments to him in their hours of need in the primitive manner of superstitious man since the first Medicine Man pranced about in his war feathers to scare away the spirits of evil.

The original wooden image, which became known as Tecumseh, was created to serve as the figurehead of the wooden line-of-battleship *Delaware*, built between 1817 and 1821 and destroyed at the Norfolk Navy Yard in April, 1861, to prevent her from falling into the hands of the Confederates. The figurehead was salvaged and brought to the Naval Academy in 1866. It was supposed to portray the great Indian chief Tamanend of the Delaware tribe, a lover of peace and a friend

54

of William Penn. But this conception failed to seize the imagination of the midshipmen of the period, who variously dubbed the image Powhatan, King Philip, and later "Old Sebree," because of the alleged resemblance to Midshipman (later Rear Admiral) Uriel Sebree, of the class of 1867. Finally some inspired soul called it Tecumseh and the name stuck.

For forty years the weather-scarred god kept his stern vigil in the Yard, until the winds and the sun and the rain at last began to take their toll and he began to disintegrate. In 1906 he underwent a face-lifting operation; with the aid of cement, putty and paint the signs of age were temporarily removed. But when again the ravages of time threatened, the challenge was met by the class of 1891, which raised a fund with which to immortalize the old fellow in bronze. The delicate task was done at the United States Naval Gun Factory, which employed in the metal composition certain old captured ordnance material. The members of the class of 1891 assembled in the factory on December 3, 1929, to attend the ceremonies of casting; in the following spring the statue, mounted on a pedestal of Vermont marble adorned with the Naval Academy seal made from the brass of the torpedo tubes of the USS *Washington*, was erected on its present site, from which the grim old warrior gazes eternally toward the main entrance of Bancroft Hall.

The "God of 2.5" derives his name from the passing mark of 2.5 on the scale of 4.0 which is demanded of the midshipmen in their academic studies and in conduct as well as in many of their drills.

The evolution of the now famous 4.0-system of grades at the Naval Academy (4.0 = "A" or "100") may be traced in the manuscript pages of the "Record of the proceedings of The Academic Board of the Naval School," written in the careful hand of the secretary of the board, William Chauvenet, the first professor of mathematics and a founding father of the Academy, who is credited with being the man who did most in making the Academy a reality. The entry in the Record for July 20, 1850, reads in part: "The Board then took into consideration the *scale* upon which recitations are hereafter to be marked. It was the unanimous opinion of the Board that the scale from 10 to 0 was too wide. After discussing the merits of a scale from 5 to 0 and of one from 4 to 0 the subject was postponed for future consideration." The scale of 10 to 0 had been in effect since the founding of the "Naval School."

Ten days later, on July 30, the consideration of the scale of merit was resumed and the following scale was adopted:

Scale of Merit

Very good	4
Good	3
Indifferent	2
Bad	1
Very bad	0

Quite possibly Chauvenet may have been responsible for the scale adopted since it was the one in effect at his alma mater, Yale, from which he had graduated in 1840. Today at the Naval Academy the scale is subdivided into tenths, with 2.5 the lowest passing grade.

Figured on the scale of 100 in common usage in educational institutions, the passing mark of 2.5 is equivalent to 62.5 per cent. While this figure is lower than the passing mark established by numerous other institutions, such a comparison is theoretical and not actual, as no real basis of comparison is possible in view of the wide variations in the methods of allotting recitation marks. A passing mark of 50 in a college of high rating may well be infinitely more difficult of attainment than a mark of 75 that still prevails in many schools of low rating and lax discipline. Snap judgments on the relative merits of a college on the basis of the academic marks they give are likely to prove as fallacious as judgments on the merits of restaurants on the evidence of their printed menus. Values are not determined quite as simply as that.

The number of plebes dropped for academic deficiencies is fairly large. During the four-year course about a quarter of those who enter the Naval Academy fall by the roadside, most of them during their Fourth class year. Expressed in official language, the "rate of attrition" fluctuates around 25 per cent.

All midshipmen take essentially the same course leading to the degree of Bachelor of Science, but they may accelerate or expand their program of studies in three ways: (1) by "validating"; that is, by being given credit for courses comparable to college-level courses they have already had and excelled in, and moving up to the next sequential course in the subject; (2) by taking electives as substitutes for validated courses, or as additional courses; and (3) by meriting placement in advanced or accelerated sections. A qualified midshipman of high scholastic ability may major in any of the principal academic disciplines.

In the computing of a midshipman's final standing in each subject following the examinations, his daily recitation marks are counted for three fifths and his examination marks as two fifths of the total; in this way a man whose examination mark may fall slightly below the 2.5 minimum may pull his average up by a good mark in his daily recitations. Should a man's marks fall below the required 2.5, and thus indicate doubt of his ability to maintain the standard established, he is called before the Academic Board. Those whose marks in any one course are only slightly below 2.5, and whose records are otherwise good, and who show reasonable promise of pulling themselves up as well as a determination to do so, are likely to be accorded a re-examination. In some cases, particularly deficiency caused by extended illness, a midshipman may be "turned back," to do the year's work over again with the next lower class. Many of the midshipmen enter the Naval Academy from schools that furnish rather sketchy preparation and have not inculcated proper methods of study; these are factors which the Academic Board takes into consideration. Another factor is the midshipman's attitude toward a career in the Navy. In one case the midshipman was asked:

"Is it your purpose to remain in the Navy when you graduate?"

"No, sir," was the reply.

That proved to be his exit cue. Like some of his fellows— and again some are too many—he had looked upon the Naval Academy merely as a means of obtaining an education at the expense of the taxpayers without any serious intention of rendering any service in return. As the cost of educating a midshipman at the public expense approximates $29,000, Uncle Sam has a reasonable expectancy that this sum be wisely invested and that he derive some benefit from it.

The courses of instruction are constantly undergoing modifications and changes to meet the ever-shifting conditions of naval warfare. In general it may be observed that the greatest emphasis in the first two and a half years is laid upon mathematics, as is to be expected in a curriculum that is essentially scientific. During his plebe year, Midshipman Gish concentrates his efforts on five subjects: mathematics, engineering drawing, chemistry, English, and one foreign language.

In mathematics he recites five days a week. During the first term he takes plane trigonometry, algebra, calculus, analytic geometry; in his second term he continues analytic geometry and also calculus. His course in the Science Department (the "Juice" Department) comprises general chemistry (known as "Skinny") supplemented with laboratory work. In marine engineering he receives basic indoctrination during the summer in the assembly and disassembly of aviation and marine internal combustion engines, pattern making, foundry practice, the use of hand and power tools, and gas and electric welding; then for the next two terms he learns engineering drawing, and finishes with statics and descriptive geometry. Courses in marine engineering are commonly lumped together in the term "Steam." The course in English (known informally as "Bull") starts in the summer with lectures on naval history, readings in naval orientation and tradition, indoctrination visits to the library and the museum, and exploratory examinations. When the academic year begins, the regular course in American and English literature with composition is taken up. These topics, together with the foreign language (commonly called "Dago") he has been assigned to take after an interview with language instructors, constitute the entire academic curriculum of the midshipman during his plebe year.

While a detailed summary of the academic curricula of the midshipmen may appear as formidable and dry as the outline of the courses in any educational institution, the section-room work is augmented by a vast amount of practical activities in the various laboratories, machine shops and model rooms, as well as by inspection tours, drills (as much of the laboratory instruction is called), gunnery practice, ship-handling and by practice cruises. Some of the courses are distinguished by educational features that are as original in conception as they are unique in observance.

When young Lieutenant Jones or (later) Admiral Jones attends a luncheon or a dinner or a ceremonial occasion of some kind, especially if it is a formal affair where guests are likely to be called upon for a few well-chosen words, the naval officer in uniform is a marked man. He represents the Navy, and in deference to the Navy the master of ceremonies is apt to ask him to say a word or two, perhaps to respond to a toast. Should Lieutenant Jones bashfully refrain or give expression to a few inept remarks, not only his own personal prestige would be affected but also the prestige of the service he symbolizes. The ability to rise promptly to his feet and make a few graceful observations without embarrassment is a part of a naval officer's professional equipment.

So the art of after-dinner speaking is incorporated in the regular curriculum of the Naval Academy.

Public speaking is not taught as a dry, academic topic studied from textbooks and expounded by lecturers; it is not made the subject of a thesis to be marked and graded. On the contrary, the midshipman learns how to talk in public exactly as he learns how to sail a boat and fire a gun—by actually doing it.

Four times a week, during the First class year of Midshipman Gish, a formal dinner is served in each of two private dining rooms off the mess hall. The setting is that of a dining room such as is customarily engaged for a private dinner at a club or hotel. The long table down the center, which accommodates a couple of dozen guests, is laid with a special set of chinaware, and is embellished with small lamps. Before the guests are seated, the conventional cocktails are served, made unconventionally with tomato juice only. The food is the same as is being served in the mess hall, but the service is much more elegant and leisurely. The guests include about twenty First classmen, all of whom appear in full-dress uniform; also in attendance are a representative of the faculty of the English, History and Government Department and a guest-of-honor, who are accompanied by their ladies.

The occasion? Well, it may be almost anything; it is more likely to be a genuine than an imaginary one. Perhaps an officer who has been serving at the Naval Academy has been ordered away to other duties; in that case the affair is a farewell dinner to him. Perhaps a new officer has just arrived to assume his duties; if so, this is a dinner of welcome. The toastmaster is a midshipman; presiding at post-prandial exercises is as much a part of the course as responding to a demand for a speech. Each midshipman guest is apprised well in advance of the nature of the function and is told that he must come prepared to make a short talk appropriate to the occasion. During the academic year every First classman attends several of these dinners.

In all sorts of midshipman extracurricular activities the midshipmen are encouraged to rise to their feet and to participate in a variety of committee discussions. Such impromptu talks give the midshipmen self-confidence, teach them "to think on their feet," and to talk sensibly and well on any topic up for discussion. The ability gained in this way to participate in public discussion is one of the chief values of these extracurricular activities.

Development is indeed the keynote of the Academy's program of instruction, as incorporated in the formal statement of its mission: "To develop midshipmen morally, mentally and physically. . . . " Though most midshipmen take the same basic subjects throughout their four-year course (except for their choice among six languages: French, Spanish, Italian, Portuguese, German and Russian), there is broad opportunity for the gifted, the energetic, and the well prepared to pursue special interests and inclinations and to achieve as broad and intensive an education as their intellectual powers warrant. The quaint notion cherished by all too many of the casually misinformed that the Naval Academy is not much more than a glorified boot camp could not be further from the truth.

The Validation or Advanced Placement Program enables the capable student, particularly one who has had some college work, to take up his academic work at his own proper level, without having to repeat work he has already excelled in. For example, at least sixty plebes each year are given credit for "Freshman English" if they can demonstrate that they can read perceptively and write efficiently, and are allowed to take

Third Class work. Midshipmen of proved academic aptitude may also take alternate or additional elective courses and graduate with a major in some highly useful specialty. It is as foolish and futile to attempt to strait-jacket all midshipmen into exactly the same program of academic instruction as it would be to assume that they all wear the same size in shoes or caps. Thus, in the words of the *Catalogue of Information*, "The overall program assures all midshipmen of the educational benefits of the basic curriculum and at the same time provides the opportunity for fuller development of individual talents."

In the social sciences and humanities, such as English literature, where individual tastes and differences of opinion may not only vary widely but run rampant, the utmost freedom of thought and of expression is encouraged. Indeed, the stimulation of creative, analytical and interpretative thinking, unguided by instructors who insist only upon holding the midshipmen down to factual premises upon which to base their conclusions, is one of the characteristic attributes of the Naval Academy section room. The result is that a class in English, for example, consisting of about sixteen men from as many States and representing as many shades of opinion, assumes less the aspect of an academic recitation than that of an informal discussion and interchange of ideas in a gentlemen's club.

In a typical class in American literature, for example, the subject under consideration for the day is inscribed on the blackboard:

Franklin's techniques of self-improvement

For the first ten minutes the students write their comment on this topic; in preparation they have read the assigned selections from Franklin's *Autobiography* in their textbooks, along with the biographical, historical and critical material which accompanies the text, and have kept an eye on the explanatory footnotes as they read. Their papers are then collected by the section leader, to serve as the basis for their recitation marks for the day. Then the general interchange of ideas and information begins. One man rises to ask just how Franklin went about the task of improving his literary style—the midshipman didn't quite understand the details of it. Another midshipman to whom it seemed clear enough raises his hand; the instructor calls on him to explain. Another man wonders whether Franklin's system would be feasible today, and, if so, what authors would furnish good models to follow. The instructor allows others to express their opinions on this point, and adds some ideas and suggestions of his own. Discussion is free and informal; the instructor intervenes only to see that the ground is covered, that questions are given, if possible, a definitive answer, and that the discussion is kept within the bounds of the limited time available.

To avoid the likelihood that the personal equation might influence the marks, the instructor is switched about and the personnel of the section is changed at intervals. Each midshipman is expected to know his lessons so thoroughly that he can recite upon them impersonally to anyone.

The Naval Academy is particularly proud of its faculty and of the depth and breadth of the subject matter they are capable of teaching. It is the only one of the three largest service academies which staffs its academic departments primarily with professional civilian instructors. Quite properly, the departments in the Division of Naval Science, the Command, Weapons and Naval Hygiene Departments, and the Executive Department under the Commandant of Midshipmen, are made up almost exclusively of Naval Officers. None are better qualified than these officers, fresh from fleet service, to devise the courses and techniques and specify the equipment needed to teach the very latest in seamanship, navigation, Naval leadership, Naval operations, weapons, missile systems, and Naval organization and procedure. But quite properly, also, those best qualified to teach such subjects as the humanities and the social sciences— foreign languages, history, government, economics, English composition, literature—and the pure and applied sciences are those who have made a lifetime professional career of these specialties.

In May of 1962 the Secretary of the Navy, Fred Korth, instituted a policy to effect the gradual replacement of officer instructors in all departments but those teaching strictly professional subjects with civilian professors. This was no attempt to "civilianize" the Academy but rather a sound, progressive step toward the best of all possible Academies—one in which every subject and technique is taught by those who have the most intensive and comprehensive knowledge and experience in it.

The officers assigned to teach professional subjects or to fill administrative poets are specially selected by the Bureau of Naval Personnel working in cooperation with the Naval Academy. Members of the civilian faculty are chosen only after a careful process of consideration of their academic and personal background, and screenings by examination and interview. Minimum requirements for the rank of assistant professor are a master's degree and a successful record of college teaching. Many of the faculty hold Ph.D. degrees or are studying to attain them. Many are distinguished scholars whose textbooks or research studies are widely recognized and used. Faculty members are entitled to sabbatical leave for further study and research, and every effort is made to provide travel abroad.

To state that the instruction given at the Naval Academy aims at thoroughness is but to paraphrase the trite claim commonly found in every school catalogue. Like the printed set of rules that used to hang on the wall of the city news room of the old New York *World*, the insistent classroom demands made upon the midshipmen may be reduced to "(1) *Accuracy*, (2) *Accuracy*, (3) *Accuracy*," not merely because that quality is desirable in itself as a general principle and is conducive to straight thinking, but more particularly because in so many of a naval officer's duties—navigation and gunnery, to cite two illustrations—it is a prime requisite. A miscalculation of a fraction of a point in determining position or range may, and often does, spell the difference between success and failure, between victory and defeat. A careless reference to a mathematical formula, an error in a radio message or in the use of the flag signal code may cause the loss of a multi-million dollar ship and thousands of human lives.

The intensity with which the Naval Academy focuses on the training of midshipmen is illustrated by its system of dividing the classes into small sections, averaging fifteen men each. Except for occasional digressions (such, for example, as special tests and examinations), every man recites, orally or in writing

—and receives a mark—almost every day in every subject. Thus it is possible to give each midshipman personal attention and to keep a close and constant tab on him.

The sections are made up according to arrangements determined by the heads of departments, and the mechanical details of assigning men to the proper sections are accomplished by the amazingly efficient electronic sorting, calculating and printing machines in the Machine Records Office. The resulting section lists are posted in Bancroft Hall and also copies are distributed to the instructors. Members of each section serve in monthly rotation as section leaders, who have military charge of the section and are responsible for reporting absentees to the instructor and also to Bancroft Hall.

Every effort is made to keep midshipmen's heads above water academically and to rescue them if they should go under. Those who go "unsat" are counseled by their instructors and the committee chairman, and even by the head of department should the difficulty be prolonged. There is a very beneficial psychology in all this: no midshipman ever need feel that he is lost or adrift in an indifferent academic world if he is having his troubles; on the other hand, if Midshipman Gish has become just a bit lazy or careless, perhaps, this counseling serves to remind him that he is not getting away with anything and that he had better get with it. Extra instruction is also provided to help the weak and weary over the academic bumps. Anyone who really wants help can get it in abundance.

During Third class, or "Youngster," year, the midshipman continues in the same departments in which he worked during his plebe year at the Academy. In Steam, he acquires a basic knowledge of engineering materials and of the strength of engineering materials and their behavior. In Math he completes his work in calculus and proceeds to differential equations and mechanics. He gets endless workouts on the slipstick, that indispensable calculator he will use the rest of his career—his slide rule. The Youngster course in the Juice Department is physics. The Bull Department gives him a course in modern European history the first term and in U. S. foreign policy the second. He pursues his second and last year of study of his language, though he may continue to improve his language skill

*E*lectronics is one of
*the most important subjects
*at the Naval Academy.

*L*aboratory time was important sixty years ago, and it is even more important in today's highly technical Navy.

A conference with the
Superintendent, and working
out problems in physics
and electricity.

Life at the Academy is varied. Studying in the Brigade Library, participating in an intercollegiate conference on foreign affairs, and a visit from Secretary of the Navy Fred Korth.

*M*idshipmen from foreign
navies enjoy being shown around
the Naval Academy.

throughout his last two years, if he wants to, by attending elective courses given by the Language Department. He continues his practical work in seamanship with drills in the rules of the nautical road, communications, recognition, and fleet operations, and lectures on aviation and submarines to prepare for summer cruise.

By the end of Third class year and Youngster Cruise, the midshipman is well on his way toward planning his career in the Navy as a dedicated way of life. And it is a dedication, just as entering on a career in holy orders, or medicine, or teaching is a dedication. He can't make a fortune for himself; he must assume, often, tremendous responsibilities; his work is essentially dangerous; he can seldom, if ever, take things easy. But, of course, as with other dedicated lives, there are enormous rewards and satisfactions which no material yardstick can measure.

Next to pride of service, the chief among these satisfactions is the knowledge that he will lead an interesting, varied, and useful life, the horizons of which are ever expanding. His career impinges upon many areas—naval command, science, education, engineering, diplomacy, public relations, administration—and sometimes on all of these at once.

There is also exciting variety within the realm of the strictly professional. He may choose a career in amphibious, anti-submarine or striking forces, or in naval aviation, or nuclear science and engineering, or submarines. Outside of line duty, he may choose to enter the Supply Corps or the Civil Engineering Corps, or become a Marine. In all of these fields of service, there will be the opportunity for graduate study and continued professional advancement. Officers are frequently ordered to universities for advanced studies and the master's or doctor's degrees. The Navy, of course, also has its own professional schools: the War Colleges, the Naval Intelligence School, and the U. S. Naval Postgraduate School at Monterey, California.

In Second class year, the midshipman continues his work in some departments that are by this time old friends. The English, History and Government Department presents courses in U. S. government and in economics; the Math Department teaches spherical trigonometry and differential equations. In the Science

Department he begins a long course of study called, comprehensively, Electrical Science, and will before he graduates burn a great deal of midnight oil over such matters as these: "Fundamental concepts of electric and magnetic fields. Laws of the electric circuit and introduction to network analysis. Principles of electrical measurements. R, L, C, and M as fundamental circuit parameters, transients; alternating currents and voltages; phasor representation and complex algebra; single phase transformers. Theory and principles of electronics. Fundamentals of electron emission and ballistics in vacuum and gas-filled tubes; tuned circuits and filters; transients and wave-shaping circuits; voltage stabilizers; transistors; radio and audio frequency amplifiers; cathode ray tubes and oscillographs." He is introduced to the mysteries of basic thermodynamics and fluid mechanics. He begins the vastly important studies of piloting and navigation and learns, in actual practice afloat, the fundamentals of celestial navigation, including the use of the sextant, as well as electronic and inertial navigation.

He also begins intensive study of another subject vital to all naval officers, naval weapons and their control systems. (Of course he has already worked under the Weapons Department during plebe summer when, on the rifle range across the Severn, he learned how to care for and fire the service rifle and the pistol. At this time it was possible for him to qualify as Expert Riflemen or Expert Pistol Shot and be eligible to wear the ribbons that signify those qualifications.) For two years he will go into all the science, art and technique of "the fire control problem": how to shoot at a ship, submarine, plane or missile —and hit it. At his disposal will be an imposing array of naval guns, missile mounts and fire control equipment lined up along the harbor seawall in what must be one of the finest modern naval ordnance drill areas ever constructed.

The Academy is particularly proud of its two-term course in naval leadership, a pioneer course in practical psychology as applied to the solution of leadership problems. It has prepared its own text, *Naval Leadership*, which not only analyzes the whole phenomenon of leadership, but contains actual problem situations which the upper classman is asked to consider and cope with. Thus he is made aware of the great responsibility he will assume as an officer with authority over others, and given a chance to acquire some vicarious experience before he is faced with the awesome problems of leadership in his actual career.

A very special feature of Second class year is the series of "Exchange Weekends" with West Point. Started in 1946, this system provides that, over a course of about six Thursday-to-Sunday weekends beginning in February, groups of midshipmen go up to the Military Academy at West Point, New York, while comparable groups of cadets come down to Annapolis, the process continuing until all members of one second class have visited the institution of the other. While at West Point, each midshipman is the guest of a cadet host and attends classes, drills, Chapel Service, athletic events and weekend social functions with him, and, of course, each cadet is similarly entertained at Annapolis. These weekends are not only great fun, but promote greater understanding and friendship between the two Academies, in preparation for the day when the graduates of the two schools will work side by side with each other in the service of their country.

First class year is a very busy one (not that the others aren't!) in which, perhaps, the midshipman comes closest to the practical concerns of the naval officer as he considers a wide variety of material on Naval organization and combat procedures. In the Command Department he is instructed in naval operations, including tactics, CIC (Combat Information Center) procedures, military planning, and the principles of naval warfare, with drills in shiphandling and tactics aboard the YP's. He is introduced to military law and international law, and to the all-important subject of meteorology—the weather. In Weapons he learns about missile systems, antisubmarine warfare, naval gunfire support procedures, mine warfare, and submarine and aircraft weapons systems. The course in electrical science continues the midshipman's intensive consideration of circuits, systems, controls and measurements he must master in that field. In engineering he proceeds to applied fluid mechanics and applied thermodynamics. He considers the importance of Naval Hygiene. (By the way, hygiene is the only course which Congress actually requires to be taught to midshipmen.) For his first term's work in the English, History and Government Department he reads naval history from texts written by the department's own Naval History Committee, which proudly and appropriately includes among its members several of the country's most distinguished naval historians and biographers. In the second term he reads representative European literature, and demonstrates his ability to read and write efficiently by a final substantial project in composition, an extended term paper based on his own research. His professional knowledge and his grasp of the affairs of the world are enhanced by a series of evening lectures delivered by distinguished scholars and other authorities in international affairs and professional subjects.

It is obvious that any professional training in such a highly specialized field as naval warfare cannot remain static. It must move forward to keep pace with new inventions, new discoveries, new techniques, new methods. The curriculum is subjected to a continuous flow of additions, modifications and deletions; courses that are vital today may be obsolete tomorrow. No other policy would be possible if that proud tradition of the Navy is to be preserved:

"The United States Navy has had only four fleet actions (before World War II), but in every one it has captured or destroyed every enemy ship."

These four fleet actions were the battle of Lake Erie in 1813, the battle of Mobile Bay in 1864, the battle of Manila Bay in 1898, and the battle of Santiago in 1898. Just for good measure one might well include the battle of Lake Champlain in 1814, even though the naval experts scratch their heads when they pause to decide whether the American forces in that decisive action should be technically classified as a fleet or as a squadron.

The Naval Academy does not propose to let that tradition fail through any deficiency in its curriculum.

Chapter 7

Organization
of the Brigade

The Officer of the Watch, on duty in his office at Bancroft Hall, was reading over the newly issued orders of the day. He turned to the Midshipman Officer of the Watch and observed:

"There will be no recitations or drills this afternoon from after noon meal until evening meal formation at 1830."

"Aye, aye, sir."

"In that case we will probably get visitors here during liberty hours. See that the reception room is in readiness and extra chairs provided to set out in the rotunda; we might need them."

"Aye, aye, sir. That has already been done, sir."

The Officer of the Watch shot a glance at his informant. Like all the Midshipmen Officers of the Watch, this one had been selected in rotation from among the brigade, regimental, battalion, and company staffs; that means he was not only a First classman but one who stood well up in the military organization of the brigade. The Watch Officer made mental note that his young assistant had anticipated his orders and taken appropriate action on his own initiative. His observation checked up with his previous impression of the young man; he had on other occasions demonstrated his capacity for anticipating needs. His papers were neatly and accurately kept. The Watch Officer liked the cut of his jib and decided that he was worth watching. Maybe some day, when he would be in command of a vessel himself, the Watch Officer might like to have this young man as a junior officer on duty with him.

When the Officer of the Watch—who when he is not serving in this 24-hour capacity is on duty elsewhere with the brigade—accumulates enough favorable impressions of the midshipman to impel him to do something about it, he gives the young man an "aptitude mark," using for the purpose a special form bearing the title "Aptitude Evaluation Report." Upon these aptitude reports are based the aptitude ratings of every midshipman, and these aptitude ratings determine the military status of all the First classmen in the brigade. He whose aptitude rating is the highest and who consequently rates tops, is the Number One man; by virtue of that fact he may become midshipman commander of the brigade, better known as the "Six Striper" because he alone, of all the 3900 or more midshipmen, wears on his sleeve the six thin stripes of gold braid that are the insignia of his rank. His official position corresponds to that of colonel in command of a regiment in the Army. He is to the Naval Academy what the "First Captain" is to the Military Academy at West Point.

Thus an aptitude rating assumes a vast importance in the life of every midshipman. It is a form of personal estimate that will follow him the rest of his life. It will decide his professional rise or fall in the Navy. Unless he demonstrates by his character and temperament as well as his training, that he has an aptitude for the service, his usefulness will be limited and his advancement checked. No matter how brilliant a scholar he may be or how high he may rank in his academic work; no matter how renowned he may be as an athlete; no matter what his social background is or what his financial resources are, unless he has an inherent or acquired aptitude for the service his career as an officer of the United States Navy will be curtailed before he sends his uniform coats to the tailor to have the four broad gold braids sewn upon the sleeves as the insignia of his rank as Captain.

Aptitude ratings are awarded to all the Fourth classmen throughout their Fourth Class year, but this aptitude rating is not counted as part of their overall standing for the year. Because they are newcomers, less mature than the other midshipmen and not yet fully familiarized with the life at the Naval Academy, they are merely held under general observation pending their further development. In the meantime, of course, their academic and conduct records are steadily being accumulated and tabulated; their marks in both of these subjects, in combination with the aptitude marks that they will receive later, will become factors when their final class standings for the four-year course are computed.

The aptitude mark increases rapidly in importance as the midshipman proceeds with his course. In his Youngster year it is given a coefficient of 4; in his Second class year its importance is increased and is given a coefficient of 8. In his First class year the aptitude coefficient soars to 16; by that time Midshipman Gish is expected to show what is in him and to give convincing evidence of his officer-like qualities.

The "Aptitude Evaluation Report" provides for ratings of outstanding, excellent, good, satisfactory, or unsatisfactory in the following qualities: Loyalty, Leadership, Initiative, Personal Appearance, Reliability, Participation, Judgment, Physical Fitness, Maturity, Military Bearing, Self-Discipline, Cooperation, Expression, and Social Presence. The faculty also reports on efficiency in the classroom by means of the "Academic Department Midshipmen Evaluation Report"; the midshipman student is assessed as to Attitude, Ability to Express Himself, Effort and Participation, Maturity, and Personal Appearance relative to his classmates. On both forms there is ample space for detailed comment by the authority making the report.

By virtue of Public Law 253 of the 79th Congress, approved December 11, 1945, a midshipman may, as a last resort, be discharged from the Naval Academy by the Secretary of the Navy if his conduct is unsatisfactory or if "it is determined by a unanimous decision of the Academic Board that any midshipman possesses insufficient aptitude for becoming a commissioned officer in the naval service." However, the aptitude system is designed to function positively rather than negatively: "While it is necessary to effect an occasional discharge for inaptitude, the correction and improvement of midshipmen who are low in Aptitude is considered to be of far greater importance."

According to the instructions for the use of the aptitude forms,

Aptitude Evaluation Reports are especially desired from the following sources:

(1) Coaches in the athletic program.
(2) Officers in charge of teams, organizations, and extra-curricular activities.
(3) Officer of the Watch or Assistant Officer of the Watch, for midshipmen on watch coming under his observation.
(4) Task Group Commander, Group, team or special movement.
(5) Command Department YP Drill observation.

Every midshipman is under observation twenty-four hours a day. He is being watched and appraised by his officers and by his instructors. In classroom, at drill and during his leisure hours, his capacities, his temperament and his manners, good, bad or indifferent, are contributing something to somebody's aptitude rating of him. A positive rating is in the nature of a commendation; a negative rating is in the nature of a criticism. When a midshipman is negatively reported two or three times he is summoned before his battalion officer.

"Mr. Gish," he is warned, "three times within the past few weeks you have been reported for indifference in the performance of your duties. The fact that two of these reports have come from your officers and one from an instructor, all of whom have observed the same fault, would indicate that these comments cannot be traced to any personal idiosyncrasy. As all of these reports are entered upon your record and consequently affect your standing, perhaps they point out a defect that you can correct."

Mr. Gish agrees. In the face of such conclusive evidence there is small purpose in seeking to argue or explain. Mr. Gish usually thanks the battalion officer and proceeds to watch his step.

Midshipmen, however, are not rated by their officers and instructors alone; they also rate each other. At the beginning of each term each midshipman is given a list of about 35 members of his company and asked to rank them in order of merit, according to his best observation and opinion. Ultimately these midshipman rankings and the Executive Department rankings are transferred to special cards and fed into electronic computers which automatically combine the two ratings and establish the aptitude rankings for each class by class and company.

Any midshipman who is relegated to the bottom 10% of his

class in his battalion is specially "observed, evaluated and counselled at monthly intervals" for the obvious purpose of helping him to improve his standing. The aptitude rankings are semi-annual and are established during the first two weeks in December and the last two weeks in April of each academic year.

The Naval Academy Aptitude System provides the means by which the midshipmen officers of the brigade organization are selected each year from the First Class. Actually there are three sets of officers chosen each year. The first set serves from September to the Army game; the second, from the Army game to Spring leave; and the third from Spring leave through graduation.

The third and final group of midshipmen officers, which serves from about the middle of March through graduation day, is the most honored of all, for it is largely composed of the pick of the two preceding groups. Competition among the midshipmen officers for selection to it is keen. Incidentally, it is this final group that commands the brigade during the colorful public ceremonies of June Week.

The method of selection is thus described in *Instructions for the Operation and Administration of the Aptitude for the Service System:*

Aptitude ranking is an important factor in selection of midshipman officers and petty officers as well as the conduct record and academic standing. . . .

Order of Merit lists taking cognizance of the above factors will be computed as follows:

(1) At the end of Second Class Year, to be used as a guide when determining the First and Second sets of Brigade Officers:

2 × Academic average for second class year
7 × Aptitude mark for second class year
1 × Conduct mark for second class year

(2) At the end of first term, first class year, to be used as a guide in determining the third set of Brigade officers:

2 × Academic average, first term, first class year
5 × Aptitude mark, first term, first class year

5 × Aptitude mark, special ranking for third set

2 × Conduct, first term, first class year

The Aptitude Officer will nominate the first and second set of midshipman officers, and the Brigade Aptitude Board will nominate the third set of midshipman officers, using the Order of Merit lists as a guide and considering in full the recommendations of Company and Battalion Officers, based on personal knowledge of the individual midshipmen. . . .

It is to be emphasized that the Order of Merit lists are simply guides for consideration of the Brigade Aptitude Board. Midshipman Officers are not selected by an IBM machine. They are selected as individuals, based on known performance. This is particularly applicable to the third set. . . .

The midshipmen officers of the First Class are popularly known as "stripers" in reference to the thin gold braid stripes which they wear on each sleeve to designate their ranks. The Brigade Commander ranks as a Midshipman Captain and rates six stripes and hence is known as the "Six Striper." The other midshipmen officer designations are as follows: Commander, five stripes; Lieutenant Commander, four stripes; Lieutenant, three stripes; Lieutenant, junior grade, two stripes; and Ensign, one stripe. All of these ranks are, in a very real sense, "won" by the men who hold them.

"We do not choose the midshipmen officers," a representative of the Executive Department carefully explained, "nor do we determine the aptitude ratings. We simply keep the records. And the records of the midshipmen determine their own status in the brigade."

At the top of the brigade organization stands the brigade commander, the midshipman captain, or "Six Striper," already mentioned. He has an imposing staff. First, there is his deputy brigade commander, a midshipman commander, a "Five Striper"; then there are a brigade administrative officer and a brigade operations officer, midshipman lieutenant commanders, or "Four Stripers"; a brigade adjutant, a brigade supply officer and a brigade communications officer, all midshipmen lieutenants and all "Three Stripers"; a National color bearer and Navy and brigade color bearers, all midshipmen chief petty officers.

The brigade is organized into two regiments of three battalions each. Each regiment is under the command of a regimental commander, a man with the rank of midshipman commander, a "Five Striper." He has a staff of six assisting him. First, there is the regimental sub-commander, a midshipman lieutenant commander, a "Four Striper"; a regimental operations officer, with the rank of midshipman lieutenant, a "Three Striper"; an adjutant and a regimental supply officer, midshipman lieutenants, junior grade, "Two Stripers"; and three regimental chief petty officers. Each battalion has its battalion commander, a midshipman lieutenant commander, a "Four Striper"; assisting him is a staff consisting of a sub-commander and an operations officer, a battalion adjutant, a battalion supply officer and a chief petty officer.

Each of the six battalions is subdivided into four companies, each under the command of a company commander, a midshipman lieutenant or "Three Striper." He is assisted by a sub-commander and a company chief petty officer. Each company is subdivided into three platoons, commanded by a platoon commander, a "Two Striper," who is assisted by a platoon sub-commander, a "One Striper."

Every single officer of responsibility in the brigade, from the top ranking captain to the lowest ranking second petty officer, is filled by a First classman. The First class is definitely and completely the boss. The brigade is organized, governed and commanded on the principle that any First classman ranks every under classman. And because the First class officers and petty officers are tried out in positions of military responsibility in two separate and distinct groups, plus the additions and shifts that are made in a third group, a considerable portion of the First classmen get actual experience in command.

Experience has shown that a percentage of midshipmen—a small percentage, to be sure, but even a small percentage is a matter of concern—develop slowly and do not display qualities of leadership as early as their fellows. Were they young officers on board ship, they would be looked upon as not entirely dependable. To search out and to bring up to standard these delinquents before they graduate and join the fleet is one of the important tasks of the Naval Academy officers. Some of these delinquents do not snap into maturity until they have been vested with authority and given responsibility, which is a phenomenon that has been likewise observed in business and in domestic life. Some people can and do rise to the occasion—but the occasion must be furnished to them. Thus the system of trying out two full complements of brigade officers, plus the incentive of winning the honor of attaining the third group, serves a practical purpose. It was not devised for the mere purpose of passing around offices as rewards.

A prominent industrialist who was conspicuously successful in picking out and surrounding himself with able associates, was once asked the secret of his method of selection. To express in a phrase or two any formula for success is a banal and futile effort at best; in this instance, however, the reply was unique and significant. He answered:

"I think of myself as a soldier in a trench, making a desperate last-stand fight against great odds. Then I estimate the qualities of the man under consideration, and I ask myself if he is a man I'd like to have standing shoulder-to-shoulder with me in such a crisis. If I decide that he is, I take him on."

It is not only on the drill field, aboard the boats and in the section rooms that the midshipmen are under surveillance. They are being watched by appraising eyes and listened to with appraising ears while they are both on duty and off duty in Bancroft Hall. For Bancroft Hall is organized and conducted as closely as practicable in conformity with a ship. The watches, in fact, are conducted exactly as aboard ship.

The highest authority on duty at Bancroft Hall is the Officer of the Watch.

The Officer of the Watch is a regular Navy commissioned officer; he acts for the Superintendent and for the Commandant, just as the Officer of the Deck aboard acts for the ship's commanding officer. He is detailed for this duty, in rotation, from the commissioned battalion and company officers attached to the Executive Department, and he serves a twenty-four-hour tour. He is always the senior officer on duty; usually a lieutenant-commander or commander. His headquarters are located on the first deck near the main entrance of Bancroft Hall; it consists of an office and an adjoining bedroom-and-bath on one side and the Main Office of Bancroft Hall on the other side. When he leaves his headquarters he dons his belt and sword and his white gloves, which constitute his insignia of authority. His position corresponds to that of the Officer of the Day in the Army.

Serving with him at the same time is a junior commissioned officer of the Navy, usually of the rank of lieutenant, who is designated as the Assistant Officer of the Watch. He also is detailed by roster from the officers attached to the Executive Department. The number of commissioned officers on duty with the regiment, including the staff of the Commandant, those in charge of the six battalions and the twenty-four companies of midshipmen, provide for a tour of duty for every man, as Officer or Assistant Officer of the Watch, about once every ten days or so.

In Bancroft Hall, too, the midshipmen learn how to be watch officers by being watch officers.

There are two Midshipmen Officers of the Watch on duty in the Main Office. The senior of the two is a Three-, Four-, Five-, or Six-Striper from the battalion, regimental, or brigade staff levels. The junior is always a company commander. The senior is the midshipman officer of the watch, or MOOW, and the junior is the company midshipman officer of the watch, or CMOOW. Like their superiors, they wear their swords and white gloves as tokens of authority.

In the Main Office of Bancroft Hall the routine work of the brigade is conducted. From this point all of the signal gongs are sounded throughout the building and messages distributed; here, too, the visitors are received. In charge of it are two First classmen who rotate a two-section watch (0605 to 2300) as midshipman in charge of the Main Office (MCMO). There are also three Second classmen who rotate a three-section watch (around the clock) as assistant midshipman in charge of the Main Office (AMCMO). A few plebes are initiated into this work by being detailed as messengers.

It is at this Main Office that the midshipmen come into personal contact with visitors and get their primary lessons in courtesy, patience and diplomacy in dealing with the Great American Public.

"Is there a student here named Williams?" inquired an elderly lady.

"Do you know his initials?" was the reply. No, she did not. Neither did she know what battalion or company he was in, nor in what class. All she knew was that a friend of hers out West knew a perfectly splendid boy, who lived only a couple of blocks away from her, and that she had promised to look him up. Yes, she was sure she would recognize him if she saw him because she had seen his picture somewhere.

"We have six Williamses in the plebe class; do you know which one it is you want to see?"

No, she had entirely forgotten his first name, if she had ever known it. Couldn't she look over all of them? Anxious to oblige, the Main Office rounded up the entire six.

"Perhaps you can find the midshipman you are looking for among these," the host hopefully volunteered.

"Midshipman?" was the puzzled response. "That doesn't sound quite right. You don't happen to have any *cadets* here, have you?"

The organization of the watch extends into each of the six battalions. The battalion officer of the watch (BOOW) is the senior First classman on duty with his battalion, and is the representative of and is responsible to the Officer of the Watch. His headquarters are in the office of his battalion. He is assisted by an assistant battalion officer of the watch (ABOOW). The office is in charge of the first class midshipman in charge of the battalion office (MCBO) with the aid of a second-classman assistant (AMCBO).

On each deck there is a Third classman detailed as "mate of the deck," and on some occasions a plebe detailed as "assistant mate of the deck." Right down the line the organization is modeled on the lines of the watch aboard ship. The lines of responsibility are all straight and tightly drawn, as is the way in the Navy and in the Army. Every man is directly responsible to his chief. There are no loose ends.

The BOOW and the ABOOW on these details wear their swords and their white gloves to distinguish them.

The responsibility for the command and administration of the brigade of midshipmen as a whole, with its vast multiplicity of detail and its ever new and shifting human problems, rests upon the shoulders of the Commandant. The regulations provide that he "shall be a line officer of the Navy qualified for command at sea. He shall command the Brigade of Midshipmen. He shall have the authority and function as the Commanding Officer of Bancroft Hall." He is, *ex officio*, the head of the Executive Department, that dreaded fountain-head of discipline and dispenser of rewards, which is charged with the responsibility of enforcing the rules and regulations as well as of directing drills. In its role of Nemesis it is held in much the same awe by the midshipmen as the Tactical Department at West Point is held by the cadets. It is in this office that daily conferences are held by the commissioned officers in charge of the six battalions, and where policies are decided upon, orders are promulgated, penalties are decreed, and promotions and awards are determined. No wonder that every midshipman who gets a summons to report to the Executive Officer just naturally marks it mentally as "Important" and "Rush."

In the German Navy there was reputed to be an adage that served as a guide in the selection and assignment of officers; it may be translated thus:

Divide the officers into two groups, the industrious and the lazy:

Then divide these two groups into two more groups—the savvy and the dumb:

Assign the industrious and the savvy to the General Staff:

Make the lazy and the savvy commanding officers:

Get rid of the industrious and dumb.

While this pungent formula may well be apocryphal, nevertheless it contains more than a grain of wisdom. It gives evidence, too, of the universal and continuous search for that invaluable quality of character and of mind that is separate and distinct from learning or culture or courage, and which in the United States Navy is summed up in that one word "aptitude." If in their search for midshipmen endowed with it, the Executive Department and the academic Departments between them are often faced with stern and unpleasant duties, it is because the Navy, following the procedure of old Mother Nature herself, must consider the interests of the breed as a whole rather than the interests of the individual.

Unexpected flashes of human interest sometimes illumine even the austerities of the Executive Department. An incident wholly without precedent occurred once in the mess hall. The midshipmen were standing at attention at the luncheon tables and gradually coming to that silence which is demanded before Six Striper commands them to sit down. Suddenly the air was rent by a small and comparatively obscure First classman—a "clean sleever" who had never been given any authority but whose soul was apparently bursting with a mad desire to exercise command just once before he graduated—who yelled:

"Seats!"

The entire mess hall was thrown into a riot of hilarity; the meal was almost over before order could be restored. The culprit was summoned before the Executive Officer who demanded an explanation of this extraordinary breach of discipline.

"I know it was a terrible thing to do, sir," the panic-stricken midshipman reported. "I don't know why I did it. I guess I must have been wanting to give that order for four years, and this time it just popped out."

The Executive Officer controlled his smile. Perhaps he knew that impulse himself; he had been a midshipman once, too. The penalty meted out was light; whatever it was, the crime was worth the cost. The midshipman had had his moment of glory.

*E*ating a square meal is
one more trial for the plebes
to live through.

M*arching in formation is a good*
thing to do on a fine day in the spring.

*P*lebe summer
watch squad inspection.

Chapter 8

The Iron
Hand of Discipline

By an ironic twist of fate, it was the hanging of a mutinous midshipman in 1842 that proved to be one of the factors which led to the establishment of the Naval School three years later. The incident was preceded and followed by a chain of circumstances symptomatic of the problems which confronted the naval service of the time and which are not wholly without significance today.

Philip Spencer, the scapegrace son of John C. Spencer, the Secretary of War in the cabinet of President Tyler, in order to avoid the jail penalties hanging over him as the result of his escapades, was forced upon the Navy through the political influence of his father. He was appointed acting midshipman and assigned to the training ship *North Carolina*. Resentful of the efforts of Lieutenant William Craney to discipline him, young Spencer turned to his paternal sponsor, with the result that Craney was so persecuted that he was eventually driven out of the service.

In the meantime, Spencer had been quickly shifted to the *Potomac* and thence in turn to the *John Adams*, where he was forced to resign "for disgraceful and scandalous conduct." Again the ominous figure of politics rushed to the rescue, and the now thoroughly discredited youth was again appointed acting midshipman and assigned to the *Somers*, a 126-ton brig, mounting 10 guns and carrying 120 officers and men. Under command of Alexander Slidell Mackenzie—father of the Mackenzie to whose gallant life and death a memorial in the Chapel pays tribute today—this small vessel had just been ordered to the African coast with dispatches for Commodore Matthew C. Perry's squadron. Mackenzie tried to have Spencer detached from his command, but political influence decided otherwise and Spencer went on the fateful cruise.

Upon the return trip to New York, a Mr. Ward, the purser's steward, got word to Mackenzie on the night of November 26 that Spencer had tried to induce him to join a mutiny; he claimed that twenty men had already pledged themselves to the enterprise. The sullen behavior of the crew for several days had caused anxiety to the officers; recent acts of insubordination, too, tended to give the semblance of truth to the report, and young Spencer was summoned to confront the captain. As a result of this interview, Spencer's sword was taken from him on the spot and he was handcuffed and placed in double irons; because the *Somers* had no brig in which to confine him, he was chained to a chest on the deck while his effects were being searched. In his razor box was found a list of names of the crew; against 32 of them had been written notations in Greek letters but in English words; four members of the crew were marked "certain," ten were marked "doubtful," and eighteen were marked "to be retained nolens volens." Boatswain's Mate Samuel Cromwell and Gunner's Mate Elisha Small were involved as ringleaders; both were immediately placed in irons.

For a day and a half the court of inquiry remained in session; when it ended, all of the crew were summoned to quarters. In full dress uniform, Captain Mackenzie commanded Spencer, Cromwell and Small to be brought before him. The verdict of the court was, he announced, that they were guilty of mutiny, that the penalty of mutiny was death by hanging, and that the penalty would be inflicted within ten minutes. During that brief period Spencer confessed that he had entertained similar mutinous ideas while serving on both the *Potomac* and the *John Adams*.

The national ensign was hoisted. To quote from the old records, "a brazier of hot coals was brought and then applied to the tube and priming of a long cannonade; on the report, the drums rolled; the command was given, the crew hauled lustily on the tails, and the three bodies, still manacled and with their heads enwrapped in pea-jackets, swung from the mainyard." Captain Mackenzie read the service for the dead. The ensign was half-masted and the church pennant was raised above it. In a rough sea and by lantern light, the three bodies were committed to the deep.

The news of the execution of Spencer exploded in Washington like a bomb, as was to be expected; the execution of his partners in crime, Cromwell and Small, neither of whom had political backing, was of slight consequence. The full power of the Secretary of War was hurled against Mackenzie; attacks that were as cunning as savage in their intensity were launched to wreck his career; among those enlisted in the campaign against him was the famous novelist, James Fenimore Cooper. This persecution did succeed in crippling its victim financially, but professionally Mackenzie was cleared by a board of inquiry which he demanded and obtained.

The Spencer affair had one important and far-reaching effect; it centered public attention upon the demoralizing practice of forcing into the Navy occasional unprincipled young rascals, without training, whose only qualification was political pull. In this way it helped to pave the way for the establishment of the Naval School, from which the United States Naval Academy of today has grown. The new Naval School raised a barrier against the intrusion of midshipmen who were unfitted for their duties; the standards of admission have been steadily rising since.

Still, in a military organization, good discipline is absolutely essential for efficiency, and erratic conduct cannot be tolerated. Hence the Naval Academy has drawn up a very explicit schedule of offenses which cannot be tolerated and a precise list of appropriate punishments to be meted out to the offenders. All offenses are classified in two categories: Class A and Class B. Class A offenses are the more serious ones, ranging from dishonorable acts, such as lying, to those breaches of discipline, such as unauthorized possession of an automobile, which the authorities wish to curtail and which, accordingly, are given heavy punishment. Forty-five such offenses are listed. It should be noted that not all Class A offenses necessarily imply moral turpitude. There are many fine officers in the Navy who received Class A's in midshipman days, took their punishment, and ultimately transcended their faults.

A midshipman who is "put on report" for Class A offenses

is furnished with a copy of the charges against him, and is required to submit a written statement in his defense, through his battalion officer, within twenty-four hours. If there are no extenuating circumstances, he may state that he will make no defense. Until the Commandant has investigated each case and the Superintendent has acted upon it, the delinquency is not entered upon the conduct report; while this routine is in progress, however, the midshipman is restricted to Academic Limits and is not permitted to attend athletic events or entertainments of any sort, or to visit officers' quarters. The extreme punishment for a "Class A" is dismissal from the Academy by the Secretary of the Navy upon recommendation of the Superintendent.

In the early days of the Naval Academy the ceremony of dismissal was public and dramatic. The midshipmen were drawn up in formation and the offender was called "front and center"; the Superintendent then read to him the official order. Immediately his insignia were stripped off the uniform which he had dishonored and an armed guard stepped forward to escort him off the reservation to the beat of drums; he was literally "drummed out of camp," never to return. Today the order of dismissal is merely issued and distributed in the customary routine; the offender receives his official copy and makes his exit.

Dismissal is the penalty of gross violations of the Naval Academy regulations. Midshipmen have been dismissed, for example, for violating the regulation against marrying, which is specifically prohibited. A few years ago a couple of midshipmen were dismissed for bringing two young women, partially disguised in midshipmen caps and jumpers, into the mess hall during the Sunday evening supper period; both offenders appealed to their Senators and Representatives, who instituted a Congressional Inquiry. The findings supported the action of the Naval Academy authorities.

"All midshipmen are on probation," a representative of the Navy Department asserted at the hearings. "They are here to demonstrate that they are good material. The burden is on them to show whether they are good material or not."

Class B offenses are those "of a less serious nature, involving comparatively minor infractions of discipline," and there are a host of these, ranging from "Authority, Unwarranted Assumption of" to "Tobacco, Unauthorized Use of." These are some of the things for which a midshipman may incur a penalty:

Studying in unauthorized place
Non reg ash tray
Meeting, unauthorized, calling or attending
Animals, introducing or having without authority
Button off
Wall, attempting to climb
Whistling or yelling at girls
Salute, failing to render
Absence, unauthorized
Conduct, unmilitary
Conduct, unseamanlike
Duty, improper performance or neglect of
Manners, poor, in mess hall
Orders, slow in carrying out
Room in disorder
Playing cards or games during study hour
Turning in after once having turned out.

Violators of the regulations are punished in seven ways (exclusive of dismissal): demerits, extra duty, restriction to quarters, restriction to academic limits, deprivation of leave, deprivation of privileges, and reduction in rank.

The number of demerits which the members of each class may incur before they are rated as unsatisfactory in conduct follows:

	Demerits
First classmen	150
Second classmen	200
Third classmen	250
Fourth classmen	300

A midshipman may be merely dropped—as distinguished from the more drastic dismissed—for deficiency in conduct, just as for deficiency in his studies. If he exceeds the maximum number of demerits allotted to the members of his class, out he goes, even though he commits no major offense. An accumulation of demerits for a series of minor offenses indicates a military weakness; failure to correct them reveals a character unsuitable for command.

More strict observance of the regulations is naturally demanded of Midshipman Gish each year as he ascends in the academic scale. By the time he becomes a First classman he is not only better informed and more experienced but he is also relieved of competition with his fellows who have proven less amenable to discipline and have been weeded out. Extra Duty consists of marching, under arms unless the weather is inclement, and is assigned by the hour. First classmen do not serve extra duty except by restriction.

For a relatively trivial offense, say "Laundry Bag, correct room number not marked on," the punishment will be "five and one," that is, five demerits and one hour of extra duty. For more serious matters, say "Drill, deliberately skipping," the cost will be thirty demerits and seven days restriction to quarters.

Who reports the midshipmen for their delinquencies?

The midshipmen are put on report by all officers, by civilian instructors, and by midshipmen themselves, for offenses that come under their observation. The delinquency reports are forwarded to the battalion office of the midshipman who is reported, and here it is logged. The delinquent initials the report and indicates, in the space provided, whether or not he wants to make a statement in explanation. Reports, statements, if any, and battalion office demerit record cards are then sent to the appropriate company officer by 0815 the next day for further investigation and consideration. The company officer indicates on the reports his recommendation of demerits and punishment and forwards them to the battalion officer, who does the same, and forwards the reports to the Conduct Clerk. The Conduct Clerk makes up the Daily Report of Conduct for each battalion and conveys each one by 1200 on the same day to the proper battalion officer, who checks, signs and returns them. After approval by the Commandant, the Daily Reports of Conduct are posted for a day and the punishments go into effect.

Numerous stories exist—who can say whether true or apocryphal?—of the plight of midshipmen involved in the conduct system.

In one instance a harassed lad who had got his dates mixed and was confronted with the insurmountable problem of playing the host at the same hop to two young ladies, each unknown to the other, saw no escape except to the sick bay. Fortifying himself with a long soak in a scalding bath and quantities of hot water taken internally, he staggered to the medical officers with complaints of fever and of violent pains in his stomach; he was instantly prepared for an emergency operation for acute appendicitis and escaped only by frantically protesting his hoax. A more circumspect midshipman, determined that his simulated ailment should conform to the most approved scientific formula, obtained from a dubious doctor back home a complete set of symptoms that he had reason to believe would succeed in having him placed under observation. His case was gravely considered by the medical officer who finally announced his diagnosis:

"Well, Mr. Gish, if all the symptoms you describe are correct, you are pregnant."

But there is a sympathetic understanding on the part of the medical officers, too, of the nerve-racking anxiety that besets a low-standing midshipman just before an examination period, and of his genuine need of a chance to concentrate upon his studies without molestation. Even if the records do not show it, there has very likely been more than one instance of a perturbed midshipman whose career in the Navy hung in the balance, and who has succeeded in having himself placed under observation for a day or two upon a frank statement of his situation.

The most common delinquency is being late for formation. Next in frequency are "military offenses," such as talking in ranks, failing to keep step, and turning the head in ranks, for example. "Improper performance" of such routine details as making out report forms and passing the proper word to sections concerning the equipment (such as slide rules, for instance) needed for the coming recitation period also rank high on the list. Carelessness in arranging articles in the room in accordance with the prescribed formula entails many minor penalties. Sometimes these little slips are enlivened with an element of humor. An instance is recorded of an inspecting officer who found a jew's-harp under the bed of a midshipman; in his explanatory statement, submitted in an effort to have the demerits removed, the delinquent invited attention to the order that specified that "under the bed" was the prescribed place for keeping musical instruments in the room.

A midshipman whose footwear was strung out improperly was duly admonished in the military vernacular: "Mr. Bumbletub (if that was his name), you should place your shoes in platoon front, not in column of squads."

The annals of the Naval Academy are filled with instances when fate has cast the duty officers in roles of veritable Sherlock Holmeses and filled their victims with consternation. One adventurer who had "Frenched out" in the usual civilian garb one night and who was thumbing his way back to town was picked up by an obliging officer who was also in mufti; only the fact that the victim was wearing the regulation midshipman shoe, which of course the motorist identified, led to his delivery to the watch officer.

Under the classification of "frivolous statement" is included the classic retort of the midshipman whose boat had finally rammed the sea wall, after a series of mishaps that stirred the instructor to ask satirically:

"Can you do *any*thing right, Mr. Doodad?"

"Well," was the considered reply of the unfortunate Mr. Doodad, "I can play lacrosse pretty well and I can certainly sock a golf ball."

Just for that he got 15 demerits.

In the category of "improper language" comes the use of slang terms and nicknames in recitation papers and reports; Midshipman Gish may call the academic course in English "Bull" if he likes, and he may refer to his roommate as "wife," but he must be careful that none of these expressions creep into his official papers or official conversation.

Carelessness in contracting indebtedness is frowned upon. "Grad debts," as those debts which become payable after graduation are called, have burdened the career of many a young officer, who likely as not purchased a watch, a vanity case or a miniature class ring on the spur of the moment to win the fleeting favor of a young woman guest; more than one young officer has had to trim his financial sails in order to pay off the monthly installments due on an impulsive gift to a young woman who in the meanwhile had become another man's wife.

The *United States Naval Academy Regulations* emphatically state that *"The importance of avoiding indebtedness cannot be over-stated. . . .* Continued yielding to material wants before they can be afforded weakens the will and character. Indebtedness is known to have adverse effect on an officer's performance because of the added mental burden it imposes on him. In the naval service, the payment of just obligations is considered a point of honor; failure to satisfy one's just debts is reasonable cause for court martial."

This ruling found its inception in the old custom of some business concerns—and particularly of the tradesmen on the block of Maryland Avenue known as "Robbers' Row," near the Main Entrance—to extend credit to midshipmen, lend them money and in other ways place them under obligation, on the assurance that the money will be paid after they have left the Naval Academy. The relations between the Naval Academy authorities and the tradesmen on "Robbers' Row" have not always been on as amicable a basis as they are today.

The *Reina Mercedes* once played an important part in the disciplinary life of the regiment as a place of confinement. Known jocularly as "the fastest ship in the Navy" because it has been tied fast to its dock for over a quarter of a century, it served as the living quarters for many of the enlisted men at the station. Special quarters were provided on it for the exclusive use of its midshipmen guests. Those who had served terms aboard were duly recorded in the year book, *The Lucky Bag*, and were awarded the "black N"—as distinguished from the gold N's awarded to members of the athletic teams.

Once in 1897 the entire plebe class was confined on the ship *Santee*, which preceded both the *Hartford* and the *Reina Mercedes* as station ships, because no member would reveal the identity of the culprits who had fired explosives, contrary to regulations, on the night of July 5. The tension of that momentous mass punishment was relieved on July 12 when the names of the two offenders were posted and their classmates were relieved from durance vile.

As each new arrival reported for duty aboard the *Reina Mercedes*, he was presented with a copy of "Ship Squad Orders." This told him just exactly what he might and might not do and when he might and might not do it, the hours he must observe, where he should eat, where he should sleep, what equipment he would require, what visitors he might and might not receive (this rule was readily memorized, as he was permitted to see no guests except his parents), what uniforms he should wear and when, and what entertainments he might not enjoy. The only entertainment furnished aboard and consequently the only one he might not enjoy was the nightly movie show. Even the adventuresome midshipman who had somehow wormed his way into the projection booth to "help the film operator" was deprived of the fruit of his labor when the Captain poked his head into the window of the booth to make a casual inquiry of the operator and was confronted with the startled visage of one of his prisoners.

Except for the loss of recreation hours, life aboard the *Reina Mercedes* had its compensations. The two compartments reserved for midshipmen were comfortable. A section of the main deck was curtained off for their exclusive use; here they set up their cots at night and their mess tables at meal times. The food was the same as that served to the enlisted men aboard; even if the chinaware was a bit thicker and heavier and some of the more dainty garnishes to the food might be missing, the fare was substantial and wholesome. Instances were not lacking, too, in which the menu had been augmented by such choice viands as crabs, caught on lines dropped from porthole windows and boiled in water obtained from the washroom.

The heaviest cross that the prisoners had to bear was to be deprived of attendance at important athletic contests. One ingenious midshipman overcame even this obstacle by rigging up a radio receiving set of sorts from parts surreptitiously furnished by various obliging friends, and listening in on a broadcast of an Army-Navy game.

And, of course, the *Reina Mercedes*, as well as the current confinement to quarters, always was available as a refuge and sanctuary. The number of delinquents who have intentionally, and with full foreknowledge of the consequences, committed a midshipman sin in order to assure an unescapable alibi for sidestepping an entangling social engagement, being a strictly personal and confidential matter, will never be known.

Chapter 9

Athletic
Training and Activities

The career of a midshipman at Annapolis starts out in much the same manner as that of a movie starlet at Hollywood; they are both disrobed and photographed. Aside from this single circumstance, however, the Hollywood and Annapolis careers show no particularly striking points of similarity.

It is with no intent to build up the midshipmen into glamour boys and reveal them in their more alluring moods that they are brought before the camera; on the contrary, they are photographed for the purpose of revealing and recording physical peculiarities and imperfections for the consideration of the officers who are responsible for the physical development of the brigade.

Within a few days after the arrival of Fourth classman Gish, he is ordered to the gymnasium, where he is neatly but not gaudily costumed in a breech-clout and photographed against a graphic wall chart, divided horizontally and vertically into lines one inch apart. To avoid any possibility of error in identification, his name is spelled out in block letters and inserted in a groove on top of the chart; blank spaces are reserved at the bottom on which are recorded his exact age, his weight and his height. He is photographed from the front, back and side, on a sort of glorified Bertillon system scale. These pictures are called "posture photographs," and they mark the beginning of Midshipman Gish's critical study of his physical idiosyncrasies and his carriage, and they intimate what he must do about it.

One set of these posture photographs goes to the officers; another set goes to Midshipman Gish himself, to be pasted up inside his locker door in his room, whereby he may constantly be reminded of the necessity for habitually standing straight and tall and eliminating the defects noted by his instructor. Is his left shoulder a bit lower than his right? Has he a sway back? Is he inclined to hold his head a bit forward? If so, Midshipman Gish is due for a bit of corrective exercise. This subject of posture gets much emphasis during plebe summer.

He is informed of the major objectives of the Physical Education Department:

"1. A maximum development of strength, endurance, agility, and the basic physical skills.

2. Proficiency in aquatics and confidence in meeting emergency situations in the water.

3. A keen interest and sufficient skill in carry-over sports to the end that he will maintain the proper level of physical fitness after graduation.

4. Confidence and ability in defending himself against personal attack.

5. An introduction to the principles and methods employed in organizing, supervising and conducting athletic and physical education programs.

6. Opportunities to develop those qualities of moral and physical courage, group loyalty, fair play, leadership ability, and quick thinking while participating under pressure in highly competitive situations."

While all this is going on, the plebes are being given physical achievement tests, basic instruction in swimming, boxing and wrestling, and orientation in five additional sports. The list includes baseball, basketball, swimming, wrestling, squash, boxing, lacrosse, soccer, tennis, track athletics, and of course rowing. It is during this period that the instructors begin to get a line on the athletic proficiencies of the new class, and make note of the men who appear to be heading for the plebe battalion and varsity squads. Participation in intramural competitive sports is obligatory. Aside from the fun of competitive sport, rewards are offered in the form of individual, company, and battalion prizes ranging from cups to extra liberty. With the beginning of the Second World War a comprehensive system of intramural sports was sponsored and promoted that became known as the Sports Program. This was designed to reach all midshipmen at the Academy who were not engaged in other athletic activities. This has been copied widely by civilian institutions all over the country. This Sports Program has awakened a liking for athletic sports in many a youth who never took the slightest interest in such matters in prep or high school.

It is not the purpose of the courses in physical education to fit men for special forms of athletics at the expense of their general, all-round proficiency. All midshipmen are required to participate in obstacle tests requiring the use of many muscle groups in various combinations. Their performance in these obstacle tests has become the standard measurement in agility.

The table below gives some idea of what is required of Midshipman Gish:

NAVAL ACADEMY AGILITY TESTS

(Full Obstacle Course—19 Obstacles)

| Class | Must be completed in | |
	Minutes	Seconds
Fourth.....................	3	35
Third......................	3	30
Second.....................	3	20
First......................	3	5

By the time Midshipman Gish becomes a Youngster, with the benefits of a year of physical education to his credit, a bit more is expected of him. The games in which he participates have become progressively faster and the obstacles have become progressively more difficult. But with the development of his muscles and his ability to coordinate his movements he is usually able to excel in these games.

The games in which Midshipman Gish must participate during his Second class year present no serious problem to the average young man. By this time he should have a well-coordinated, well-developed muscular system.

What happens if Midshipman Gish fails to measure up to all these requirements? He is assigned to one of a variety of special groups for training and exercise in addition to his regular drills, and sweats it out until he has acquired the strength and agility to pass the test in which he has been found deficient. If he cannot swim well, he is put in the group which goes by the ominous name of the Sub Squad, Sub being short for submarine, which vessel the poor swimmer tends to imitate by submerging instead of propelling himself on the surface. If he doesn't "stand tall" and doesn't habitually carry himself erect, he is referred to the Posture Squad. If he is not in prime physical shape, he becomes a member of the Conditioning Squad. There is even an Awkward Squad for those who just don't get this infantry drill stuff too well. The seriousness with which physical shortcomings are viewed is indicated by the fact that passing all of the required tests as they come along is a prerequisite to leave and even to graduation. Furthermore the special squads practice after hours in the afternoon when the others are normally enjoying their recreation. The prospect of these deprivations proves a powerful stimulant to effort; few delinquents ever fail to make the grade when confronted with these penalties.

During the regular academic year, those who stand in the bottom 5% of their class on the basis of the marks given by the instructors in the various drills are assigned to the Weak Squad, where they are brought up to snuff in agility, applied strength, boxing, wrestling and gymnastics.

Every midshipman is taught to swim. Some, of course, already know how, but all of these do not know how to swim correctly and in accordance with the prescribed fundamentals. They must unlearn their technique and start all over again.

There are two large swimming pools at the Naval Academy. One is the Instruction Pool, which is 90 feet by 60 feet, with a graduated depth ranging from 4'3" to 5'9". It is kept disinfected with chlorine; when midshipmen complain that it stings their eyes, they are reminded that chlorine is not only a tonic for the eyes, but also kills the germs of colds. It is here that the plebe receives his official introduction to the art of natation. Around the walls of the gallery of this pool, incidentally, is the Naval Academy athletic Hall of Fame, or All-American Gallery, row after row of pictures of Academy athletes who have won championships or All-American recognition.

Beginning with talks given by the instructor to small groups, the plebes are put through the more simple paces. Before Midshipman Gish is released from these duties he must be able to swim 100 yards without stopping; in addition he must demonstrate his capacity to swim 20 yards in each of the standard kinds of strokes—the crawl, the backstroke and the left-side or right-side strokes. About 15 per cent of the men of the entering class are able to qualify upon entrance; these thereafter assist in teaching their less proficient classmates. About 70 per cent are classified as mediocre swimmers; it is from this group that the faulty methods must be eliminated. The remaining 15 per cent are non-swimmers, and must start to learn from scratch.

During Youngster year the midshipmen must swim 160 yards in four minutes, comprising 40 yards in each of breast, back, side and crawl strokes.

The test for the Second classmen includes swimming forty laps in the pool at a point a lap; that is, if he can swim forty laps, his grade is the maximum 4.0. He can just make it with 25 laps, since the lowest passing grade in the Academy's marking system is 2.5. There is also instruction in life-saving: how to tow a man in the water, how to break the strangle holds, and how to resuscitate an unconscious victim. About 18% of the class qualify as Red Cross Senior Life Savers, and about 5% as Instructor-Examiners in life-saving. Diving does not constitute a compulsory part of the course, but every man is taught how to "get over the side into the water" from a height of 25 feet—a contingency which every officer is likely to face. And he must swim for 20 yards under water after he jumps, without coming to the surface. Drill in swimming concludes with Second class year.

The large pool, used only for qualification and competition purposes, and for the use of experienced swimmers, occupies a special building of its own, the Natatorium; it is connected by a passageway with the gymnasium, Macdonough Hall, where the Instruction Pool is located. The tank in the Natatorium is one of the largest and finest in the country; its length is 150 feet, its width 60 feet, and it is 10 feet deep throughout. The water is obtained from artesian wells, and is chlorinated. The building contains 1200 seats for visitors, and of course is equipped with the most approved types of adjustable diving boards. Large, permanent score boards contain the Naval Academy record of each swimming event, as compared with the intercollegiate and national records. The pool is dedicated as the Norman Scott

Natatorium, in honor of Rear Admiral Norman Scott of the class of 1911, who was instrumental in introducing swimming as a sport at the Naval Academy. He was awarded the Congressional Medal of Honor for heroism at the battle off Savo Island, 12–13 November 1942.

Sailormen who live cooped up at close quarters with each other over periods of weeks at a time just naturally get on each other's nerves now and then. In the good old days of iron men and wooden ships, when Sailor Biff got fed up with the looks of Sailor Stiff, he would proceed to alter the objectionable countenance in that direct and primitive manner which is the inheritance of the brute male. To clarify the atmosphere aboard and to systematize the brawls that enlivened the long cruises, bouts were staged at intervals, to such vast delight of all concerned that they came to be known as "happy hours"; and that term has come down to the present day. Our Navy, like all the other navies of the world, schedules boxing matches aboard ship as a matter of routine; they are a stimulant to athletic training as well as an important feature of the recreational programs. These bouts are conducted under the prescribed rules and are directed by the officers of the ships. Consequently some knowledge of the noble art of self-defense has become a part of the equipment of a naval officer.

Experience with the gloves comes to the plebe immediately upon his arrival at the Naval Academy and continues during the entire first summer. It starts with mass instruction to groups of a hundred or more at a time and develops into individual practice bouts under the supervision of the gymnasium instructors, of experienced officers, and occasionally of upper classmen. This instruction extends over the first three years; the midshipman is relieved of further duties in the ring only after he has satisfied the instructors that he has learned the basic principles of boxing. The more capable boxers voluntarily continue their training during their liberty hours and compete for the plebe class championships, which are decided at a gala tournament late in August. From these boxers come the Naval Academy champions.

Intercollegiate boxing was discontinued in April 1941. Prior to that date an intercollegiate boxing meet in Macdonough Hall

*T*rack and intercollegiate boxing
are but two of the sports in which
midshipmen participate.

*W*orking out in the gym is part of a midshipman's regular routine for keeping the body fit.

was a combination athletic and social event. Full dress was *de rigeur*, and the affair was conducted with all of the polite formality that distinguishes boxing exhibitions held in the more exclusive sporting clubs of England. One of the practical reasons for demanding full dress was the necessity of cutting down on the demand for tickets; the attendance was limited to the more ardent fans who not only owned evening clothes but were willing to go to the bother of putting them on. The matches were held before the evening hops began on Saturday evenings— which explained why so many "drags" in evening wraps and walking shoes carried packages containing their dancing slippers, for use later.

The ring in which the bouts were conducted was the one used when Gene Tunney won the world's heavyweight championship from Jack Dempsey; the Naval Academy bought it for $700. (Or so Coach Spike Webb said!)

There are three boxing rooms, one of which contains two standard-sized rings. These rooms are used for training purposes by midshipmen during their liberty hours as well as for instruction. Boxing is still very much alive at the Academy, and the Brigade boxing championship bouts in February of each year form a big and well-attended event. The plebes always do well in this—the heavyweight champion of a few years ago was a plebe.

It is not entirely by accident that the room devoted to boxing opens directly into "Misery Hall," the apt name given to the first-aid station where injuries from splinters in the finger and black eyes upward are treated. This department is equipped with rubbing-down tables, couches, steam tubs for treating strains and bruises, and medical supplies. Here 95,000 treatments a year are given; most of them, however, are merely protective dressings given to athletes.

Up to 1909 the Naval Academy boasted but one wrestling champion. He won his honors by defeating all midshipmen claimants. While this system of determining the Number One man was simple and conclusive, it tended to discourage the smaller chaps; consequently eight classes of wrestlers were established on the basis of weight. Today a champion of each division is crowned every year.

The plebe is given three lessons in wrestling during his first summer, and nine more during his first academic year. He is taught the rules and rudimentary holds, as well as the prescribed methods of breaking those holds when his opponent applies them to him. He is shown the dangerous bone-breaking holds which are forbidden. These twelve lessons constitute the required course, but a call for volunteers for the plebe wrestling team (and later for the battalion and varsity teams) always brings forth plenty of material. Battalion teams that win championships get personal awards in the form of insignia. Members of the varsity teams who participate in three-quarters of the intercollegiate meets are given the major N.

The annual champion of each division is awarded the honor of having his name emblazoned on a permanent tablet, and the captains of every team are memorialized by framed photographs that adorn the walls.

So proficient has the wrestling instruction been that the Naval Academy has had a representative on most recent United States Olympic teams—with the notable exception of the team that was sent to the games in Nazi Germany. Coach Ray Swartz, of the Naval Academy, was coach of the United States Olympic Wrestling Team in 1952.

Under the arched roof at the north end of Macdonough Hall is the Fencing Armory; this too is hung with tablets bearing the names of all past Naval Academy champions in each of the three weapons used in intercollegiate contests, the foil, the épée and the saber; several of the Academy champions went on to become national champions as well. Gold, silver and bronze medals are awarded every spring to the midshipmen who excel with each of the three weapons; they are provided from funds bequeathed by the late Col. Robert M. Thompson, of the class of 1868; members of the plebe and varsity teams are awarded insignia in addition. One of the notable characteristics of the fencers is their high academic standing.

"We never lose a member of the fencing team because he is bilged for going 'unsat' in his studies," the fencing instructor reports. "That is one handicap we don't have to worry about."

The main gymnasium floor of Macdonough Hall, where general instruction in setting-up exercises and gymnastics is given, measures 100 feet wide and 200 feet long; it is completely equipped, of course, with all the needed apparatus. It is here that the sports program and intercollegiate competitions are held in gymnastics and wrestling.

The intercollegiate basketball games draw such large numbers of spectators as to demand the larger space available in the new field house, completed in 1957. Incidentally, all sports at the Naval Academy are major sports. Varsity sports letter winners are awarded "N" sweaters; three awards rate a blue and gold "N" blanket; "N" men also receive a silver or gold medal.

With the coming of spring, the members of the baseball squad emerge and begin their outdoor practice. Intercollegiate contests are held at Lawrence Field, just across the creek from the parade ground—Worden Field—and opposite the long, stucco building, Halligan Hall. The uncovered grandstand seats 7670 people.

With the approach of spring, candidates for the various racing crews congregate at Hubbard Hall, the boat house, which is located across the creek, directly south of Lawrence Field. The Naval Academy began competing with outside crews back in 1870; since then its crews have traveled a long way; in 1920, at the Olympic games in Berlin, the Navy boat not only won first place but set the world's record for the 2000-meter distance. The walls of Hubbard Hall, built in 1927, are hung with many trophies as well as shields that bear the names of former crew heroes; among its other features are the rowing tanks where the crew candidates do their training, a shop where the shells are repaired and refitted, and the beautiful "N" Room, where the annual dance is given in honor of the athletes who have won their coveted letter in the fields of sport. Navy crews frequently competed in the Poughkeepsie and Henley regattas; in 1938 the Navy crew not only won the varsity eight-oared race at Poughkeepsie but broke the course record.

Again in 1952, the Navy crew was Olympic Champion. From 1952 to 1955 Navy varsity crews won 31 consecutive races, a record-breaking performance.

Navy football has also received nationwide recognition in recent years. Invited to the Sugar Bowl classic on New Year's

Day, 1955, Navy soundly trounced Mississippi, 21–0. Navy's mighty mites, the 150-pound football team, have compiled a fabulous record, the best sports record of any team at the Academy. Organized in the fall of 1946, the team, through 1953, won 35 games, tied one, and lost only one. They were Eastern Intercollegiate Champions in all but one of those eight years.

Since the Naval Academy is located in the heart of the "Lacrosse Belt," it is appropriate that it should excel in this rugged but exciting sport, along with its neighborhood rivals, Johns Hopkins and the University of Maryland, and its arch rival Army. The Naval Academy lacrosse team was crowned Class A Champions in 1962, an award tantamount to recognition as national champions, after a collegiately undefeated season. Hardly a season goes by without at least one Navy player among the All-American selections, and the loss of a single game is a phenomenon hardly to be believed.

To be eligible for any Navy team, the candidate must be satisfactory in each subject of his academic work, in his aptitude marks and in conduct. If he is behind in his studies, or if he has exceeded the speed limit in the matter of demerits, he is out of luck. In addition, he must conform to the intercollegiate eligibility rule, which limits him to a total of three years of intercollegiate competition. This restriction bars many a famous athlete who comes to the Naval Academy from another institution.

The Naval Academy Intra-Brigade Sports Program was established as that part of the competition for the Color Company under the supervision of the Department of Physical Education. It has for its special mission the athletic training of every midshipman in the brigade. It not only teaches Midshipman Gish the skills required by the various sports but also gives him recreation and teaches him to work with others and to become an integral part of an organization with a specific goal to attain. Such training is of special value to a future officer of Uncle Sam's Navy. One of the great advantages of the program is that a beginner in athletics has no difficulty in finding an opportunity for practice and competition. This is because the range of competition is so wide that the "expert athletes" are distributed to a thinness that does not embarrass the beginner. The program attempts to reach every midshipman not engaged in intercollegiate athletics, and in general all midshipmen must participate in one sport in each of the three sports seasons.

The sponsors of the program believed that it should provide not only for healthful recreation and physical development but should help to develop those physical and mental traits which are essential to Joe Gish's naval career. The program should assist in giving him courage, determination, self-assurance, and the will to win.

During his junior years in the Navy an officer is very closely associated with his men and must take part in the organization and administration of their athletics. His success in other phases of his profession may depend on his ability as a leader of athletics among the enlisted men. In order to prepare a midshipman for his duties in the Fleet, the program aims to give him the greatest possible experience in organizing and coaching athletic teams and in officiating in contests held under the program. During the academic year 1944–1945 members of the First class organized and coached 384 different teams and officiated at the 2094 contests which made up the sports program competition for that year.

Sixty-five per cent of the entire midshipman body that year participated on an average of 3.7 hours each week through the entire year.

The activities of the program are carried on through the three seasons of the athletic year. Competitions are held in 21 different sports, giving Joe Gish the widest possible choice for his athletic proclivities. Here is the intramural sports program by seasons:

FALL

Battalion

Basketball	Handball
Boxing	Swimming
Crew	Tennis
Fencing	Wrestling
Football	

Company

Cross Country   Volleyball
Soccer

WINTER
Battalion

Handball   Squash

Company

Basketball   Touch Football (150-pound)
Cross Country   Touch Football (Unlimited)
Fieldball

SPRING
Battalion

Badminton   Tennis
Gymnastics   Track
Lacrosse   Water Polo
Soccer

Company

Softball   Volleyball
Squash

Midshipmen who have been awarded varsity or plebe insignia on any team automatically contribute points to their battalion and company in that sport.

Foremost among the personal awards to athletes ranks the Naval Academy Athletic Association Prize, a sword presented annually during the June Week Presentation of Athletic Prizes "to the midshipman who has personally excelled in athletics during his years of varsity competition."

Whoever wins this coveted prize is immortalized in bronze when his name is added to the large tablet (hanging at the right of the main entrance to the Field House) which keeps the record of the fame of Navy athletic heroes since 1893. On the wall nearby hangs its companion memorial, which similarly immortalizes the winners of the Thompson Trophy Cup presented November 6, 1895, to the Navy Athletic Association by Col. Robert M. Thompson, class of 1868, as a trophy "on which to inscribe each year the name of the midshipman declared by its Athletic Committee to have done the most during the year preceding for the promotion of athletics at the Naval Academy." A miniature of the original Thompson cup is presented to each winner—also at a June Week ceremony.

A check-up on the naval records of the winners of these two athletic awards has revealed that a strikingly large percentage have won distinction through feats of experiment and daring, particularly while serving in aviation and submarine duties.

The Trophy Room, located on the ground floor of the gymnasium, is open to visitors from 9 o'clock in the morning until 5 o'clock in the evening. Its main entrance at the north end of Macdonough Hall is marked by a 24-pound gun captured from the British flagship *Confiance* at the battle of Lake Champlain, September 11, 1814, by Commodore Thomas Macdonough, in honor of whom the gymnasium is named. The dent in the muzzle of the gun has an interesting origin; it was made by a shot fired from one of the American vessels. The shot caused such a violent recoil as to kill the British Commander, George Downie, who happened to be standing near.

Immediately at the right of the main entrance hangs a small portrait of Commodore Thomas Macdonough, together with a brass tablet that summarizes his career; it is a duplicate of the brass tablet on *Destroyer No. 331*, which bears his name.

Thomas Macdonough was born in Delaware in 1783, became a midshipman at the age of sixteen, and served under Preble and Decatur in the War with Tripoli, participating in the daring adventure of the burning of the frigate *Philadelphia*. In the War of 1812, while in command of an American flotilla of 14 vessels, with 86 guns and about 850 men, near Plattsburg on Lake Champlain, he met and destroyed the British flotilla of 16 vessels, with 95 guns and about 1000 men, on September 11, 1814; it was a victory so unexpected, so timely, and so decisive as to cause the abandonment of the British plans to invade New York, and it turned a desperate defensive campaign into a triumph. Macdonough died at sea in 1825.

"Down to the time of our Civil War, Macdonough is the greatest figure in our naval history," is the estimate placed upon him by Theodore Roosevelt in his book *The War of 1812*.

The place of honor in the Trophy Room, directly in the center, is occupied by a large, glass-covered display case in which is preserved what must rank as the largest and most ponderous granddaddy of all record books; it is the *Athletic*

Year Book of the United States Naval Academy, better known as "The Athletic Bible." It is open at the page, several feet square, containing the typewritten record of all athletic awards made to all midshipmen of all classes during the past year. If Junior's name appears on this record, his athletic honors are official and will be secure for all time. It is the Naval Academy's scroll of athletic fame.

"Three-to-Nothing Jack Dalton," the goat who rose to glory as the mascot of the Navy football team that defeated Army on November 26, 1910, by the score of 3 to 0, now prances eternally as a museum piece in a glass case now in the Field House. High hopes had been pinned upon him to repeat his illustrious performance for the game the following year, but, alas! his little body was found dead only a few days before the event. Fearful lest the news of the tragedy might be taken as an ill omen, the keepers surreptitiously replaced the late lamented with a brother that looked much like him. The deception fooled the regiment and apparently fooled the old war god Tecumseh too, because the substitute mascot repeated exactly his predecessor's feat, and again Navy won, on the same field and by the same play and by the same score. To believers in the jinx, omens and hoodoos, this must prove something or other, no doubt.

The wall cabinets that contain the spoils of conquest in the form of the footballs, baseballs, basket balls, soccer balls and boxing gloves actually used in intercollegiate contests, with the scores inscribed upon them, are perennial objects of interest to visitors, especially the balls used in the games with Army, which are regarded as the most valued of all athletic treasures and are appropriately painted in gold. Track victories are recorded on discuses.

Over there are tablets on which are emblazoned the names of the members of the Navy teams that were acclaimed as "national football champions" in 1926. In cabinets are exhibited a large array of big and little cups, statuettes and other trophies accumulated by individual midshipmen and by teams over a long period of years.

That banner high up on the wall honors Navy's "Intercollegiate Gymnastic Champions" consecutively in the six years from 1920 to 1925 inclusive. In the frame under the stairway is a specimen of every type of athletic insignia awarded to midshipmen—letters, numerals and monograms. And painted in Navy blue and gold upon the east wall is the permanent record of all intercollegiate championships and of all the games played with Army since the Army-Navy competitions were established back in 1890; every competition won by Navy is embellished with a star—the same star that is added to the insignia awarded to individuals who have played on teams victorious over Army or who have been members of Navy teams that have won intercollegiate meets and have "actually engaged and defeated Army entries." That N★ is the most cherished of all the insignia awarded to Naval Academy athletes; it is the emblem not only of victory, but particularly and specifically of victory over the Military Academy—the ultimate goal of every Navy athlete.

The largest and most striking exhibit in Macdonough Hall is not a trophy at all; it is the ship model mounted against the south wall of the gymnasium. It has an over-all length of 51 feet, and is believed to be the biggest, the most exact and the most expensive model in the country; Macdonough Hall, indeed, had to be built up around it. While the building was still a boat shed and used for instruction in seamanship, this model was used because its rigging was just about perfect. It is a scale model of the *Antietam*, a full-rigged, double-decked steam sloop of war, mounting 24 guns.

Among the athletic notables whose pictures have hung in Macdonough Hall are Midshipman Vaulx Carter, who organized the very first Navy football team in 1882 and is hence honored as "the father of Naval Academy football," and Midshipman Joseph M. Reeves (later admiral and commander-in-chief of the U. S. Fleet), class of 1894, who invented a very important piece of football equipment. Young Reeves once injured his ear so badly that he was forbidden to play, but he overcame his handicap by devising the headgear that proved to be the forerunner of the helmets used today. (Among other contributions made by the Naval Academy to football might also be mentioned the laced canvas jackets, made out of sail cloth originally, which were the prototype of modern body protection gear.)

The Reception Committee plays a most important part in spreading good will toward the Academy to civilian institutions all over the country and incidentally to the folks back home. Visiting teams are met at the No. 1 Gate by the Midshipman Officer of the Watch or the Company Midshipman Officer of the Watch. The MOOW or CMOOW escorts the visitors to the Visiting Team Dormitory and turns them over to a member of the midshipman Reception Committee. When the team is comfortably settled and has found its bearings, the midshipman watch officer escorts the coach, manager, or whoever is in charge to the commissioned Officer of the Watch for an official welcome to the Academy. The member of the Reception Committee in charge of the team takes over from there. He gives each team member an identification card and button which enable him to get about in Bancroft Hall and in the Yard as a privileged guest. He assigns the athletes their room and bunks, and sees that they are supplied with soap, towels, blankets, and all the other paraphernalia of hospitality during their stay. He informs them of the meal schedule and is their host in the mess hall. He is responsible for getting the team to the scene of the athletic event on time. So gracious is the Academy's sense of social responsibility that a watch is posted in the visitors' dormitory to care for their wants.

The officers in the Executive Department are particularly anxious that each athletic visitor should be treated with the utmost courtesy and consideration. They exhort the midshipmen on the Reception Committee to keep ever in mind that all visiting teams are guests of the Academy and that the committeemen are their hosts. Every committeeman is told that, if possible, he should be on hand when the visiting team to which he has been assigned arrives or departs, he should eat his meals with the team, and see them as often as possible during their stay. For the young athlete coming from some small, inland college his first entrance into the huge mess hall with his young midshipman host is something always to be remembered.

The Reception Committee and their recruits have an important function to perform and they do it gracefully and tactfully. A visiting athlete after his brief sojourn at the Academy, whether his team wins, loses or draws, takes back to his college pleasant memories of his visit and becomes a good will ambassador for the Academy through the thoughtfulness and courtesy of the Reception Committee.

Chapter 10

The Navy Goat
Meets the Army Mule

Three times a year the old Indian chief Tecumseh dons his war paint in preparation for battle with his traditional foe, the Army; before the Army football game, before the weekend in which Navy meets Army in winter sports, and before the weekend in which Navy meets Army in spring sports.

Every November, shortly before the Army-Navy football classic that marks the climax of the athletic season, the bronze figurehead of the scowling old warrior blooms forth in gaudy colors, after the custom of his race. This supercolossal facial betokens the fact that his tribe of midshipmen are about to take the warpath again and propose to come back with the scalp of the enemy. Fantastic streaks of red, yellow and white adorn his countenance; the feathers in his war bonnet are painted the color of blood; in case the impending conflict demands a special hex, his tomahawk, knife, and pipe may be painted too. The marks of beauty-parlorification are never wholly erased, as the observant visitor may see for himself. Neither, for that matter, is the memory of the latest game played nor the anticipation of the game just ahead.

This football battle is without doubt the most colorful, the most brilliantly staged and altogether the most exciting, as it is the most sought-after of all the intercollegiate contests in the world. No stadium ever built could accommodate more than a fraction of the hordes who clamor for tickets; not only is every Army-Navy game invariably a complete "sell out" but a sell out in a great big way.

Entirely aside from the game as a spectacle, with its parade into the stadium by the Brigade of Midshipmen and the Corps of

Cadets, each group headed by its own massive band of picked musicians; aside from the rhythmic beat of drums and the martial music that sets the blood tingling; aside from the unusual character of the host of spectators, which resolves itself into something of a reunion between old friends in the services; aside from the comedy contributed by the Navy goat and the Army mule mascots, the cheers and yells and songs and all the countless things to see and hear at once, this contest is marked by an intensity and illumined by a fire that even the torrential storm, in which it is too frequently held, cannot dim. You see, this particular game is important—terribly important—to midshipmen and cadets alike, important to all former midshipmen and cadets, and to all Navy and Army men everywhere.

Just why this Army-Navy game should be so different from other games was told by the sports writer, Richards Vidmer, in the following words years ago:

> On a certain Saturday during the current football campaign, a certain college coach was standing outside the gymnasium at Annapolis, gazing out across the green lawns and silvery waters of the Severn as he waited for his players inside to get into their uniforms.
>
> Middies in blue coats, the buttons glistening in the sun, were marching in little squads to and from classes, their shoulders back, their chins up and their eyes straight ahead. They were at strict attention as they paraded with books beneath their arms, and so it was all the more startling when spontaneously, suddenly, intermittently, each group broke forth with a wild yell:
>
> "Navy, Navy, Navy! Fight, fight, fight!"
>
> They neither turned their heads to right or left, nor missed a step as they marched along. Just a sudden wild shout, then the rhythmic beat of their feet on the hard cement walks again. The coach turned and shook his head.
>
> "That's why it's always tough to beat a Navy team. Or an Army team for that matter. These two schools are different from any other college or university. To them a football game is everything, and all the players on the field realize that they are playing not just for themselves, their coach, their teammates and their academy, but for every living graduate and undergraduate of Annapolis or West Point.
>
> No member of the Brigade of Midshipmen, no member of the Corps of Cadets would think of missing the game. No graduate

of either academy would consider staying away if it were possible for him to get there. And in far-off China, the Philippines or Hawaii every officer of either service will be waiting by a radio for the result. And as they wait they will remember games of other years and the heroes of the past. Those men were heroes on the football field and in the eyes of all service men they are heroes still. And those men who go forth on the gridiron today, whether in Navy blue or Army gray, will go with the conscious knowledge that whatever they do will be remembered down through the years, throughout their careers at home and abroad.

. . . No matter what his team has done through the season, no matter how great the odds may appear against it, facing the Army or the Navy every man will rise to supreme heights and play just a little harder, just a little faster with just a little more determination than he ever has played before.*

To the Naval Academy Athletic Association, (NAAA) football season is the time to hang out the sign, "This is my busy day." Incidentally, it is also the period during which enough football tickets are sold to keep all nineteen sports at the Naval Academy supported in the manner to which they have become accustomed. Not one of them—except football—supports itself. Football also provides the funds for maintaining all the other squads. Without this help, all intercollegiate contests would be stopped dead in their tracks. To sell tickets without stirring up cries of protest and acrimonious charges of favoritism is a yearly task that stimulates the sales of pills for That Tired Feeling.

Yet the blame for this deplorable situation does not belong to the Association at all. It is partly the fault of the City of Philadelphia, which built a puny Municipal Stadium that seats a mere handful of 102,000 fans instead of the half million or more demanded by the Army-Navy game, and partly the fault, too, of the Intercollegiate Football Rules Committee, which inconsiderately provides only one 50-yard line on which the aforementioned half million fans may all sit together in amity and accord. Until somebody rectifies these oversights, the "N-Triple A" will have to struggle along somehow and dipose of its allotted 51,000 seats to clamoring and insistent applicants as best it can.

* By courtesy of the New York *Tribune*, Inc.

How does the NAAA distribute its Army-Navy football tickets?

First of all—and properly enough—it gives the opportunity to buy tickets to its own dues-paying members. It allots them not in the order in which the applications are received, but in the order of seniority of the applicants; in this way an old Admiral who has been paying his dues for forty or fifty years gets a better seat than the young ensign. The allotment is made on the date set as the "deadline," which is on or about November 1. After the demands of its members are met, applications from non-members are considered in the order of receipt. The Army-Navy game is invariably a complete sell-out (the Association could sell about five times the number of tickets it has at its disposal). Non-members can usually be accommodated for all other Navy games.

There are about 11,000 members enrolled in the NAAA. Membership is restricted to present and former officers of the Navy and of the Marine Corps, to graduates of the Naval Academy, to its civilian professors and instructors, and to non-graduates who have been midshipmen for at least two full years. The initiation fee is $10.00 and the annual dues are $3.00 thereafter—with the privilege of buying two preferred tickets a year to the Army-Navy game. In addition, all midshipmen are classed as "undergraduate members," at present paying no dues, and are entitled to admission to all games. In theory, each of these members may buy as many as four tickets each; in practice, however, they may be cut down to the number of tickets that may be available after all the applications are in and the supply is prorated to meet the demand. In addition, there are the members of Congress, who are classed as "honorary members." They pay no initiation fee and no dues, but they have the privilege of buying as many tickets as dues-paying members.

Altogether, this unique association has on its records about 16,000 members, who are privileged to buy, in theory, a total of 60,000 or more tickets out of the maximum of 50,000 that are available, and that is a problem that takes more than a slide-rule to work out. (The other 50,000 tickets, of course, are disposed of by the Army.) That is why the tickets have to be prorated, so as to insure an equitable balance between the supply and demand, and prevent any member from being left out entirely.

Over 20,000 names of non-members are kept in the files; any citizen in good standing may get his name on the list by making application. It may not help him get in to the Army-Navy game, but it will help him get in to other Navy games. If any tickets for other than Army games are left over after this demand has been met, they are turned over for public sale to the regularly accredited and licensed ticket agencies. In the effort to keep tickets out of the hands of speculators, the Association has the cooperation of the local police and the Office of Naval Intelligence officers. All tickets issued in the names of Congressmen are mailed to them personally to their homes. And to discourage counterfeits, the tickets are printed at the last minute in four or five colors, on paper that is protected by a "safety center," thus making the job of imitating them on short notice impractical.

The members of the football squad, upon whose broad and willing shoulders rests the responsibility for providing their fellow midshipmen with athletic facilities, take their rewards in the form of hard work, hard knocks, and glory—the glory of making all intercollegiate sports at the Naval Academy possible, of establishing their alma mater in a proud place in the intercollegiate sun, and of contributing substantial sums to athletics to boot. Though football uses up only 25% of the Athletic Association budget, it contributes 84% of the total income. (Other sports bring in only 1.5%.)

Here are some of the ways in which the Association adds to the sum total of human happiness:

It pays the cost of the midshipmen's participation in 19 intercollegiate sports.

It contributes to the support of the Brigade's 21-sport intramural program.

It pays the salaries of some of the coaches who also assist with the work of the Physical Education Department.

It covers the deficits incurred when expenses of away games exceed the guarantees.

It pays the guarantees due visiting teams.

It transports the Brigade and the Naval Academy Band to out-of-town football games.

It buys thousands of dollars worth of athletic gear.

It has contributed almost a million dollars to "special projects" for the improvement of the Naval Academy—floodlighting of athletic fields, improvement of athletic facilities indoors and out, purchase of the new stadium site. It even helped build the Museum, on the upper floor of which it has its offices, and paid for the furniture in Memorial Hall, and for the new Steerage.

Rear Admiral Colby M. Chester, of the class of 1863, really started something when he organized the Association back in 1892. He set a Good Samaritan on the road to the Naval Academy.

For days before the game the cry "Beat Army" echoes through Bancroft Hall. Placards bearing this slogan appear at unexpected places; "Beat Army" is inscribed on the curtains of the showers, on discarded bed sheets; if tradition is to be believed, the words were once painted on the rump of the Admiral's favorite white horse. The large placard over the west entrance of the gymnasium is changed daily to record the approaching event, "40 days to Army," "28 days to Army," "6 days to Army." The midshipman dance orchestra, the NA-10, bursts forth at pep meetings in Smoke Hall, and the band is brought into the mess hall—not so much for the purpose of arousing enthusiasm as to furnish an outlet for it. Sections proceed to classes to the rhythmic chant of cheering enlivened with an occasional marching song. And when at last the fateful day actually arrives and the brigade marches out of Bancroft Hall to board the buses, the midshipmen render a left-hand salute to old Tecumseh and cast pennies toward him in tribute, "just for luck." Not that they really believe that he can help them put the Indian sign on the Army, or are superstitious, you understand—but after all, who are they to ignore an old custom?

A hundred buses or more are needed to transport the Brigade on its excited 125-mile trip to the Municipal Stadium in Philadelphia. The loading operation in the Yard on the morning of the game is as carefully planned and smoothly executed as an invasion (which it is). Spare buses go along in case of a breakdown. (Nobody can miss this game!)

The entrance of the brigade into the stadium to the stirring

*T*he rally before a varsity
football game is a happy time for
midshipmen.

*F*ootball has long been
one of the favorite sports at
the Academy.

*W*est Point exchange
officer at the Army-Navy game rally.

march "Anchors Aweigh!" brings the vast crowd to its feet in an ovation. The formation on the field breaks up as the lines of midshipmen file into the rectangular section of seats reserved for them—a section which thereafter appears as a blue and white highly articulate patch upon the packed grandstand. The band settles itself on the ground seats, ready for action. Lithe, slender cheer leaders dart out with their megaphones and call for cheers and songs, which they themselves punctuate with a series of acrobatic tumbles in unison.

This is the cue for the entrance of Bill the Goat—the traditional mascot of the Navy team.

Bill is greeted with such an outburst of approval—especially when he faces the crowd and bows his head in a menacing gesture that is characteristic of his breed when challenged, but which the crowd interprets as acknowledgment of applause— that his two stalwart midshipman escorts become as inconspicuous as the gentleman who escorts a reigning queen of the films. But these two stalwarts are no mere valets to a goat; on the contrary, they are First classmen who are football heroes themselves, and have been given the coveted duty of escorting Bill as the reward of long and faithful service to the team, the only reward that they are eligible to receive. Under the rule which prevents any varsity player from engaging in intercollegiate contests for more than three years, these two Goat Keepers (sometimes they have been famous gridiron stars before they came to Annapolis) may expose their persons to the various forms of mayhem that are practised in scrub games at home, and may lend their time and experience to their fellows, but the honor of representing Navy and the glory of playing in a game against any opponent is forever denied them. The privilege of serving as the personal attendants to Bill, and of traveling with the football squad, is the Naval Academy's way of giving these two boys a great big hand. They deserve it.

What is outwardly visible of the game itself, with all its pandemonium and exaltations and drama and heartbreak, has been recorded in countless millions of printed and broadcast words, and will continue to be thus recorded. Whether the contestants rank high or low in the season's rating is wholly immaterial; when Navy beats Army, the season is a success, regardless of the outcome of earlier games. Only rarely, as a matter of fact, is any mythical national "championship" involved, as it was, for instance, in that historic duel in Chicago in 1926, which ended in a 21 to 21 tie and gave Navy an undefeated season with a claim to the national title.

When the ball is not in motion on the gridiron, the blue patch of midshipmen stuck against the grandstand on one side of the field and the gray patch of cadets stuck against the grandstand opposite, take up the slack. These patches are technically known as the "cheering sections," and they consist of the entire undergraduate personnel of both service institutions.

The Navy cheers are drilled into the midshipmen from their earliest plebe days, beginning with the gatherings in Mahan Hall during their first summer. There the plebes are instructed in the technique of the yells and in the appropriate occasions for each. During the regular athletic season there are normally six cheerleaders, preferably two from each of the three upper classes, selected after competitive tryouts by the Brigade Activities Committee. During the summer practice sessions the plebes try to visualize a ball game; "the team comes out upon the field"; "Gish is about to kick off"; "Navy scores a touchdown"; "time out for Army"; "Door comes out and Jones goes in at center"; "end of first quarter." The suitable yell and the suitable song for each circumstance are duly rehearsed.

The most important Navy yell, as well as the oldest, is the "4-N," so-called because each letter of the word Navy is repeated four times. This is reserved for the team as a whole; only as a special tribute is it given for a player who has covered himself with glory or for a coach. Here it is:

> Navy! Navy! Navy!
> N-N-N-N
> A-A-A-A
> V-V-V-V
> Y-Y-Y-Y
> Navy!
> Fight! Team! Fight!

Another popular cheer goes by the curious title of the "Whisper Cheer," but it soon belies its name as the yell develops. It starts out *pianissimo* but rises in *crescendo* to a fierce roar and is a sure bet to bring on a sore throat when attempted by those without proper voice training:

> (softly) NA- NA- NA-V-Y!
> (louder) NA- NA- NA-V-Y!
> (very loud) NA- NA- NA-V-Y-!
> Navy, Navy, Fight! Team! Fight!

A good deal of the noise-making at the games is accomplished by what might be called "informal" cheering. Certain quasi-primitive chants become popular and are generated by the midshipmen themselves in the stands and repeated as if they were incantations. One of these is a four-note affair in a minor key followed by an exhortation, and it goes something like this:

> Yay-
> Ay-   Oh-
>   Yo-
> Come on, Navy! Let's go!   (Repeated *ad infinitum*.)

Another involves the insistent repetition of the assertion: "We want it!" "We want it!" with the antecedent of the pronoun generally understood.

No list of Navy yells would be complete without the "Long N," familiar to many midshipmen generations. It may be represented thus:

> N-
> A-
> V-
> Y-
> NA-VY
> Fight! Team! Fight!

Every once in a while, of course, new combinations of words and noise are strung together and tried out; once in a while, too, special yells are created for special occasions. For years a yell so personal as to be almost intimate was given just before the start of a game to the beloved little man who tended the hurts to flesh and spirit of Navy athletes for many midshipmen generations, and who always sat on the players' bench with his boys; it was known as "Doc's yell." When the years took their toll and Doc had to retire on a pension, his place on the bench was one day found vacant.

"Where's Doc?" the cry went forth. At last they espied him, sitting alone and desolate up in the grandstand, just like an ordinary spectator. Friendly hands led him down to his accustomed place on the players' bench; to start a game without Doc there and without "Doc's yell" was unthinkable. It is big, heart-warming yells like that which make little paragraphs like this.

When the timekeeper's final whistle has blown and the announcers have yelled in their microphones the familiar phrase "And the game—is—OVER!" bedlam breaks loose. The midshipmen rise and with bared heads sing "Alma Mater," accompanied by the band, win, lose or draw. When Navy beats Army, the brigade tears across the field and the midshipmen crowd before their cadet rivals to taunt them with such gestures and grimaces as the ingenuity and facial muscles of the individual midshipmen permit. And what are the cadets doing all this time? They are staying right in their places and taking it. It is all part of the code. After all, the day of reckoning will come, and when it does, the midshipmen will stay in their places, too, while the cadets regale them with "Good Night, Navy," and give a demonstration of the new line of faces that West Point is turning out this season. It's all part of the game.

During World War II special trains were no longer used to transport the midshipmen because of transportation restrictions. The midshipmen were sent by steamer to Baltimore and Philadelphia.

In former days when special trains deposited the flushed and happy midshipmen back in Annapolis, the town turned out in hilarious welcome. With swinging steps the brigade marched home in triumph through the gates, headed by its band beating out the tempo of the songs the midshipmen were singing. How such a homecoming stirred one young woman who happened to observe it from the shadows, has been recorded in these words:

> One of the most vivid and wonderful memories I have of the Academy was gotten one night when the brigade was returning from Baltimore. I almost felt as if I was watching something I wasn't meant to see. The midshipmen marched in behind the band, singing and cheering. The moon had just come up and

shone on the tile roof of Bancroft Hall, and shrouded the figure of Tecumseh in a silver mist. The song came nearer and nearer, and after the midshipmen had passed, the sounds gradually faded away, as if into the shadows. . . . It was like looking through a window and seeing something one never knew existed. I wish that every Navy drag could have seen the brigade as I saw it that night.*

The ceremony that completes the traditional celebration of a football victory over Army is the ringing of the Academy's victory bells which stand on either side of the steps leading up to the main entrance to Bancroft Hall, the old Japanese bell on the left and the bell from the carrier *Enterprise* on the right. The former is rung only after a football victory over Army, by anyone who chooses to bang on it. The only exception to this tradition is that this bell was rung, appropriately enough, on VJ Day, September 2, 1945, when the force of the excited blows cracked the bell, perhaps not without symbolic significance. The *Enterprise* bell is rung for a victory over Army in football or soccer, or for a majority of victories in winter or spring sports over the ancient foe. The captains of the winning teams are the first to ring this bell when the teams return.

The Japanese bell, which is very old (dates as far back as 1168 have been given), was presented to Commodore Matthew C. Perry by the Regent of Napha, one of the Lew-Chew Islands, part of what is now known as the Ryukyu Islands, then a dependency of Japan, when that American naval officer was on his historic treaty-making visit to Japan in 1845. In compliance with Perry's wish, the bell was presented to the Naval Academy upon his death and was set up in 1858 in its Oriental framework, in which it now hangs. The *Enterprise* bell was brought to the Academy in 1950 by the then Superintendent, Admiral Harry W. Hill.

A close inspection of the old bell reveals that its surface is inscribed with Japanese characters, which tell that the bell was cast to memoralize a "prayer of benevolence for the people" in the reign of King Lew-Chew. Following a lengthy and

---

* From *The Log*. March 25, 1938.

flowery introduction, the real text of the bell comes down to business with the following message:

> This beautiful bell has been founded and hung in the tower of the temple. It will awaken dreams of superstition. If one will bear in mind to act rightly and truly, and the Lords and Ministers will do justice in a body, the barbarians will never come to invade. The sound of the bell will convey the virtue of Fushi, and will echo like the song of Tsuirai; and the benevolence of the Lords will continue forever like these echoes.

Upon the return of the midshipmen from a victory over Army, this bell is surrounded. On the terrace in front of Bancroft Hall, a cry is raised for the captain of the Navy team; his appearance is met with thunderous cheers from more than four thousand midshipmen throats. To this new hero of the gridiron is accorded the honor of being the first to tap out on the bell the score of the game.

"One! Two! Three! Four! . . ."

One by one, each member of the victorious team steps up and repeats this happy formula. Perhaps the clarion notes do indeed, as the inscription proclaims, "awaken dreams of superstition"; after all, did not the sacrificial pennies cast before old Tecumseh prove efficacious? And has not the prophecy come true that "the barbarians will never come to invade"?

But perhaps that is because the game is nearly always held in Philadelphia.

Chapter 11

Songs of the Brigade

It is the day of the Army-Navy football classic at Municipal Stadium in Philadelphia. The Brigade of Midshipmen, headed by the Naval Academy band, has now come to a halt with the head of the long column resting at the players' entrance to the field. An air of expectancy and suppressed excitement pervades the ranks. The climax of the season, the approach of which has been heralded day by day on the huge bulletin board over the west entrance of the gymnasium, checked off on calendar pads and served as a primary subject of speculation for months, is now actually here at last; the very hour is striking. Football history is in the making.

"Atten—tion!"

The command echoes down the line. The ranks stiffen. The drum major raises his baton. With a blare of trumpets and a crash of drums the brigade marches onto the field, to the stirring music of what has come to be regarded as perhaps the best, as it is the most popular, of all the college marches in the country, "Anchors Aweigh!" The appearance of the midshipmen is greeted by a roar of welcome from over 102,000 throats.

Millions more are watching on television, or listening on radio as the game is broadcast all over the world to far-flung Naval ships and stations. Movie cameras will record every detail of the action.

"And that," has admitted more than one midshipman, "gave me the biggest thrill I ever had at the Naval Academy. I felt that the responsibility of the entire parade was on my shoulders, that every eye was upon me personally."

"Anchors Aweigh!" is not only the one outstanding march of the Naval Academy, but it has taken its place among the outstanding marches of the nation. It is probably played more often than any college march ever penned. The music was composed

119

in 1907 by the famous Charles A. Zimmerman, who for thirty-four years served in the capacity of leader of the Naval Academy band and for a part of that time as organist in the Chapel; the affectionate regard in which he was held is attested by the monument to his memory which has stood in the cemetery since 1916, "erected by his midshipmen friends."

The composer dedicated this work to the class of 1907, in accordance with the custom of writing a new march each year for the graduating class. Its inspiring strains are heard at the opening of many official ceremonies, at brigade parades, and at the "march on" at all football games; so proficient has the Naval Academy band become in rendering it that it can play it extemporaneously in any key. Its inception was found in a three-stanza verse written by midshipman Alfred Hart Miles of the class of 1907, while he was leader of the chapel choir. He also collaborated on the music. Two of these stanzas follow:

> Stand Navy down the field,
> Sails set to the sky!
> We'll never change our course,
> So Army, you steer shy-y-y-y!
> Roll up the score, Navy,
> Anchors aweigh!
> Sail Navy down the field
> And sink the Army; sink the Army gray!
>
> Get under way, Navy,
> Decks cleared for the fray.
> We'll hoist true Navy blue
> So Army down your gray-y-y-y!
> Full speed ahead, Navy;
> Army heave to.
> Furl black and gray and gold
> And hoist the Navy, hoist the Navy blue!

Both of these stanzas were obviously composed with the Army game specifically in mind; it was sung less appropriately at other football games, and a need was felt for words that would be suitable for occasions other than contests with the cadets. This demand was met twenty years later by Midshipman Royal Lovell of the class of 1926, who contributed this concluding stanza:

Blue of the Seven Seas,
  Gold of God's great sun—
Let these our colors be
  Till all our time be don-n-n-ne.
By Severn's shore we learn
  Navy's stern call;
Faith, courage, service true
  With honor over, honor over all.

But "Anchors Aweigh!" as a gem of poetic literature is hardly destined to attain such fame as it has won as a swinging, throbbing military march that puts rhythm in the feet and fire in the heart. As such, it takes its place among the great.

During the practice cruise of 1932 on the USS *Wyoming*, Lieutenant William R. Sima, the Naval Academy bandmaster, conceived a melodious, whistlable march tune that was later set to some conventional words of admonition to the old team to "fight on down the field" and to "hold the foe at bay," put together by Midshipmen William M. Collins and John C. Martin of the class of 1933. The band tried out the march one evening, under the title of "Navy Victory March," at a movie show aboard ship; it found immediate favor. Since then it has come to rank as a march second only to "Anchors Aweigh!" It is nearly always played by the band that furnishes music at the basketball games, boxing meets, and other athletic events.

This band, by the way, is a pretty versatile sort of aggregation and plays a very important part not only in the military life of the midshipmen but in their athletic and social activities as well. It is made up of eighty-five enlisted men, the leader and the assistant leader, and most of them play at least two instruments; in the parlance of the profession, most bandsmen "double in strings." This means that in addition to a band instrument, most musicians can play a stringed instrument that is used in an orchestra. This array of talent makes it possible to convert the organization into two full military bands of about forty men each when occasion requires (such as when events take place simultaneously on Farragut and Worden Fields, for example) or into several dance and concert orchestras. In anticipation of just such contingencies, the band can furnish a symphony orchestra, two dance bands, and three small "combos." It is not at all unusual for all of them to be in demand on the same evening.

During the examination periods in January and also immediately preceding June Week—and only on these occasions—the band plays, or used to, a medley of traditional and beloved Navy airs in march tempo, as its contribution to the celebration known as "No More Rivers." In midshipman parlance, that word "river" means a semi-annual examination in academics. During the four-year course, accordingly, the undergraduate must cross eight of these obstacles, but as no midshipman was in former years permitted by custom to indulge his lyric fancy by singing this song until he had completed his plebe year, the maximum number of crossings celebrated vocally was six. As each examination period was successfully passed, the number of rivers to be crossed was reduced by one, and the words of the song were altered to fit the occasion.

In recent years, the singing of "No More Rivers" had become more of a pre-graduation ritual. The first class (or the plebes for the first class) sang it as they took their last two sets of term examinations. On the completion of each examination, one "river" is dropped until there are "no more rivers to cross."

"No More Rivers" is a medley made up of bits from "Life on the Bounding Main," the Naval Academy's own "No More Rivers," followed by "The Girl I Left Behind Me," "The Mermaid" (one of the most famous of the old sea songs), and the immortal "Auld Lang Syne." The first stanza states a simple fact in the following mildly profane terms:

> We've got a hell of a way to go,
>   Hell of a way to go, hell of a way to go,
> We've got a hell of a way to go—
>   Six more rivers to cross.
> Six more rivers, there's six more rivers to cross,
>   Six more rivers, there's six more rivers to cross.

The upper class modifies the first three lines by reiterating to the world that they are "Almost out of the wilderness"; not until the final academic examination is over and the exuberant First classmen, secure from further academic persecution, pour out of their last class room to indulge in their newly won freedom do they "Thank God we're out of the wilderness" with "No more rivers to cross."

"No More Rivers," is also the name given to the series of sketches, usually pointedly satirical in content, which the midshipmen present on a stage in the Field House at the conclusion of the final examinations in May. These sketches are good-natured take-offs of persons and conditions at the Academy which have amused (or tormented) the midshipmen during the previous academic year. If an officer of the Executive Department has been just a bit too "regulation" to suit the midshipmen's taste, or a Bull prof has fussed too much about misplaced commas, they are likely to see themselves caricatured in a lively skit that pokes fun at their foibles. The sketches are usually ingeniously staged and the performers ludicrously costumed, much to the delight of the midshipman audience, which enjoys to the limit these harmless, but soul-satisfying, lampoons.

During the fall, spring, and summer, weather permitting, the band plays at 11:00 every morning (10:30 during the summer) in the bandstand in the Yard. During the morning concerts it adapts its programs to the processions of sections proceeding back and forth between Bancroft Hall and the recitation halls, when it breaks into military marches to which midshipmen may keep step. It has made recordings. It plays for many of the drills during plebe summer and supplies the musical accompaniment to innumerable social and official functions. It furnishes the music for motion pictures based on Naval Academy life; included among them have been such films as "Navy Blue and Gold," "Shipmates Forever," and "Annapolis Salute." It plays at track meets, baseball games, lacrosse games, the concert series, and theatrical performances given by the Masqueraders. It follows the football team wherever it goes and supplies music for all the home games.

As a result of all these agreeable duties, membership in the band is looked upon as a very desirable berth. Members of the Naval Academy Band are drawn from the bandsmen of the naval service, who in turn qualify as musicians in the Navy by auditions and courses of instruction at the Naval School of Music in Washington, D. C. The musical library of the Naval Academy Band contains more than 5000 pieces; of these, 2500 are marches and the rest are concert and dance numbers. There is probably no aggregation of musicians in the service—and few anywhere else—that is more proficient in dance tempos and rhythms, in which the band takes special pride.

After the band has headed the parade of the brigade into the playing field to the inspiring strains of "Anchors Aweigh!" and settled itself on the chairs provided at the foot of the midshipmen's section, it opens its program with the college air of the opposing team, as a complimentary gesture of hospitality. From that point on it confines itself pretty much to the job of accompanying the midshipmen in the Navy's own songs.

Most of these songs are directed specifically at the ancient and honored rivals of the midshipmen, the West Point cadets. Like all college football songs, they seek not only to inspire the home team but also to hurl defiance at the opponents; consequently modesty does not exactly loom as a distinguishing attribute. Were all the demands met to rip, tear, sock, sink and otherwise commit mayhem on the opposing teams, only a rake and a shovel would be needed for cleaning up the field.

Perhaps the most popular of these songs of challenge is "The Service Boast," the words and music of which were both contributed by the versatile Mr. Anon. It consists of the following lone stanza:

> Oh, you've heard of the Navy and the men who sail the seas
>> For the glory of our country's colors fair.
> For the glory of the Blue and Gold our team is here today,
>> And we'll cheer them as through Army's line they tear.
> Oh, there'll be high elation on the far China Station,
>> From Crabtown to ships at Timbuctoo,
> And we'll drink a merry toast to our team, the Service boast,
>> And the wearers of the good old Navy blue.

The "far China Station," it may be explained, includes all Navy ships as well as naval stations in the Far East, while "Crabtown" is the nickname of Annapolis.

A gay bit of clowning is contributed in the brief but pungent "Army Mule," dedicated to the traditional mascot of the West Point team. This is rendered to the familiar air of "Tammany," and is climaxed with the mule's bray accompanied by a massed waving of fingers with thumbs stuck in the ears; at the last note, all hands are raised into the air. The words go:

> Army mule, Army mule,
> You can kick and balk and bray,
> But football you cannot play,
> Army mule, Army mule,
> On-kee, on-kee, on-kee, on-kee,
> Ar-my mule!

To the bucolic tune of "The Old Gray Mare She Ain't What She Used to Be," another lyric outburst that in its sentiment bears no special quality in common with the blushing violet, is "We Are the Old Ny-vee." This is usually repeated ad lib until something—perhaps the resumption of play after a brief intermission—checks it. Various stanzas of a more or less ribald nature have been added to the one original verse used in public, which runs thus:

> We are the old Ny-vee;
> We are the old Ny-vee.
> We don't have to march like the infantry,
> Ride like the cavalry
> Shoot like th' artillery.
> We can lick your whole damned Army,
> We are the old Ny-vee!

An irate Congressman who once scathingly denounced the midshipmen as "the spoiled and pampered pets of Uncle Sam" served as the happy inspiration for the words of the sprightly song "There's an Aggregation"; here they are:

> There's an aggregation known throughout the country,
>   Always ready for a frolic or a fray;
> From their high and mighty station
> They are known throughout the nation
>   As the boys from down in Crabtown-on-the-Bay.
> Each year they sally forth to face the Army,
>   And turn the Army mule into a lamb;
> In the midst of scrap and scrimmage
> You will see the busy image
>   Of the spoiled and pampered pets of Uncle Sam.

CHORUS

So round the ends and through the line we run,
Show those Graylegs how the deed is done;
Navy Blue, we'll see you through—
Here's HOW! to the boys of the Navy blue!

The final line is dramatized by a brigade raising of hats in salute.

One of the more striking of the fighting songs, inspired, like so many of those in the Navy repertoire, by an overwhelming desire to "lick the Army," is the famous "Up and At 'em, Navee!" which, though it seems to be guilty of a mixed metaphor in urging the stalwarts in Blue and Gold to *sail* down the football field, has been a favorite for a considerable number of years in an area of vocal activity where tastes change whimsically and yesterday's favorite song goes by the board today:

Up and at 'em, Navee!
Let's go sailing down the field;
Tear right through 'em, Navee!
Our old line will never yield.
Fight! Fight! Fight!
Touchdown after touchdown,
Man for man we're back of you.
Victory for us today,
Now we're getting under way,
Navy Blue—Let's go through!

Because one of the songs employs as its opening phrase "We will forge ahead," it has been pertinently dubbed "The Blacksmith Song." Because eight of the sixteen lines of another song consisted of the command "Sink that Army gray," it was appropriately enough given the title "Sink that Army." Indeed, in the whole galaxy of the more familiar football songs, there are only three—"A Cheer, a Cheer for Navy," "Gangway for the Navy Blue," and the ever popular sentimental ballad "Song of the Navy"—that do not prophesy more or less dire disaster to all and sundry Army teams. From this circumstance the uninformed outsider might well jump to the (correct) conclusion that the one consuming object of the midshipmen is to defeat the cadets. But he would be a rash outsider indeed who would also conclude that because of this rivalry, either institution likes to see its brother-in-arms defeated by anyone else. To "beat Army" is an accomplishment that the midshipmen want to reserve exclusively for themselves; it is a strictly family affair. That is why, when an Army team is reported ahead in a game with an outsider, the news is greeted by the midshipmen with cheers.

When victory appears in sight, the midshipmen haul out of their repertoire the classic dedicated to the mascot of the Navy team, entitled "The Goat is Old and Gnarly." This is sung to the air of "The Battle Hymn of the Republic," perhaps more widely known under its name of "John Brown's Body." The one and only stanza is marked by a controversial reference to the epicurean diet of Bill the Goat, and its chorus is punctuated with a spoken interpolation in the spirit of the occasion. Here they are:

> The goat is old and gnarly
> And he's never been to school,
> But he can take the bacon
> From the worn-out Army mule.
> He's had no education
> But he's brimmin' full o' fight,
> And Bill will feed
> On Army mule tonight!

Chorus

> Army, Army, call the doctor!
> Army, Army, call the doctor!
> Army, Army, call the doctor!
> You're all in, down and—
> (*Spoken*) Whoa! Any oats today,
> lady? No? Giddap!
> Army, Army, call the doctor!
> You're all in, down and OUT!

Other fight songs heard repeatedly at all the games are the "Navy Victory March," "Up with the Navy," and "Eyes of the Fleet" ("Fight, Fight, Fight, Fight for the Navy!")

During a summer practice cruise to Europe some years ago, the visiting midshipmen were called upon to sing some of their representative Navy songs. They obliged.

"They are enormously entertaining and awfully jolly," was

the opinion of the delighted audience, "but now won't you sing something that isn't about the Army? Sing something just about yourselves!"

It was this unexpected request that focused attention upon the need of a real, 100 per cent Navy song, a song that does not challenge the cadets or even celebrate football at all. Through *The Log* a call was broadcast for both words and music for a Naval Academy Alma Mater song, a real midshipmen's hymn.

Among the texts received in response one came anonymously "from an officer of the fleet." Dozens followed. But the anonymous text proved to be the best, and it was selected pending the receipt of a suitable musical setting. Numerous scores were submitted, but none of them clicked. At last the former Chapel organist and choirmaster, Joseph W. Crosley, came forward with "some new music I have just found." The Glee Club tried it out before a group of officers.

"That's what we want," was the verdict.

It was first sung in public at the spring concert of the Glee Club in 1926, under the title "Navy Blue and Gold." It not only made an instant hit, but gained favor so rapidly that in 1927 it was officially designated as the Alma Mater song and rules were promulgated for its use as such. Not until the song had been accepted on its own merits was the name of the composer revealed. It was Joseph W. Crosley himself.

Today the midshipmen stand and sing "Navy Blue and Gold" with bared heads, at the end of every football game, win, lose, or draw. They sing it at ceremonial occasions, including the Baccalaureate during June Week. It is the last song sung by the First classmen after they are handed their diplomas, as a farewell to the brigade in which they will march no more. It has become in fact as well as name the midshipmen's hymn— the one serious song, charged with sentiment, around which memories and traditions cluster with the years. The words are by Commander Roy de Saussure Horn, USN (Ret.) of the class of 1915 and are here given:

> Now, college men from sea to sea
> May sing of colors true;
> But who has better right than we
> To hoist a symbol hue?

*V*olleyball teams are formed
within the Brigade each spring.

*N*aval Academy midshipmen
are justly proud of their crew.

*O*nce the grass gets green, *it's*
time for golf clubs *and* baseball *bats.*

For sailor men in battle fair,
   Since fighting days of old,
Have proved the sailor's right to wear
   The Navy Blue and Gold.

Four years together by the bay
   Where Severn joins the tide,
Then by the Service called away,
   We're scattered far and wide;
But still when two or three shall meet,
   And old tales be retold,
From low to highest in the fleet
   We'll pledge the Blue and Gold.

All of these songs and many more are available in a handsome volume published by the United States Naval Institute and called *The Book of Navy Songs*.

The familiar hymn of benediction "God Be with You Till We Meet Again" was for many years incorporated in the impressive services in the Chapel on Graduation Sunday. It is an eminently serious religious composition and its use on such occasions was fraught with deep sentiment. But the solemnity of its reception began to come under an uneasy suspicion years ago, by an outbreak of sniffing and furtive blowing of noses that lacked certain earmarks of conviction. With the years, these audible signs of grief increased in volume until the occasion came to be known as "Sob Sunday." The climax to the rising tide of sorrow over the pending departures came on one epoch-making service when towels supplanted handkerchiefs and tears squeezed from water-soaked sponges splashed upon the floor and ran off in rivulets down the church aisles.

The next day orders were issued that "God Be with You Till We Meet Again" was out. It has never been played in the Chapel since.

Back in 1860 a terrible storm swept the Mediterranean Sea, bringing death and destruction in its train. Among the ships imperiled was one bearing as a passenger an English clergyman, the Reverend William Whiting. So profoundly was he stirred by the spectacle as well as by his miraculous escape that he penned the hymn originally entitled "Travelers by Sea and Land," destined to become more generally known as "For Those in Peril on the Sea." A year later it was set to music by

John B. Dykes; in time it became a favorite with seafaring men throughout the English-speaking nations. Today the first stanza of that hymn is sung at every service in the Naval Academy Chapel; from this custom has grown a similar use of the hymn on many of the ships of the fleet.

> Eternal Father, strong to save,
> Whose arm hath bound the restless wave,
> Who bidd'st the mighty ocean deep
> Its own appointed limits keep;
> Oh, hear us when we call to Thee,
> For those in peril on the sea!

At the opening notes, the congregation kneels, facing the altar. For a few fleeting moments the thoughts of the midshipmen and of the congregation reach out to comrades and friends who face the God of Storms, and whose duties—like their own that lie so shortly ahead—are faced with the uncertainties of the elements.

It is peculiarly appropriate that from the Chapel of the Naval Academy should emanate every Sunday this reverent hail and benediction

"For those in peril on the sea."

Chapter 12

What Every
Drag Should Know

Annapolis drags eat more than West Point drags. That is due to the fact, no doubt, that there are more of them. There are more of them partly because the Naval Academy has several hundred more midshipmen than the Military Academy has cadets, and partly because Annapolis is easier of access than West Point.

On Saturday afternoons and evenings, and on Sunday afternoons, the three upper classes take up society in a big way. These periods are largely given over to the entertainment of young women guests, whose status ranges all the way from only a sister up to an O.A.O. These initials, the visitor is assured, stand for "One-And-Only," although an occasional cynic may point out that they also stand for "One-Among-Others." The influx of femininity begins Saturday morning and the exodus starts about suppertime on Sunday. This social phenomenon, however, leaves the plebe practically untouched. Plebes are not permitted to escort what *Reef Points* calls "young, unrelated, female guests." Dragging is an upperclass rate, and any attempts to beat the system by plebes are not considered cricket. Until recently plebes were permitted to drag only to the very last social function of the academic year, the Farewell Ball. But in the fall of 1955, the Superintendent, Admiral Boone, convinced that the social development of midshipmen could not start too early, shattered a long tradition by establishing the Plebe Sunday Informals, where Fourth classmen could meet and dance with girls of their own ages and begin to acquire that social poise so necessary in an officer.

One of the distinguishing features of Annapolis life is the Saturday morning arrival of the young ladies. They troop in

131

droves through the narrow streets of this quaint old Southern town, their high heels clattering over the uneven brick walks, carrying their suitcases, on their way to the rooms that have been engaged for them by their midshipmen hosts, perhaps at Carvel Hall or (more likely) at the various less expensive private homes and rooming houses where week-end paying guests are welcomed. They come by busses from Washington, 33 miles distant, and from Baltimore, 27 miles distant. Annapolis is the only State Capital in the country which has no railroad or airline service.

To the more affluent and self-indulgent drags, a modest supply of taxicabs is available but shanks' mare is the usual mode of locomotion.

Drags who arrive in town before the midshipmen's midday meal can expect no hosts to greet them; liberty to "visit Annapolis," as the regulations so euphemistically term permission to go outside of the Yard, does not begin until after luncheon. The usual hospitality midshipmen extend to their fair guests is to carry their luggage and escort them on foot to their destination—as far as the parlor only. Going to the guest's room or even going upstairs at all is definitely out. This regulation applies not only to Carvel Hall, where both midshipmen and guests are under the eyes of the hotel staff, but also to all private houses, and there are several dozen Mrs. Bonifaces who are watchful to observe that this regulation is enforced, too. If it is not, the house of Mrs. Boniface is likely to be stricken from the approved list, and her revenue from that source stopped in short order.

There are certain modifications to this rule. A midshipman is permitted to visit the room of his mother, father, legal guardian or male officer. In such cases the term mother is interpreted in its strictly technical sense, and does not include ladies who are palpably no older than their ingenious if improbable "sons."

But it is on Saturday evenings on which hops are held—and they average about three a month—that the social life of the midshipmen bursts into full splendor. For it is then that those who "drag," as escorting fair ladies is called, take their guests out to dinner and later to the large and colorful formal hops.

The rambling, historic brick mansion, Carvel Hall, that two

and a half centuries ago served as the home of the Colonial aristocracy, becomes suddenly alive with youth and beauty and romance. Midshipmen in their trim, close-fitting full-dress uniforms appear with girls who but a few hours before had appeared merely as inconspicuous young women in traveling garb, but who now have become miraculously metamorphosed into colorful and sparkling ladies of fashion.

Along about nine o'clock the diners begin to fumble with wraps; within half an hour they are broken up into couples and are strolling back through the Academy gates. The armory, Dahlgren Hall, is all lighted up; toward its entrance leisurely lines of humanity are moving. It is the night of a representative Saturday hop, and that means that midshipmen of all the three upper classes may attend, with or without drags. The angel faces peering over the rail of the surrounding balcony belong to the plebes.

If the dance floor of Dahlgren Hall is not the largest in the country, it must come fairly near to it. The building is 600 feet long and 100 feet wide; practically all of its width and most of its length is clear dance space. The proper military atmosphere is provided by the massive gunmounts and by the long rows of rifles secured in the racks which line the walls, and by the state flags overhead. In the far distance, behind a semitransparent curtain of bunting, metal tables and chairs are set for those who care to smoke; beside the tables are arranged massive brass gun shells, filled with sand, as reminders to cigarette addicts that ash trays are not always just "things to put butts in when the room hasn't any floor."

The great hall is lighted by globes suspended high overhead, but not brilliantly lighted; for some dances, indeed, the lights are dimmed low. The decorative scheme varies with the energies and ingenuity of the Hop Committee, but it nearly always includes pillars of bunting, illumined from below, that shed a mystical and colorful glow over the scene. And if any of the couples should appear even as prematurely as the time when the hop is scheduled to begin (which is usually nine o'clock), they will find the sixteen-piece Naval Academy dance orchestra all set and waiting to play for them.

A hostess receives the guests at all formal hops. She is

selected from among the wives of the officers on duty at the Naval Academy. None, however, serves more than once during the season, with the exception of the wife of the Superintendent, who ranks as First Lady, and the wife of the Commandant. Custom decrees that the Superintendent's wife be accorded the honor of presiding over the first formal hop of the academic year, held on the first Saturday after the return of the three upper classes from summer leave, and also over the last festival hop of all—the Farewell Ball, held on the eve of graduation day. At all hops the hostess takes a position under the palms set near the entrance to the dance floor; she is accompanied either by the chairman of the Hop Committee or by his representative, who introduces the midshipmen and their guests by name. It is customary, too, for the hostess to entertain at dinner her midshipman aide, together with his drag, if any. Four women are also engaged by the Naval Academy to act as chaperons; officially they are designated as "hostesses" at all social affairs at the Academy where girls are present. They also inspect all rooming houses offering accommodations to "drags."

By half-past nine o'clock the hop is in fairly full swing. Any upper classman who is not undergoing a punishment tour or otherwise removed from circulation is free to attend if he wants to; the only obligation is that he must be on hand promptly at the start, and only First classmen may leave before the hop comes to an end at 12:00. Stags are rare at hops (the golden-moments are too precious to share with non-draggers), and there is very little cutting-in or exchanging of dances during the course of the evening. The dance draws to a conclusion in appropriate sentimental fashion as the couples turn to the slow strains of "Navy Blue and Gold," and ends with all hands at attention as the orchestra plays "The Star-Spangled Banner."

At the conclusion of the hop, little time is wasted in hanging around; the number of minutes allotted to the midshipmen for escorting their drags home are reduced to a schedule, and they do not provide for elaborate leave-takings. First classmen are permitted 60 minutes to report back to the Watch Officer on duty at Bancroft Hall and to sign in; Second classmen are allowed 50 minutes, and Youngsters 40 minutes—a system that would appear to be designed to develop the younger lads into fast workers. The minimum penalty for being late is about ten demerits, though midshipmen are fast runners and are seldom late.

While all of the formal hops do not follow the exact formula of the one described here, only on occasions do they depart from it. Especially popular are the costume hops where midshipmen can capitalize on the rare opportunity to get out of uniform and into some ludicrous get-up suitable for a "Shipwreck" or Halloween Hop. The ladies too are in costume appropriate to the occasion.

Once a year, in the excitement of June Week, the "N" dance, in honor of the athletes who have won the right to wear that coveted bit of insignia on their chests, is held in Hubbard Hall, the boat house, located on the banks of Dorsey Creek. Chairs and tables are set out upon the float, refreshments are served under the Chinese lanterns, and special souvenir favors are included among the attractions. These affairs are all very picturesque and romantic in their setting and add a colorful touch to the June Week festivities.

Sometimes, particularly at the conclusion of a successful Saturday in winter sports against Army, the regular hop may be designated a "Victory Ball." In previous years, before the Army-Navy football game moved to Philadelphia in all senses of the word "moved," "Victory Balls" were held in Dahlgren Hall to celebrate triumphs over Army, and what gay and excited and altogether happy celebrations they turned out to be! Among the stunts devised for such events were souvenir awards to the members of the football squad, perhaps taking the form of large Roman fasces, each bearing the name of one of the athletes, lowered from the balcony one at a time, with the spotlight focused upon it. Following the football victory of 1937 an illuminated sign at the far end of the huge hall flashed congratulatory messages, one at a time, to all of the twenty-nine members of the squad: "Well done, Jarvis!" Even the wife of the Superintendent danced with the members of the team.

At intervals during the year, too, a hop may be raised to the dignity of something a bit out of the ordinary by being designated as a special "Christmas Hop" or "St. Valentine's

Dance"; aside from the scheme of decoration which these names suggest, however, they do not differ materially from all other hops. But there is one hop of the year about which traditions have been growing and over which, more than any other dance —with the possible exception of the Farewell Ball—the aura of sentiment hovers. That is the Ring Dance.

The Ring Dance has grown out of the sentiment attached to the class ring, one of the most treasured of all a graduate's possessions. So deep has this become that when the Naval Academy, at the time it was arranging for its ninetieth anniversary celebration, undertook to make a loan exhibit of all class rings extending back to 1869, when the custom originated, it met much difficulty in persuading some of the owners to let them out of their possession at all.

"I cannot lend you my ring," replied one old admiral, "because it has not been off my finger for fifty years."

Under promise that the loan collection would be placed in a glass cabinet and set in the Museum under an armed guard, the exhibit was at last completed. That case probably held such a load of sentimental value as has rarely been assembled in one spot.

While these rings maintain the same general character, showing the Naval Academy seal on one side and the class seal on the other (the choice of stone or crest is optional with each owner), the designs differ in detail with each class. The ceremonies of distributing them have undergone many changes over the years; the boisterous custom of hurling the new owners into the waters of Dewey Basin, clothes and all, was abruptly halted in 1924, when Midshipman Leicester R. Smith, of the class of 1925, was drowned, just how no one knows; probably his head struck a boat and the blow knocked him unconscious, and in the turmoil and darkness his absence was not immediately noticed. Since that tragedy the class rings have been distributed at a hop that has grown into one of the most picturesque of all the midshipman functions. Because the ring may be worn only by midshipmen who have successfully completed three full years at the Naval Academy and are in good academic standing, the hop is held—by the Second classmen only, of course—in various places, even afloat, on the Saturday evening preceding Graduation Day.

*P*erhaps the most memorable gala
of a midshipman's four years at the Academy
is the Ring Dance.

*The climax of the Ring Dance
occurs when each midshipman is ceremonially
presented his class ring.*

The Ring Dance is distinguished by several very extra special features that set it apart from all other hops at the Naval Academy. In the first place, it is preceded by the Ring Dance Dinner, a unique function in that it is the only occasion during the year at which midshipmen are permitted to entertain their ladies at dinner actually in the mess hall. Each drag finds at her place an orchid corsage, a dainty souvenir of the occasion, say a pin or a compact, and two lengths of narrow ribbon, one blue and one gold. The ribbons will later be part of a very important ceremony. For the time being, she takes her host's ring, strings it on the ribbons, and thus hangs it around her neck. Then, of course, comes the dinner itself, with sliced ham and turkey as the principal fare.

The music is furnished by some nationally famous orchestra engaged for the occasion, as the Naval Academy orchestra plays for the hop for the other classes in Dahlgren Hall. All these items are paid for by a substantial class assessment, and this means, in turn, that the guests are chosen with a fine discrimination; it is the one event to which each midshipman is pretty sure to ask his most particular O.A.O.—or as near to that as he can come. It has been pertinently observed that the girl who is invited to the Ring Dance "must fulfil all the qualifications of a Navy wife."

But the crowning event of the evening arrives when each couple mounts the carpeted dais and passes through the large gilded replica of the class ring, surmounted by a glowing globe of crystals that simulates the jewel.

As each couple approaches this archway, the lady takes her host's ring, suspended from the silken ribbons, and christens it by dipping it into a binnacle containing water from the Seven Seas, which symbolize the journeyings that lie ahead. She then places the ring upon her host's finger, kisses him, and together they pass through the archway. It is a moment fraught with real romance, especially if the lady is presented with a miniature class ring for her own wear, for that is generally accepted as equivalent to an engagement ring.

And what if the couple are not sentimentally attached?

Well, of course no girl is compelled to attend a Ring Dance if she doesn't want to; even if she does, it may not mean anything—much. Nor is there any regulation that forbids a midshipman to take his own sister through the ceremony. And once in a while, too, a midshipman takes his dad's old sweetheart through the ring . . . Yes, indeed; a great deal more than mere gold is spun into the texture of a class ring.

And this is a good place to report that there is a greater demand for photographs of this ceremony than for any other scene at the Naval Academy.

Informal hops are interspersed through the week-ends as opportunities permit; they are held only in the afternoons, and they differ from the formal affairs in that street or sport clothes are permitted. The only informals that are held regularly are in Smoke Hall on Saturday and Sunday afternoons between four and six o'clock; the music is usually supplied by radio tuned to the Academy's station WRNV, although the midshipmen's dance orchestra, the "NA-10," volunteer their services once in a while, just for the fun of it. Any midshipman of the three upper classes may bring one drag and no one else; even parents are taboo. And no cutting in is allowed, either. Refreshments may be had in the new and handsome Steerage, which is attended by the Naval Academy hostess during the periods when it is open to guests.

Informals are held occasionally in Carvel Hall on Saturdays and Sundays between two and six o'clock. And during the football season, too, informals are held in Smoke Hall after the home games, between 4:30 and 6:00 o'clock; the music is usually furnished by the Naval Academy dance orchestra.

Like all good things of life, these social festivities must be paid for out of somebody's pocket; as the pockets of the midshipmen are neither very deep nor very well lined with what-it-takes, the expenses of a week-end are usually shared by the host and his drag—especially by his drag—on the basis of economic necessity backed up by custom. The "economic necessity" in this case is the polite term that refers specifically to the midshipmen's allowance of spending money, which is all defined in the regulations, and which comes within the classification of what every drag should know.

The midshipman who replied to the question, "How much money do you get?" merely stated a bare fact clothed in the proudest terms he could summon when he answered, "Five dollars a day—once a month." Five dollars a month is indeed all the spending money that a plebe gets. It is referred to as the "monthly insult."

But as a plebe is not allowed to attend hops, he has little occasion to entertain drags; not until he attains the dignity of Youngster does the problem of meeting the costs of entertainment become pressing. To meet this rising obligation of rank, Uncle Sam raises the monthly ante to nine dollars. By the time he gets to be a Second classman, he is allowed eleven dollars a month, and when he reaches the proud estate of First classman, he runs haywire on as high as fifteen dollars a month. After deducting the small sums that may be spent on cigarettes, an occasional soda or magazine, and a few postage stamps, there is not a vast amount left on which to assume the role of big-hearted playboy on the scale that the proverbially generous sailor impulses might dictate. A midshipman who plays the host to a week-end drag, therefore, pays for the pleasure of her society by denying himself many of the little comforts dear to the heart of youth. Even though his offerings be modest, they constitute a big part of what little he has.

The drag's share of the expenses always includes all transportation expenses going and coming.

The host's share of the expenses always includes the costs of dinner for two on the Saturday evening of the hop. The customary cost of dinner is between $3.00 and $5.00 plus tips. Truly devoted couples who are saving up together for the future may dine at the very inexpensive places without losing any caste whatever; it is not at all unusual to see a young couple in evening dress munching a sandwich together in refreshment parlors only one degree removed from the joints with sawdust on the floor.

No fixed rule covers other expenses of a week-end; to quote the old Navy phrase, "all depends on circumstances." In most cases the drag pays for her room, which is reserved for her by her host. A room may be had for about $5.00 in a private home and for between $7.00 and $9.00 at Maryland Inn or Carvel Hall. In many cases the host pays for the Sunday dinner—if he has the money. In cases he hasn't and the guest has, tactful arrangements may be made with the major domo for putting the charge on the guest's account.

Ordinarily, too, the guest pays for her own Sunday breakfast and for her own Sunday evening supper, in case she stays over —which she seldom does.

Thus the midshipman who invites his drag to both Saturday evening and Sunday noon dinners and pays only the low price of two dollars a meal apiece, plus tips, is thrown back on his financial heels to the extent of $9.00 anyway, which is as much money as a Youngster gets in an entire month. If he squanders as much as three dollars on each dinner and throws in a one-dollar corsage besides, his finances get an acute attack of fallen arches. And spending more than a month's income on a girl within twenty-four hours is a great big splurge for any playboy to make, even on the Great White Way.

And what does the midshipman expect in return for his hospitality? First and foremost, he expects a companion who is having a perfectly swell time and is not afraid to show it. The drag who is happy and cheerful and natural stands at the very top of the list by all counts.

Mere beauty is not enough in itself to insure popularity; as a matter of fact, beautiful girls are so often spoiled that they are regarded with a bit of suspicion—and with a lot of suspicion if they assume an air of hauteur. Austere and aloof drags rank well down on the list. When Midshipman Gish drags, he wants a comrade who is merry and uncomplaining, who adapts herself to conditions and to the rules and regulations as she finds them, and who finds them good. If she is an intellectual—well, that is all right too, provided that she keeps her mental attainments and her esthetic tastes under restraint and gives her attention to the pleasures immediately at hand. Of all the classifications into which the midshipman has relegated girls—the Regal Girl, the Childish Girl, the Athletic Girl, the Coquette—the girl classified as the Natural Girl rates Number One.

And how is this Natural Girl defined by midshipman standards?

The answer may be found in the words of the midshipmen themselves, as revealed at various times in the pages of *The Log*: In appearance, she is of medium height, with brown hair and white teeth; in temperament she is naive, truthful, modest, sincere and straightforward. It is a good formula.

From various undergraduate sources has been compiled a list of helpful hints for the guidance of drags generally—tips from the midshipmen themselves concerning what they should and should not do. Here are some of them:

DON'TS FOR DRAGS

Don't keep a midshipman waiting. (Liberty hours are too precious to waste.)

Don't chew gum in public. (The midshipmen don't like it—and besides, the regulations forbid them to chew it themselves.)

Don't suggest anything that cuts into your host's bankroll. (He's putting up the best show he can on the little money Uncle Sam lets him have.)

Don't try to induce your host to violate any regulation. (Remember that it is he and not you who pays the penalty.)

Don't smoke in the Yard, on the street or on the dance floor. (Special compartments are set aside for cigarette addicts.)

Don't bring liquor into the Yard and don't offer your host any at any time. (Serving drinks to midshipmen is a felony in Annapolis, and no reputable restaurant will serve it to anyone at a table at which a midshipman is seated.)

Don't indulge in loud actions or in daring or eccentric clothing. (Drags have been ruled off the dance floor for both offenses—and your host is held accountable for your conduct.)

Don't wear anything that sheds. (The hairs and fuzz come off and mess up the blue uniforms.)

Don't suggest that your host take you to places. (If he is allowed to take you to them, he will ask you himself—if he wants to.)

Don't hold hands in public. (Unless they are your own.)

First among the useful bits of information that every drag should have is one that concerns her clothing.

If you expect to attend an evening hop or any other formal evening function (and what girl does not?), you need a long or short formal. If you expect to attend an afternoon informal, proper attire should also be included in your wardrobe.

If you plan to attend an outdoor athletic event that requires you to sit in a grandstand—especially a football game that is held in the fall—you should provide yourself with ample warm clothing.

You will usually know beforehand any plans which call for sports clothing. It is possible that you may need a bathing suit, though, curiously enough, facilities for swimming in and around Annapolis are limited. If you know you are going sailing, be sure to bring bermudas or slacks, and topsiders (tennis shoes).

Be sure to bring along a pair of comfortable flat shoes for walking, whether you go hiking or not; high-heeled shoes are particularly ill-adapted to the uneven brick sidewalks of Annapolis. These brick sidewalks are cordially detested by almost every Annapolitan, no matter how proud he may be of his city's antiquity. (This advice has been given for years, but with no noticeable results.)

Rain coats have saved many a gown from ruin. The light and compact emergency rain capes of cellophane or plastic are especially useful, as they are easily carried about—and the distances to go in Annapolis are not great. From the western boundary of Annapolis to the Naval Academy sea wall is less than a mile and a half, and most of the hotels and rooming houses are within a half-mile radius of the Academy.

And a small, light suitcase is preferable to a large and heavy one, whether you carry it yourself or your host carries it for you.

There are many odd bits of information that women guests will find useful; some of them may be summarized thus:

USEFUL TIPS TO WOMEN GUESTS

Of all the outdoor recreations available to drags, sailing is far and away the most popular during the fall and spring seasons. Qualified upperclassmen are permitted to take guests sailing in various units of the Academy's sailing fleet: 30 Gannet dinghies, 30 small sloops called "knockabouts," 12 44-foot yawls, the sloop *Norderney*, the yawl *Royono*, the cutter *Highland Light*, and the schooner *Freedom*. (The famous staysail ketch *Vamarie* was destroyed in a hurricane in 1954.) Daytime sailing trips of several hours' duration with midshipmen acting as crew and their drags as passengers constitute one of the major attractions of week-end parties.

Should you ask what those cute little gray boats are, with the big letters YP painted on their bows, you may be told by your host that they are yachts that belong to his rich uncle. They do; but the uncle is Uncle Sam, and the boats are his 80-ft. patrol boats used for instruction purposes by the First classmen only.

Strolling through Lover's Lane (which was once surrounded by a high hedge) has no sentimental significance whatever—and don't let any midshipman tell you differently.

A canvass of the brigade has revealed that what a drag does during the week makes little if any difference to her midshipman host, although a girl who works for a living, a coed or a debutante has a slight edge over the high-school lass.

The same canvass reveals that 85 per cent of the drags smoke cigarettes and that 75 per cent of the midshipmen wish they didn't.

The forfeit for putting on a midshipman's cap is a kiss. If you ask for it, you're likely to get it.

Stand at attention when the colors go by at parade, and also when the flag is lowered at retreat in the afternoon, from the pole in front of the Administration Building, in case you are within hearing distance of the bugles. "Standing at attention," for a woman, means merely standing upright and in silence, facing the colors, with arms at the sides.

If you are a student at a college or girls' school within a weekend radius of Annapolis, find out if the authorities have a list of approved rooming houses at Annapolis. Many of them have.

Among the conveniently located eating places, where excellent meals may be had, are the Anne Arundel Coffee Shop, Carvel Hall, the Cruise Inn, Doherty's, Harbour House, the Red Coach Inn, the La Rosa Restaurant, the Little Campus, the Treadway Maryland Inn, and the Royal Restaurant. Scattered about, too, are several drug stores, and hamburger-and-hot-dog emporiums where snacks can be had at reasonable prices.

About three miles outside of Annapolis, on U. S. 50 East which leads to the Chesapeake Bay Bridge—second longest bridge in the world—are the Annapolis Terrace Motel, Charter House Motel, and Howard Johnson Motor Lodge, all of which—plus the nearby Captain's Table—offer dining facilities.

Type	How She Looks	Why Do We Hate Her	Why Do We Like Her
THE REGAL GIRL	Brunette, serious face—heavy rouge—very neat.	She's vain—has terrible line—talks too much.	She's a good companion—has pretty eyes—is an excellent dancer.
THE CHILDISH GIRL	Small—no make-up—has adolescent skin.	She always chatters—bores one—scatter-brained.	She's charming at times—and is a great social worker.
THE CLINGING VINE	Blonde—dainty—moderate makeup—flowy clothes.	She can't open doors or light cigarettes—she has a good line.	She's good-looking—is a good dancer—is easy to please.
THE MATRON	Long hair—colorless face—no makeup—serene.	She simpers over babies—is too quiet—looks older than her age.	Has common sense—is considerate of others—is kind—and generous.
THE ATHLETIC GIRL	Tall, tanned and muscular—little makeup.	Leans over bars—too mannish—beats men in sports.	She's healthy—clear-eyed—and candid. She's an excellent companion.
THE PERSONALITY GIRL	Pleasant looks—startling makeup—cleverly dressed.	She always gets in your hair—she won't let you forget her.	She respects others—she's intelligent—friendly—never catty.
THE BEAUTIFUL-BUT-DUMB GIRL	Blonde hair—heavy makeup—very, very pretty—brightly dressed.	Disgustingly ignorant—shallow—vain—can't talk well.	She's an excellent date if you want to impress your friends.
THE COQUETTE	Small size—brown hair—neat—wears a lot of white.	She's inconstant—fickle—and tells all the boys the same things.	She has good manners—is intelligent—and is an able speaker.
THE NATURAL GIRL	Brown hair—innocent-looking features—bright teeth.	She's hard to get next to . . . !	She's naïve—truthful—modest sincere—and straightforward.

SIZE UP THEIR DRAGS

By These Words Ye Shall Know Her	Is She Worth the Time and Trouble	The Successful Wooer Will—	And This Is How It Will End
"Do you think my nose is shiny, John?"	See her without makeup before you decide anything.	Tell her that she is divine—that her teeth are like stars—etc.	You will go broke buying her new nylons.
"John dear, please don't drink tonight."	Yes, if you go in for baby talk.	Arouse all her reforming instincts by traveling the road to ruin.	She will put you on a cigarette and cocktail ration within a month.
"Oh, gracious, John! How strong you are!"	(Censored) no!	Treat her rough in the true style of the caveman.	She will henpeck you the rest of your life.
"John, why don't we stay home tonight!"	Yes, if you are a family man.	Impress her by kissing strange little babies on the street.	You'll be an old and tired husband before you're thirty.
"Goodness, John, you aren't tired already are you?"	Yes, if you can stand her beating you in every sport.	Appeal to her on an intellectual plane.	You will stay home with "baby" while she's out playing golf.
"Say, John, did you hear the one about . . ."	Absolutely, if you have the time and money.	Be straightforward and real.	You'll be the happiest and the most popular couple on the avenue.
"Shall we talk about each other?" (she means herself in this case)	Yes, if you have a yen for useless ornaments.	Tell her that she is beautiful, at least every five minutes.	She'll be fat and ugly when she's thirty—and you'll go broke buying her beauty aids.
"Let's slip away from the crowd, shall we, John?"	Yes, if you are not jealous by nature.	Show her plenty of excitement.	She will charm your friends and leave you in the background.
"I don't love you, John, but can't we still be friends?"	Nice work if you can get it!	be natural—gay —truthful and candid—and own a sense of humor.	It will end like all marriages should —IN HEAVEN!

—Courtesy of "The Log."

The legend that the statue of Tecumseh will draw one of the ten arrows out of his quiver and shoot a drag who has always been true to her midshipman sweetheart is a base canard; don't believe a word of it.

If you have a friend who is desirous of attending a hop at the Naval Academy but does not know any midshipman to invite her, you may ask your own midshipman to provide a host for her—sight unseen. The midshipmen are naturally a bit cautious about taking a chance on a "blind drag," partly because it entails expense and partly because it may expose them to the embarrassments of a "brick party." And a brick party, which is almost always inspired by a blind-drag date, is spectacularly unique and wholly indigenous to the Naval Academy.

Sooner or later, every drag who appears more or less regularly at midshipmen functions is given a rating on the same 4.0 system as that on which academic marks are given; nothing formal, of course, and certainly never a matter of record; the ratings are intended just to give a fellow a rough idea about how the drag stacks up. While you and Brigitte Bardot and Gina Lollobrigida all rate tops at 4.0 flat, no doubt, other girls may have a somewhat more slippery hold on feminine charms; unless they attain the passing mark of 2.5, they are mentally pigeon-holed as "bricks." And that is what an occasional blind drag turns out to be. Every once in a while a blind drag shows up as—well, just as someone who does not quite fit into the midshipman picture. Perhaps she is a bit uncouth in her manners; possibly she does or says something that just isn't done or said. When such accidents happen, the midshipman who brings her is sticking his neck out, and he is likely to be given a boisterous hint, wholly lacking in finesse, that whoever induced him to drag blind pulled a fast one and that the joke is on him. Brick parties are purely battalion affairs.

So it was Midshipman Whosis who dragged that Miss Wzzxhsch last evening, was it?

Word is passed down the line after Sunday morning breakfast for certain plebes to assemble in a certain room on the first deck —a room far removed from that occupied by Midshipman Whosis on the fourth deck and consequently not under suspicion. A mere handful of plebes, under the direction of upper classmen, are enough to get the event under way; once it starts, it accumulates like a snowball hurtling down a mountainside during a spring thaw.

The procession that forms in the corridor has the appearance of a circus parade gone mad. At the head march the outriders in such weird combinations of uniforms and underwear as their fancy dictates, carrying mop handles for spears; close behind comes the clown band, whose unrehearsed efforts may or may not be supplemented with drums but which otherwise consists of such instruments as shower clogs, battered trumpets, jew's-harps, tin pans and hair combs. After that marches the Bearer of the Brick, clad in a bath-towel turban, trunks, boots and modernistic decorations inscribed upon his person in colored chalks; he bears before him a pillow on which the uncoveted masonry reposes, all tied up in nice tissue and ribbon and perhaps covered with a silk guidon flag; behind him come the wild animals—elephants with gray-blanket hides and stuffed-stocking trunks, and other nightmare beasts more difficult to classify. And somewhere marches the Maker of the Presentation Speech, who may be an oriental potentate if suitable costume effects are available, or perhaps just a plain American Indian, wrapped in a blanket, with a headdress consisting of a broom, and smoking a long pipe of peace.

As this aggregation moves forward on command, the band breaks into a noise that would make the sound-effects producer of a television station run around in circles. Grinning faces appear at open doors; half-clad figures emerge and fall in line, led by curiosity. Down one corridor the laughing mob wends its way, up the ladder (stairway to you) to another deck, gathering numbers as it progresses. When it halts before the door of the victim, the ranks open and the Bearer of the Brick makes a majestic entrance, followed by the Maker of the Presentation Speech; the rag-tag and bobtail crowd in behind.

The victim has no alternative but to grin and like it. He hails his visitors jovially.

"Speech! Speech!" the visitors cry.

The audience cheers his efforts. Candid cameras click from the tops of tables and radiators. The party melts away. It is all over within a few minutes.

"But what if he really knows and likes the drag?" a visitor may ask.

In that case brick parties are definitely out. Never are feelings knowingly hurt. Any girl who has the affections of a midshipman rests secure under the protecting wing of every man in the brigade. And that is the way it ought to be.

Moral: "Never drag blind and you'll never get bricked."

There's a good deal to this dragging business, and to help out the ladies, particularly those who have never before been guests at the Naval Academy, the staff of the midshipmen's humor magazine, the *Log*, publish a very useful as well as amusing guide called *The Drag's Handbook*, available at modest cost. Many a girl who has read it in advance of her visit has felt much more at her ease when she got to Annapolis by reason of this clever little pamphlet.

TIME OF DAY IN THE NAVY

(for the benefit of the uninitiated).

Civilian Time	Navy Time
1:00 A.M.	0100 ("oh one hundred," etc.)
2:00	0200
3:00	0300
4:00	0400
5:00	0500
6:00	0600
7:00	0700
8:00	0800
9:00	0900
10:00	1000 ("ten hundred," etc.)
11:00	1100
12:00 Noon	1200
1:00 P.M.	1300
2:00	1400
3:00	1500
4:00	1600
5:00	1700
6:00	1800
7:00	1900
8:00	2000
9:00	2100
10:00	2200
11:00	2300
12:00 Midnight	2400

Chapter 13

Midshipman Practice Cruises

BY DON D. THORNBURY

Cruises for the practical training of midshipmen antedate the Naval Academy itself. The first one of record was initiated by the Navy without the aid of Congress, in 1817, twenty-eight years before the Naval School was established. It was undertaken at the suggestion of Commodore William Bainbridge, who obtained the United States brig *Prometheus* for a cruise along the Atlantic coast. It is a long cry from that primitive but successful experiment to the highly organized practice cruises of today.

The mission of the practice cruise of eight weeks is "to train midshipmen of the First and Third classes in practical work afloat." A secondary mission is to expose the midshipmen to such cultural opportunities as may be afforded by meeting foreigners on their home grounds.

The itinerary of the trip is carefully planned, of course, long in advance. It is customary for the squadron to visit Europe, where it usually stops at two ports. In the selection of these ports several factors have to be taken into consideration. The ports must be free from epidemics and in a good state of sanitation. They must have adequate facilities for obtaining food, fuel and supplies. They must have adequate anchorage facilities and should be reasonably secure from sudden storms. And the ports must be under the control of nations which are on friendly terms with Uncle Sam and where, consequently, a reception of the midshipmen is not likely to be marred by unfortunate incidents.

When the plans of the practice cruise are finally drawn and approved by the Superintendent, they are forwarded to Naval

Operations in Washington. From that point they go to the Secretary of State, who communicates with the foreign governments that control the ports of call and obtains their consent and approval. This provides plenty of time in which to arrange for receptions, entertainments and short tours for the midshipmen.

The first port of call is Norfolk, Virginia, where the squadron stops to embark Naval Reserve Officers Training Corps midshipmen from civilian colleges throughout the country. Naval Academy and NROTC midshipmen are embarked together in each ship as a single integrated unit, thereby creating a close relationship and the opportunity for making friendships which will last throughout their careers. Out of this integration comes a homogeneous Junior Officer group, graduates from each source aiding in broadening the outlook of the other.

The duties of the midshipman on his first, or "Youngster," cruise are closely associated with those of the enlisted men, and introduce him to life aboard a man-of-war. To insure that the Training Squadron does not become a militarily ineffective group of "school ships," each midshipman is integrated into the ship's battle organization as a member of a closely coordinated team. In addition to his permanent battle station assignment, he is also assigned to various stations and watches under instruction as he rotates through the three phases devoted to Operations (which includes navigation), Gunnery, and Engineering, respectively. He will stand watches such as lookout, lifeboat crew member, burner tender in a fireroom, or assistant in an engine room; and learn the basic arts of loading, pointing, and firing the ship's main and anti-aircraft batteries.

The practical training of Second class summer consists of indoctrination in amphibious warfare, and a three-phase introduction to all phases of naval aviation, generally referred to as "aviation summer." On the day the First and Third classes leave for their practice cruise, the Second class embarks in an APA (attack transport) for Norfolk, Virginia, where they board buses for Little Creek, site of the Naval Amphibious Base. Here they participate for two weeks in a highly realistic venture called TRAMID (TRAining of MIDshipmen), the climax of which is an actual amphibious attack landing, complete except for the serious shooting. The program begins with movies and classes on the management of amphibious gear. The midshipmen are taught how to pilot the LCVP's (Landing Craft, Vehicles, Personnel) and how to get into them over the side of the attack transport, accomplished by means of "dry net" and "wet net" drills. In the "dry net" drill the midshipmen climb up a tower rigged with a huge rope net down which they clamber; they graduate from this to the "wet net," which implies of course scrambling down the net actually rigged against the side of a ship. They also witness some demonstrations of the latest Navy frogman underwater tactics.

At the end of the second week they "hit the beach," shoving off from their APA in their LCVP's and "fighting" their way inland after a preliminary bombardment of the beachhead. The attack is made as authentic as possible, even to the issuance of K-rations for the noon meal.

The Naval Academy Phase of aviation summer comprises flight and aircrew indoctrination in training seaplanes and multi-engine amphibians, and instruction and lectures in all phases of flight operation, including that of the helicopter. The midshipmen do not actually pilot the planes, the purpose of the course being not to train pilots, but to demonstrate the important role of aircraft in the modern American Navy. There is also a trip to Patuxent for a really fast ride in a jet.

The Field Trip Phase includes a five-day visit to naval installations in and around Philadelphia and a trip to the Glenn L. Martin Aircraft Factory in Baltimore. A hot time in Philly is provided by a big oil fire which the midshipman learns how to extinguish in the safest and most effective manner.

The last phase of aviation summer is the carrier cruise, a three-week cruise in a first-line aircraft carrier, which usually makes a run to Halifax and back. The midshipmen serve in enlisted and officer billets and stand watches as they do on the other cruises, but of course there are lots of new things to see and learn and do aboard this very special type of combatant ship. The big thrill comes in the flights from and landings on the carrier deck, by both day and night.

On his final, or First class, cruise, the midshipman is assigned duties more closely approximating those of a Junior Division Officer or senior Petty Officer. Again he has a permanent station in the overall battle organization, generally requiring a higher sense of responsibility and degree of training than in his Youngster Cruise. Also, he again rotates through the three phases of training; although this cruise finds him performing practical celestial navigation and piloting, standing watch as Junior Officer of the Deck, Junior Engineering Officer of the Watch, Communications Watch Officer, and CIC Watch Officer, among others. His gunnery training progresses to the study and operation of the complex surface and anti-aircraft fire control systems.

Instruction while at sea takes two forms. One consists of lectures and classroom work conducted by the officers of the Naval Academy; the subjects covered include electrical and steam engineering, ordnance, gunnery, seamanship and navigation; in case a civilian instructor happens to be aboard, talks are given on the literature and on the people and customs of the countries about to be visited. No study is required, but the midshipmen must keep notebooks. The lectures are supplemented by gunnery drills; in order to familiarize the midshipmen with the different types of guns, they are rotated among the different gun stations. While not thus engaged, all except those who are standing watches are given general ship's work until 4:00 o'clock in the afternoon. From then until suppertime the midshipmen may relax completely and enjoy their recreation hours.

The most popular pastime during recreation hours is reading. Outward bound, some write letters home; on the homeward course, letters addressed to misses, frauleins, mademoiselles and senoritas who live in the ports recently visited make up a suspiciously large proportion of the ship's mail. Some of the midshipmen spend their leisure time pasting up scrapbooks; others indulge in athletic exercises and such ship's games as volley ball and quoits played with rope rings. On many ships trap shooting from the fantail is held on Saturday afternoons. Another diversion, appropriately enough, is the fashioning of curious knickknacks from sail, twine, canvas and similar material found aboard, under the guidance of obliging old tars; many of the midshipmen show extraordinary skill and ingenuity in weaving fancy belts. So popular has this industry become that

Making a navigational fix of a ship's position during a summer cruise.

*U*p and out of the hatch.
*Midshipmen not only get their sea
legs during summer cruises but
also become familiar with other
aspects of life aboard ship.*

the ships' stores now carry supplies of belt buckles to meet the demand.

A mimeographed "Plan of the Day" is distributed to all hands early each morning while under way. It clearly sets forth the work and training schedule for that day, as well as indicating the watch standers and making general announcements. Part of an actual Plan of the Day for a heavy cruiser upon arrival at a foreign port on a recent practice cruise is shown below.

Uniform of the Day:

Officers and CPO's:	Service Dress Khaki
Midshipmen:	White Working Dress, Charlie
Enlisted Personnel:	Undress White ABLE

Uniform of entering Port:

Officers and CPO's:	Service Dress White
Midshipmen:	White Working Dress, Charlie
Enlisted Personnel:	Undress White ABLE

Uniform for liberty and shore leave

Officers:	Service Dress Khaki or Civilian clothes
Midshipmen and CPO's:	Service Dress, Khaki
Other enlisted:	Undress White ABLE with neckerchief

0100	Voice Communication Drill (Exercise No. 53) OCE:WOOD. Set all clocks ahead one (1) hour to zone minus 1 (ABLE) Time.
0200	Flashing Light Drill (Exercise No. 21) OCE:MACON.
0400	Voice Communication Drill (Exercise No. 53) OCE:LEARY.
0511	Sunrise
0545	Reveille
0600	Turn to. Pipe sweepers. Scrub down all weather decks. Muster all restricted men. Breakfast for watchstanders, 1st Class Petty Officers and Anchor Detail
0615–	
0715	Breakfast
0700	Set the Anchor Detail
0735	Set the Special Sea Detail
0740	Be prepared to receive Pilot either side by Jacob's Ladder.
0745	Quarters for muster and entering port.
0800	Fire National Salute.

0815 Turn to.
0820 Sick call.
1100 Liberty commences for section three of the crew to expire on board at 0100 for enlisted men. Liberty expires at 2400 for 1st class Midshipmen and at 2330 for 3rd class midshipmen. Liberty expires at 0200 for CPO's. Liberty expires at 0730 for officers.
1130 Pipe sweepers. Dinner for watchstanders and 1st Class Petty Officers.
1145–
1245 Dinner
1300 Pipe sweepers. Muster all restricted men. Commence Holiday Routine.
1330 Shore Patrol Muster and Depart.
1540 Pipe sweepers.
1600 All hands shift into the clean uniform of the day.
1615 "Muster Fire and Rescue Party do not provide."
1630 Supper for watchstanders and 1st Class Petty Officers.
1645–
1745 Supper
1800 Pipe sweepers
1815 Muster all restricted men.
1915 8 o'clock reports.
2000 Movies
2004 Sunset
2115 Muster all restricted men.
2200 Taps.
2400 Liberty expires on board for 1st class midshipmen at 2400: for 3rd class 2330.
0100 Liberty expires on board for enlisted men.
0200 Liberty expires on board for Chief Petty Officers.

NOTE #1 We used 26.1 gallons of fresh water per man yesterday. We should not use over 20 gallons. Let's make every effort to reduce this waste.

NOTE #2 The fueling of the DD was Well Done. All concerned are to be commended.

NOTE #3 The contributions to the Orphan's Party total about $300. This generous attitude on the part of the crew exemplifies fine spirit. Thanks for putting these parties over.

NOTE #4 Currency exchange lines will be run on Saturday, June 19, to exchange U. S. currency into Spanish currency. The port line will form outside the Disbursing Office. The starboard line will form aft of the passage, which enters into the Personnel Office.

Word will be passed concerning the starting time. One American dollar is worth 38.95 pesetas. One peseta is worth 2.567 American cents. Based on the best information money will be exchanged in increments of $4.00 for which you will receive 155 pesetas and 2 cents.

While the midshipmen are placed in positions of authority, and while they do actually perform the duties, the responsibilities they assume are nominal rather than real, and they perform the duties as understudies. Uncle Sam is not so naive as to assume that his youthful proteges can officiate as officers—yet. After all, the lives of from 300 to 3000 officers and men may be at stake, to say nothing of many millions of dollars' worth of ship, armament and equipment.

Lurking somewhere in the background behind every midshipman who is standing an important watch is a commissioned officer or an experienced enlisted man selected because of his even temper as well as for his abilities. Always is he observing, guiding, appraising, ever ready to step forward and assert his authority in case of need. The First classman who is standing an important watch is in much the position of an aviation cadet who is flying a plane with his instructor-pilot standing by at a dual set of controls; as long as he is doing all right he is left alone. Just because First Classman Gish is acting as a junior officer in charge of the Youngster detail on the signal bridge, for illustration, it does not follow that he will be allowed even accidentally to make an error that might lead to trouble. The supervision over him is too alert. The folks back home need have no fear concerning Junior's safety merely because the ship on which he is traveling is turned over to the midshipmen.

"Field day" aboard ship is a deceiving and double-faced term. In its less happy sense it means that "general cleaning-up day" which comes on Friday—every Friday. Between 8:00 in the morning and 4:00 in the afternoon every bit of paint work must be washed by the Youngsters, every bit of metal work polished, every bit of canvas from hatch covers to gun covers scrubbed, in preparation for the especially rigorous inspection of the upper decks by the Captain on Saturday mornings. The same term is also used to designate the couple of days during the cruise devoted to sports; one of the days is always the Fourth of July. These festive affairs are enlivened with such amusing contests as the limitations of the ship and the ingenuity of the midshipmen permit; they include such old stand-bys as sack races, potato races, obstacle races, dressing races, rope-climbing races and boxing matches astride a spar. The rules of this latter unique and precarious contest provide for the use of a boxing glove on only the one hand which is used to sock the other fellow, while the unclad fist is put to excellent service in hanging on to the perch. These fields days traditionally end up with a tug-of-war between representatives of the ship's divisions; the winners are rewarded by bringing extra shore liberty to their comrades.

Musical smokers are staged about three times during the cruise, between 7:00 and 9:00 o'clock in the evening. The midshipmen assemble on the main deck, where boxing bouts, wrestling matches, vaudeville acts, and musical entertainment are presented.

As soon as the squadron drops anchor in a foreign port, representatives of a travel agency come aboard and change American currency into the coin of the local realm. The average turnover for each ship on the day of arrival is about $6000.

These travel agencies are awarded contracts for this service by the Naval Academy authorities long in advance. The business goes to the lowest bidder, as is customary with Navy contracts. All of the group tours provided for in any one port are awarded to one company; usually several short tours are made available to the midshipmen who choose to make them—at their own expense—while on shore leave. A fixed sum of money is required for each of these leave tours; this sum is sufficient to cover all necessary expenses; any midshipman who takes it should be able to do so without a cent in his jeans. To make sure that this may be done in fact as well as in theory, the Naval Academy authorites insist that the following services be rendered by the travel agency:

Only Class A or Class B hotels shall be patronized. (The uniform should be seen only in places above reproach.)

A separate bed must be provided for each midshipman. (Several midshipmen may be assigned to one room, however.)

The cost of baths, not to exceed one a day, shall be included.

(Some European hotels charge their guests for each bath they take.)

Three meals a day must be provided in the main dining room of hotels or in first-class restaurants. (Sidetracking the midshipmen into auxiliary dining rooms or into servants' halls is not permitted.)

A real, honest-to-goodness American breakfast must be furnished, with fruit, cereal, bacon-and-eggs, toast, coffee 'n' everything. ("Continental breakfasts" do not rate as an American meal at all.)

All transportation costs must be included, railroad fares and, in case of need, bus fares, street-car fares and ferry fares also. As the midshipmen travel in uniform, they are sometimes accorded the special military rates as a courtesy.

All gratuities, tips, fees and other forms of tribute exacted by porters, waiters, couriers and English-speaking guide-lecturers must be included in the lump-sum cost of the group tour; also all admission fees to buildings visited.

No midshipman is compelled to go on these group tours; they are offered to him purely for his own pleasure. The costs of them are about half of what he would have to pay for similar accommodations were he making the tour on his own.

As a guaranty that the midshipmen get their information straight about the countries they visit, untainted by propaganda, bias, obsolescence or editorial errors, the Naval Academy issues its own guide-books every year under the modest title of *Cruise Ports*. This practical little volume of nearly 200 pages is prepared by experienced members of the Department of English, History and Government, who are not only extensively traveled men themselves but who keep their information up to date by participating in the practice cruises and by making explorative tours in anticipation of the cruise for the following year. In view of the quick shifts in the national, political, and racial conflicts in Europe and the changing aspects of the European map, these volumes serve a much larger purpose than merely pointing out places to visit, things to see and prices to pay; they interpret the background and the people of the countries, and explain their viewpoints and customs in terms that the midshipmen can grasp and put to immediate use.

When the weather is good while at sea, anti-aircraft firing exercises are frequently conducted, especially while en route to Guantanamo Bay, Cuba, from the last foreign port. Midshipmen man the guns, communications and firecontrol systems under close supervision of the regular ship's company. Twin three-inch fifties on the cruisers and battleships and twin turreted five-inch guns on the destroyers, cruisers and battleships fire at cloth sleeves towed at a discreet distance by a plane from an aircraft carrier. The practice cruise squadrons since World War II have been centered around the carrier. Radio controlled drones launched from cruisers and battleships also serve as targets for antiaircraft exercises.

Demonstrations, such as destroyers firing depth charge patterns as they steam down a lane formed by the cruisers and battleships, and star shell firing at night to show how enemy ships may be silhouetted against the horizon are also part of the cruise training. Man overboard drills, blackout drills, steering casualty problems, fire drills, and even simulated atomic attack conditions are conducted, sometimes without advance notice, to test the alertness of the ships' crews.

Upon arrival at Guantanamo Bay and the huge Atlantic Fleet base located there, preparations are made for the actual firing of the big eight-inch batteries of the heavy cruisers and sixteen-inch batteries of the battleships. These big guns of the fleet are never fired on the open sea; only on the Atlantic Fleet firing range in the waters off Guantanamo Bay are heavy gun exercises held.

Extreme measures are taken to insure safety; indeed, the preliminary work is devoted entirely to detailed instructions in handling both the guns and the ammunition in a manner that reduces the hazards to the minimum. Speed and accuracy of fire, important as these factors are, must ever be subordinated to safety. The scores made at target practice do not enter into the inter-ship competition, but those midshipmen whose guns attain the highest percentages receive medals from the Naval Academy. The targets are square sails of canvas mounted on floats towed by tugs; the bits of color left on the edges of the holes made by the shells indicate the guns from which the shots have been fired.

After completion of the exercises, which usually last about three days, the squadron heads for Annapolis by way of Norfolk to disembark the midshipmen. The day of disembarkation marks the beginning of the annual summer leave. Reveille comes early and is eagerly awaited. After breakfast the rapid stowing of clothing and gear and the boat ride to the dock are accomplished with dispatch. A change of uniform and departure on leave follow in rapid succession. The thirty-day leave period scatters the midshipmen to all parts of the United States, to recount the stories of ports visited and to display the purchases made in foreign countries. To no group, however, is this leave period more exciting than to the new third class. They have completed their first year at the Naval Academy and their first tour of sea duty. Not until they spot the Chapel dome on their return from cruise do they rate the designation "Youngsters."

The graduate of the Naval Academy or an NROTC institution is not a finished product upon being commissioned in the Naval Service. Rather, he is a Junior Officer with a basic education and knowledge of the naval profession, developed mentally, morally, and physically, and indoctrinated with the highest ideals of duty, honor, and loyalty. Developed in him are the capabilities and foundations for future development in mind and character which will lead him toward a readiness to assume the highest responsibilities of citizenship and government. In addition to the tangibles there is considerable evidence of the intangibles that manifest themselves in the graduate as the process of development continues.

The seeds of this development are planted early in a midshipman's career, not only in the home and during the academic year, but while on the cruise. For in addition to learning to become a man-of-war's man he is acquiring other attributes, the outward manifestations of which are not immediately apparent, but the latent forces of which are in being for the future. Thus, the importance of the Midshipmen's Cruise cannot be measured solely by simple fulfillment of the cruise objectives but also by the imperceptible contributions to the individual, the Naval Service, and Country.*

* (Quoted from *1952 General Information Book*.)

Chapter 14

Sentinels of the Valiant

HERNDON

Carved in sharp relief upon the face of an unadorned brownstone shaft in front of the Chapel, that one word stands alone in stark and eloquent simplicity. It needs further identification no more than do the names "Washington," "Lincoln," "Grant." In the annals of the sea there is but one Herndon.

This monument does more than perpetuate the name and fame of one man; it symbolizes the ideals and the traditions of the United States Navy which the Academy has taken upon itself to preserve as the heritage of all naval officers; ideals and traditions which, through the imperishable medium of stone and marble, are held constantly before succeeding generations of midshipmen; ideals of duty and traditions of honor that are woven into the fabric of the Naval Academy itself. The memorials that mark the Academy grounds are not gravestones; the bodies of the heroic dead whose names are graven upon them do not rest here; most of them have long been part of the sea. To the midshipmen of today these silent sentinels bear a message, indefinable, intangible, from gallant officers and gentlemen who won the noblest of all accolades:

FAITHFUL UNTO DEATH

The drama behind the Herndon monument constitutes one of the great epics of the sea. Commander William Lewis Herndon was born in 1813, and had been an officer of the Navy several years when the Naval Academy was founded. He was the brother-in-law of Commander Matthew Fontaine Maury (after whom Maury Hall is named), who even as a mere midshipman had established himself as one of the foremost authorities on navigation. It is a matter of interest, too, that Herndon's

160

daughter, Ellen, who at the time of her father's death was a small child, later married Chester A. Arthur, who became the President of the United States.

In accordance with the laws of that period, which allowed officers of the Navy to command vessels carrying U. S. mail, Herndon was detailed by the Navy Department in 1855 to the Pacific Mail steamship *Central America*, a side-wheeler. On its fateful trip from Aspinwall (now Colon), Panama, to New York, the vessel carried a crew of 101 and 474 passengers—a total of 575 souls, of whom all but 152 were fated to die. At midnight of September 9, 1857, when just north of the ever perilous Cape Hatteras, North Carolina, the ship ran into a storm of hurricane force that marked the beginning of a desperate three-day struggle for existence. Sails were blown into shreds. When leaks were sprung that caused the vessel to list dangerously, bailing gangs were put to work, but when the incoming waters extinguished the fire under the boilers and the ship became helpless, the *Central America* faced disaster. The national ensign was hoisted upside down, as a signal of distress; the brig *Marine* came to the rescue and stood by.

But how could the passengers and crew be transferred through the gale and across the mountainous seas? Herndon had but two lifeboats with which to meet the crisis. And what assurance had he, in case these boats should miraculously reach safety, that the crews would have the courage to come back for other loads?

Not a man wavered in his duty; not a boat faltered in its mission. Each lifeboat succeeded in making two trips; each followed to the letter the ancient law, "women and children first," and nearly a hundred were thus rescued. As the next-to-last boat to leave was about to pull away, Herndon approached one of the passengers and placed his watch in his keeping.

"Give this to my wife," he directed. "Tell her—"

But his voice broke. Burying his face in his hands, he turned abruptly.

He ordered the hurricane deck cut away and converted into rafts. He directed the distribution of life belts. He supervised the sending of rockets at half-hour intervals. In the meantime the storm raged unabating and the vessel slowly, steadily, sank lower into the angry waters. One of the lifeboats, returning heroically for a third attempt at rescue, came close; so close that it threatened to be engulfed by the doomed vessel. In spite of the knowledge that this lifeboat offered the last chance of safety for himself, Herndon ordered it to keep off. It was his last command.

When it became apparent that the ship was beyond all human aid and that certain death was only a matter of minutes, Herndon made a gesture that for sheer majesty is probably unparalleled in naval history. He went to his stateroom and donned his finest uniform; from his gold-braided hat he even removed the oiled silk covering, in order that it might appear at its brightest. Buckling on his belt and sword, he stepped forth and calmly took his position on the wheelhouse, clutching the railing with his left hand. If this was to be the moment in which he was to come face to face with his Maker, he would greet Him erect and unafraid, clad in the best he had to offer—the ceremonial full-dress uniform of an officer of the United States Navy.

For a fleeting moment the awed spectators in the lifeboat were illuminated by the burst of the last rocket flare overhead. They saw the doomed ship give a last, convulsive lurch. With upturned face, Herndon uncovered, raising his hat high in salute, and disappeared beneath the waves at his post of duty.

"It was one of the sublimest spectacles ever witnessed," reads the special report to the Secretary of the Navy, made by Lieutenant Maury on October 19, 1857. "Forgetful of self, mindful of others, his life was beautiful to the last, and in his death he had added a new glory to the annals of the sea."

The monument to Herndon stands in the Yard, not because it is either impressive in size or beautiful in design, for it is neither. But from the day of its arrival in Annapolis on June 14, 1860, on the brig *A. Lawrence*, it has memorialized that uncompromising sense of devotion to duty that is the requisite of American naval officers, and which therefore has become a part of the tradition of the Naval Academy itself and an inspiration to its midshipmen.

A few paces nearer toward the sea wall and squarely in the center of the double-tracked Stribling Walk that runs straight between Bancroft Hall and Mahan Hall rises the white marble memorial that is variously known as the Mexican Monument and the Vera Cruz Monument. Each of its four sides bears the name of a single midshipman, graven in letters of gold—"Pillsbury," "Clemson," "Shubrick," "Hynson." At each corner is mounted a 12-pound, smooth-bore Spanish cannon of embossed bronze captured by the United States Navy from the Mexicans in California in 1847.

This monument was not raised by a grateful Republic; it was not even raised by a grateful Navy Department. It was not authorized by Congress nor paid for out of public funds. It was conceived and erected "by passed and other midshipmen of the United States Navy as a tribute of respect, 1848," and it was paid for out of their own meager personal allowances. Thus it becomes something a bit more than a mere memorial to the four valiant souls whose names it bears; it assumes the character of a message from the past, of a torch lit by the midshipmen of a century ago to be kept aflame and passed down to the generations of midshipmen to follow.

Passed Midshipman Henry A. Clemson was acting-master of the brig *Somers*, on duty off Vera Cruz during the War with Mexico; serving with him was Passed Midshipman J. R. Hynson. On December 8, 1846, an enemy vessel attempted to make the harbor; the *Somers*, under a press of canvas, started to intercept it. During the pursuit a norther struck the light American brig with such unexpected fury as to throw her on her beam ends, and she sank within ten minutes, carrying to death Midshipmen Hynson and thirty-seven of her crew of eighty. In the purely factual record of the disaster is found the following terse sentence; in it is packed a story that gives meaning to the term *noblesse oblige:*

> The acting-master Henry A. Clemson was struggling on a small steering sail boom with five others, two of whom could not be supported, and he left and struck out alone and unsupported.

The record concludes with the brief observation:

> He probably perished in the surf.

In an almost identical manner did Midshipman J. W. Pillsbury sacrifice his life in observance of the same tradition of the Navy. While serving on the USS *Mississippi* off Vera Cruz, a small enemy vessel attempted to run the blockade on the night of June 24, 1846. Pillsbury was directed to take command of the launch and give chase. At midnight a heavy squall of wind and rain capsized the craft, which immediately filled with water. Again the cold and impersonal report preserved the record of the knightly deed that followed:

> As there was a heavy sea running at the time, both men and officers were several times swept from their hold on the boat, but as often succeeded in regaining it, until Wingate (Pillsbury), observing that one of the men either from exhaustion or want of skill, could swim but little, ordered him to seize a more elevated situation of that frail bark by which he was supported, and sought some less desirable position. While engaged in making this change in favor of one of his men, a sea struck and carried him far from all aid . . ."

The fourth member of this little band, Midshipman T. B. Shubrick, was serving on one of the vessels participating in the joint land and sea attack upon Vera Cruz. Such eagerness did the crews express to take an active part in the military operations that General Winfield Scott assigned a place in the line to the naval forces. Three detachments were thereupon made up from the volunteers in the fleet, and Commander Alexander S. Mackenzie—he whose memorial tablet today adorns the south wall of the Chapel—was placed in command. Three 8-inch Paixhan guns and three long 32-pounders were removed from the vessels and dragged with great difficulty through the sand to the assigned position in the trenches. It was while pointing one of the guns that Midshipman Shubrick was killed.

Reaching back to the short but spectacular war with the Tripolitan pirates in the early part of the nineteenth century, the Naval Academy has claimed as its rightful heritage and added to its own legion of valor six young naval officers who found the end of the adventuresome trail to glory off the alien coast of Africa. To the honor of the men themselves and to the spirit of the Navy which they so heroically exemplified, stands the pretentious marble memorial, revealing in its conventionalized figures and ornate detail unmistakable evidence of its Italian origin, known as the Tripoli Monument. On each of the four sides of its massive rectangular base are inscribed their names—Somers, Caldwell, Decatur, Wadsworth, Dorsey, Israel.

Like the Mexican monument, this too was reared by brother officers; "as a small tribute of respect to their memory and of admiration of their valour, so worthy of imitation," the inscription reads. Its symbolic statues of America, Commerce and History, all three about to be crowned with laurel by a winged Victory who has apparently climbed to a higher vantage point from which to accomplish his purpose; its richly carved pedestal bordered with a frieze of turbaned Tripolitan heads, the whole surmounted by a shaft crowned with a coat of arms, together with a bronze plaque depicting in relief a naval battle and signed with the name of the artist Micali, was made in Italy in 1806. Two years later it was set up in the Washington Navy Yard, where it was mutilated during the occupation of that city by the British in 1814; traces of these mutilations are still visible. The memorial was restored by Congress, however, and removed to the grounds of the Capitol, where it remained until it was set up near its present site, midway between the Officer's Club and Sampson Hall, in 1860.

The first of this little company of officers to die was Lieutenant James Decatur. While in command of a gunboat in an engagement with the Tripolitan fleet on August 3, 1804, he singled out a vessel of the enemy and after a furious assault forced its surrender. While stepping aboard to take possession, he was treacherously killed by the Turkish commander—who was, in turn, almost immediately cut down himself by his victim's infuriated brother, Lieutenant Stephen Decatur, Jr., who was destined to carve a name for himself high on the honor roll of his country.

Four days later the Americans hurled a second attack upon the Tripolitan fleet, which kept close within the harbor under the protection of shore batteries. One of the more venturesome of the American gunboats, which had approached to close quarters, was hit near the magazine by a hot shot; in the explosion that followed, the vessel was sunk, carrying with it the bodies of its two young officers, Lieutenant James Caldwell and Lieutenant John Dorsey.

A naval action that for excitement, daring and spectacular scenic effects is comparable to the lurid melodramas of the Hollywood film producers, took place a month afterward. On September 3, 1804, the American squadron under Commodore Edward Preble for the fourth time attacked. In a desperate effort to strike the enemy, the appropriately named ketch *Intrepid*—the same two-masted vessel that had shortly before been captured from the Tripolitans and had been used by Lieutenant Stephen Decatur, Jr., in his historic destruction of the frigate *Philadelphia*, which had fallen into the enemy's hands —was fitted out as a fireship. She was loaded with a hundred barrels of gunpowder in bulk; on the deck immediately above were placed 150 shells and a quantity of shot. To navigate this floating mine into the harbor under cover of darkness and explode it in the midst of Tripolitan shipping was a hazardous undertaking that demanded daring and skill. Captain Richard Somers was selected to head the adventure; to accompany him he selected Lieutenant Joseph Israel and a small crew of volunteers. But another young officer, Lieutenant Henry Wadsworth, son of the doughty old captain Peleg Wadsworth of Minute Men fame, was not to be denied. He resolutely insisted upon accompanying his friends on their desperate mission, and go he did.

Disguised as a blockade runner and furnished with two rowing boats for the last-minute escape of the crew, the *Intrepid* set forth on the night of September 4, 1804. Just before she entered the harbor, however, she ran aground; before she could get free, she was discovered and subjected to the fire of the Tripolitan guns. With a flash and a roar that shook the harbor, the ketch disappeared; no soul aboard escaped. Whether Somers had deliberately fired the magazine in order to avoid capture, as many believe, or whether the combustibles had been set off by an enemy shot, no man will ever know. To the men who led this little band of high-spirited volunteers, a panel on the Tripolitan monument pays this tribute, which expresses the symbolism of the monument itself:

THE LOVE OF GLORY INSPIRED THEM,
FAME HAS CROWNED THEIR DEEDS,
HISTORY RECORDS THE EVENT,
THE CHILDREN OF COLUMBIA ADMIRE,
AND COMMERCE LAMENTS THEIR FALL.

Three years after the death of Lieutenant Henry Wadsworth, his sister gave birth to a son. His name was Henry Wadsworth Longfellow.

Across the waters of Dorsey Creek, directly north of Worden Field and on the highest point of the Naval Academy cemetery, stands a stone cairn—such as man builds for a marker in the Arctic wastes—surmounted by a stone cross to which stone icicles cling. It pays tribute to the memory of those men who perished in one of the most grim and terrible of the great sagas of the sea, the *Jeannette* Arctic Expedition.

This venture was not originally a project of the Navy at all; on the contrary, naval officers had looked askance at it from the beginning. But it was made a Navy project officially by act of Congress, as the result of the pressure applied upon the Grant Administration by the politically influential and wealthy publisher of the *New York Herald*, James Gordon Bennett. The steam bark *Jeannette* was made a naval vessel and the Navy was directed to supply its personnel.

The scheme originated with Lieutenant George Washington De Long, who carried it to Bennett. Fresh from his triumphs in Africa, where he had financed and exploited Henry M. Stanley in his explorations, the New York publisher was seeking new journalistic fields to conquer, and he lent a willing ear to De Long's proposal to reach the North Pole. Bennett purchased the *Jeannette*, equipped it, and financed the expedition.

Of the five naval officers on the *Jeannette*, the three line officers were graduates of the Naval Academy; the commander of the expedition, Lieutenant Commander George W. De Long, of the class of 1865, the second in command and executive officer, Lieutenant Charles W. Chipp, of the class of 1868, and the navigator, Lieutenant John W. Danenhower, of the class of 1870. Chief Engineer George W. Melville (in honor of whom

Melville Hall is named) and Passed Assistant Surgeon James M. Ambler, completed the commissioned personnel.

The *Jeannette* sailed from San Francisco July 8, 1879, with the intention of finding a warm current north of Behring Straits and drifting across the Pole. But the ship early encountered ice floes that threw her off her course, and De Long decided to winter at Wrangell Island. Here the vessel froze into an ice pack that carried her, helpless and in increasing peril, toward the northwest from September 6, 1880, until she was crushed and sunk June 12, 1881, leaving her crew on an ice floe in mid-ocean. From then onward the record becomes tragic; in terms of human suffering and stark horror it looms as one of the greatest of marine disasters. But out of that suffering arose qualities of fortitude, of self-sacrifice, and of indomitable courage that assumed proportions of grandeur.

Starved, ill-equipped, inadequately clad and handicapped with sickness, the little band entered upon a struggle for life during which it underwent the agonies of the damned. Realizing that their only chance of escape lay in reaching the delta of the Lena River in Siberia, 500 miles away, De Long divided the men into three groups, to each of which was assigned one of the small boats. They retreated southward over the ice, with their boats on sledges, toward the Siberian coast, reaching Semenovski Island and open water on September 10, 1881. On the eve of departure on this fateful phase of their voyage in frail shells across the open Arctic Sea, De Long held divine service; at its conclusion their rough voices mingled with the gale as they sang the Navy hymn that became a prayer:

> Oh, hear us when we cry to Thee
> For those in peril on the sea!

The next morning, September 12, 1881, the three boats shoved off. The first cutter, under command of De Long, carried Dr. Ambler and twelve men; the second cutter under Chipp carried seven men; the whaleboat under Melville carried Danenhower and nine men.

The fates were kind to the Chipp boat; it foundered the first day in a gale and all of its occupants were mercifully drowned. The other two boats became separated; each had to seek adventure of its own. The Melville boat, after incredible hard-ships, reached land; more dead than alive, the men fought their way to a tiny settlement many miles inland. But the De Long cutter faced a sterner destiny. Brief entries in De Long's diary tell of men driven to near-lunacy, of frozen hands and feet that putrified and dropped away—tales of horror that serve as a background for examples of fortitude, of bravery and of faith-fulness to duty and to shipmates. At the end of his strength, De Long finally halted with his dying comrades and sent two of his strongest men ahead to seek aid. By a strange mishap, this mes-sage was delivered to Melville; it was the first word he had re-ceived from De Long since the gale that separated them.

November 5, 1881, commemorates an act of heroism that stands near the top in the records of exploration. Weak from starvation, frost-bitten as he was, Melville deliberately turned his back upon civilization and once more disappeared into the Arctic wastes in the forlorn hope that his comrades might still be alive. Not until March 23, 1882, did he come upon the re-mains of a fire that might have been lighted by De Long. What happened has been recorded in the following words, attributed to Melville:

> . . . A few steps off, partially buried in the snow still left on that forlorn and gale-swept height, I saw a copper tea kettle. With a beating heart I started for it, then stopped short. There before me on that desolate plateau, protruding stiff and stark above the snow—was an extended arm! For an instant I gazed, aghast at my discovery, then I dropped to my knees to find that the arm belonged to Captain De Long! . . . There had the saga of the *Jeannette* ended . . . I was struck by the odd position of his left arm, upraised with open fingers as if, lying there dying, he had tossed something over his shoulder and his stiffening arm had frozen in that gesture. I looked behind him.

> A few feet away in the snow beyond his head lay a small notebook, the journal he had kept since the *Jeannette* sank. To me it seemed as if De Long, in his dying moment, had tossed that journal over his head away from the fire at his feet lest it should blow in there and be destroyed.*

* From *Hell on Ice*, by Commander Edward Ellsberg; by permission of Dodd, Mead and Co.

From that notebook has been pieced together the story of what happened. The last entry reads:

> Sunday, Oct. 30, 140th day. Boyd and Gortz died during night. Mr. Collins dying
>
> And there (the Melville report continues), on October 30th, the pitiful record ended. Before he could put a period to that final tragic sentence, the pencil dropped from De Long's nerveless fingers; with his last conscious effort he tossed his journal over his shoulder to save that record of what had happened to his shipmates, from the fire near by . . . My captain had died as he had lived—with his thoughts only on his men. Not a word on that last tragic page about himself, his sufferings or his own approaching death.

Near De Long's body was found, too, his chronometer, which is now preserved in the Naval Academy Museum, together with the wooden marker of the Arctic grave of one of the bravest of the brave, Seaman Ericksen.

The *Jeannette* monument in the Naval Academy cemetery is a replica of the rocky cairn built by Melville on a desolate cape overlooking Lena Bay in Siberia, where all that was mortal of De Long and his shipmates was laid to rest forever.

Of these four public monuments within the Yard—the *Jeannette*, the Mexican, the Tripolitan and the Herndon—not one, it may be noted, marks the resting place of the men they memorialize. They are not tombs; they are tributes to valor, standing guard to the memory of men who met great crises with great gallantry and who held duty, loyalty and honor greater than life itself.

But near the *Jeannette* monument lies the actual dust of what were once sailormen who lived and fought and died in the service of their country, in the burial ground overlooking the quiet waters of the Severn. It is the Naval Academy's Valhalla. Behind the brief inscriptions on the modest headstones lie tales of high adventure, of romance and courage; true tales of American history. Over there, in the woody dell, stand in serried ranks the gravestones of sixty men of the ship's company of the ill-fated U. S. steamer *Huron*, which was wrecked off the coast of North Carolina, on November 23, 1877, not far from the spot where Herndon went down. True, only twenty-six of these stones stand over the bodies that were recovered; the rest are merely memorials erected to those whose bodies were either not found or were not identified. Yet here, so far as was in man's power, the old shipmates have been reassembled, not without a sentiment touched with drama, as though they were lined up to answer "Here!" to the last roll call.

Here sleep midshipmen, admirals of the fleet, officers of the line, seamen, side by side; rank does not enter into the broad estates of Death. Yonder is the grave of the towering Rear Admiral Christopher Raymond Perry Rodgers (1819–1892), father of admirals, veteran fighter in the Seminole, Mexican and Civil wars, Superintendent of the Naval Academy and commander-in-chief of the Pacific Squadron, who during his term as Commandant of Midshipmen established the First classmen on such an unshakable basis of quasi-aristocracy that their authority has never been challenged since. Not far away is the humble tablet to one Seaman Thomas Taylor, drowned off the U. S. sloop *Preble* on the night of April 2, 1852, "erected by his messmates in token of regard and friendship." Under a single large granite monument lies all that is mortal of Midshipmen William Edward Traylor Neumann and Thomas Ward, Jr. "Killed in discharge of their duty on board the U. S. Battleship *Missouri* during target practice off Pensacola Bay, Florida, April 13, 1904," the inscription reads. And what is the story behind this humble stone to Kamekichi Ando, who was born in Japan and who died, aged only twenty-five, in Annapolis in 1889? Its inscription bears only the tender message:

AND HE SHALL BE AS ONE THAT IS BORN IN THE LAND.
—EXODUS 12: 48.

Drama and pathos and sentiment and flashes of nobility that stir the pulse lie behind many of these headstones. Under that white marble tablet surmounted by a cross—the standard marker for the graves of midshipmen—lies Midshipman Grigsby E. Thomas, of the class of 1911; the legend reads simply, "Who lost his life in an heroic effort to save another from drowning." But that tells only a part of the story, for his classmate Sherman M. Nason perished with him in a vain attempt to rescue the daughter-in-law of Superintendent John M.

Bowyer, when the knockabout in which the three were sailing capsized off the Naval Experiment Station on the morning of June 28, 1910.

Commander Theodore Gordon Ellyson, who died in 1928, bears on his tablet the proud epitaph that none shall ever take from him:

NAVAL AVIATOR NUMBER ONE.

And what indomitable purpose and unquenchable love of the sea shine forth from the few words that epitomize the life of Montgomery Meigs Alger, of the class of 1916, who lived but two years after graduating! They read:

FAITHFUL TO DUTY, BY SUFFERING UNDAUNTED, IN DEATH COURAGEOUS, NOT ABLE TO SAIL THE SEAS, HE GAVE HIMSELF IN BUILDING SHIPS.

A peculiarly poignant touch may be found at the grave of Commodore William Nicholas Jeffers (1824–1883), who stands Number 4 on the list of graduates, and whose name still lives in the annals of the Navy. Upon his headstone is inscribed an expression of his high-minded sense of service, beginning with the phrase:

ALL PRIVATE VIRTUE IS THE PUBLIC FUND;
AS THAT ABOUNDS, THE STATE DECAYS OR THRIVES.

Within reach of his arm is a small grave; its headstone carries the name William Nicholas Jeffers, 4th, who died when a little lad of less than eight years. But he did not fail to catch the torch passed on to him from his fathers; he was drowned, so the writ proclaims, "in an heroic attempt to save the life of a younger companion."

Over in the Naval Academy cemetery, also stand the adjoining monuments of two close friends who, tragically separated in life by the fortune of war, now rest side by side, young men together through all eternity. Behind their reunion lies a story of devotion, of loyalty and of bravery in the performance of an act that marked an epoch in naval history.

One of the monuments is the gravestone of Lieutenant Commander Charles W. Flusser, of the class of 1854, who was killed in action April 19, 1864. The other, the inscription tells, commemorates "the coolness, fortitude and heroism of a very young officer." It is the gravestone of Commander William Barker Cushing, one time a member of the class of 1862, whose racked body and tortured brain found peace at last beside his comrade in 1874—but only after he had wrought vengeance upon the slayers of his friend in a manner so brilliant, so complete and so devastating that the whole world paused to contemplate it.

As a naval cadet, young Cushing was not an unqualified success. Ablaze with the love of life, he took but scant interest in his academic studies; legends began to grow about his youthful skylarkings at the Naval Academy even before "the young man was restored to his friends" by being permitted to resign March 23, 1861. But his great love of the sea and his purpose to pursue a career in the Navy never faltered. In a letter to his sister, written in 1860 while he was still a cadet, he stated:

> I want to live on the sea and die on the sea, and when once I set foot on a good ship as her commander, I never want to leave her till I leave her a corpse. . . . I had rather be an officer on board a man-of-war than the President of the United States.

Fate began to weave his destiny immediately upon leaving the Naval Academy. Within a few days the country plunged into civil war and Cushing entered the Navy with the rank of Acting Master's Mate. He quickly won a reputation for dashing courage under fire. A long series of brilliant achievements began to approach a climax in April, 1864, when the huge Confederate ram *Albemarle* attacked the Union vessel *Miami* and killed Cushing's friend Flusser. It was this incident that proved to be the first of a chain of circumstances that led to the determination of Cushing to destroy the Confederate ram. "I shall never rest until I have avenged Flusser's death," he is reported to have said. He forthwith proceeded to plan the destruction of the *Albemarle* with that same meticulous care and attention to detail that, a couple of generations later, Lindbergh gave to the preparations for his flight to Paris.

Cushing journeyed to the Brooklyn Navy Yard to supervise the construction of two especially designed open steam launches, 45 feet long. In the bow of each was built an 18-foot spar that swung on hinges and that could be raised and lowered at will.

At the end of the spar a torpedo was to be attached; when ready for action, the spar was to be lowered and the torpedo released by means of a lanyard. This ingenious contraption was the invention of John L. Lay.

Late in October of 1864 Cushing arrived at Albemarle Sound, in North Carolina, where the Confederate ram lay at anchor near the town of Plymouth. To prevent her escape and assignment to other duties, the United States Navy was maintaining a small fleet of vessels at the mouth of the harbor. On the night of October 27, Cushing set out on his extraordinary exploit in one of the launches, with a picked crew of fifteen men. As noiselessly as possible they approached the *Albemarle*. Suddenly through the darkness a challenge rang out; when Cushing did not reply, a fusillade of bullets followed. Cushing thereupon put on full steam, dashed up the river past the ram, swept around in a circle and charged toward the enemy's bows with sufficient power to enable his small launch to hurdle the log boom that protected the vessel. At close range—he was now under the very bows of the enemy towering above him—he lowered the swinging spar and pulled the lanyard that released the torpedo a bare instant before one of the big guns of the ram, which had been depressed with frantic haste, fired at him. It was all done in a matter of seconds.

With a thunderous detonation, the torpedo tore a gaping hole in the side of the *Albemarle*. Within a short time the ram lay a a shattered hulk at the bottom of the harbor. A very small but exceedingly brilliant David had shattered a very large and greatly dreaded Goliath.

The concussion from the explosion swamped the little launch and hurled its stunned crew into the water. Two were drowned, twelve were taken prisoners, two miraculously escaped. One of the latter was Cushing. The details of his fight for life in the black waters of Albemarle Sound, of his incredible immunity to bullets (five pierced his clothing and the sole of a shoe was shot away), of his refuge in the woods, and of his eventual return to the Union fleet in an old rowboat, aided by a negro slave who befriended him, read like fiction—and not very probable fiction, either. As he had anticipated in a letter to a cousin, he did indeed receive the thanks of Congress. He received in addition the highest reward within the power of the government to bestow for heroism, the Medal of Honor. He was promoted to the rank of Lieutenant Commander, and he was given $50,000 of prize money to boot.

But the shock of his experience took its toll; broken in health and at last in mind too, his death ten years later was a merciful release. Now he is back again in the scene of his youth at the Naval Academy; at peace by his side lies his old friend Flusser. And upon his tomb is graven a single word in large, bold letters, on which his fame so largely rests, and which by strange circumstance is not his own: "ALBEMARLE."

Chapter 15

Answers to
Visitors' Questions

The Naval Academy is good-naturedly referred to by the West Point cadets, with a dash of envy, as the "Country Club." The Military Academy is good-naturedly referred to by the Annapolis midshipmen as "Hell-on-the-Hudson."

If neither of these appellations hits the bull's-eye, both are at least on the target. To the week-end visitor, especially to the visitor who is familiar with the scenic grandeur, the architectural severities and the formal austerities of West Point, the Yard at Annapolis appears to be an inviting recreation park, redolent with the amiable, easy-going spirit of the South, rather than the workshop of the exacting, modern technical school that the Naval Academy actually is.

From the moment the visitor, especially the visitor in the spring and fall, passes through the main gateway (officially designated as Gate No. 3 or the Maryland Avenue Gate), he makes an entrance upon a nautical scene that suggests a lovely stage setting, in harmony with the quaint old-fashioned Southern town of Annapolis itself. Green lawns slope gently down to the tennis courts beyond which stretch the blue waters of the Severn; white sails of small pleasure craft gleam in the sun. The nearest sizable building is the Officers' Club. Ancient cannon and figureheads of old vessels, with here and there an anchor thrown in, dress the scene and create a romantic atmosphere of the sea; young men in uniforms pass before one in easy, swinging strides. One almost expects to hear the prompter's bell signal the overture to begin and the curtain to rise, and to see bevies of lovely ladies troop forth in frills and furbelows to greet the audience; if the visitor arrives opportunely, he will, in fact, find these delights too, for a musical background is furnished by band concerts in the mornings and afternoons, and the lovely ladies arrive in bewildering bevies for the week-end festivities.

The guards are the first uniformed officials to meet the eyes of the visitor as he passes into the Yard. There are 35 of them altogether; most of them rotate in tours of duty at the gateways. As these gates are in service only at intervals during the day, the duties of these kindly guardians are not burdensome; they consist largely of answering questions propounded by Mr. and Mrs. John Q. Public and all the little Public children. How can I find Midshipman Gish? When does the parade begin? Where is Bancroft Hall? Can I park my car over there? Will you keep my dog here until I get back? Why are all the midshipmen running; is there a fire? Have you seen my wife? What time is it when the ships' bells strike three? Can I hire a boat here? When does this gate close for the night? No wonder the guards are picked out because they are patient and friendly.

Here are some of the answers to the less personal queries, set down in much the same haphazard forms as the questions themselves are asked.

Visiting hours are from 9:00 A.M. to 5:00 P.M.; most buildings close at 5:00 P.M. Anyone who seeks admittance at other hours is asked to give his reason; usually it is to call socially upon someone who lives in the Yard. On Saturday evenings and on special occasions when hops and other entertainments are held, the gates are open as late as the situation demands. Right here, at the Main Gate, stand the two oldest Academy buildings. Both are unpretentious plain brick structures, painted gray; they constitute the sole relics of the institution as it was before the renaissance that began at the turn of the present century. The building at the visitor's left, built in 1881, now serves as the gatehouse and headquarters for the guard; the one at the right, built in 1876, serves as the ladies' waiting room.

Is the visitor a stranger in these parts? If so, he is welcomed with a printed pamphlet that will tell him what he might like to see and how to get to it.

Historic Annapolis: The Setting of the Naval Academy

The Naval Academy could scarcely have selected a better place in which to become distinguished and honorable: it grew up at the edge of Annapolis, one of the country's most distinguished and honorable—and venerable—cities. Rich, cultured, splendid and free, it was renowned in colonial times and the days of the early Republic as the Athens of America. It is now one of the great national shrines of colonial culture and American liberty. Three of the four Maryland signers of the Declaration of Independence are intimately associated with Annapolis: Charles Carroll of Carrollton was born here, and the mansions of Samuel Chase and William Paca are two of the most notable of its architectural gems.

The original town, first called Providence, was founded in 1649 by Protestant Nonconformists persecuted by the Anglicans in Virginia, from which religious intolerance Cecilius Calvert, the second Baron Baltimore, and proprietor of the colony of Maryland, offered refuge. A treaty with the Susquehannock Indians, supposedly negotiated under the Liberty Tree on the campus of St. John's College, enabled further settlement of the area, and the town grew rapidly as an important shipping and commercial center, being established as an official Port of Entry in 1668. It became the capital of Maryland in 1695, and in the following year King William's School, the ancestor of the modern St. John's College, was established. The flourishing city became known as Annapolis (after Princess and later Queen Anne) officially when its city charter was granted in 1708.

Annapolis is so rich in historical lore that it is hard to summarize even the main occurrences in its long existence. The oldest newspaper in the country, the *Maryland Gazette* (still being published), was first printed here in 1727. Patriots of the town put on their own special "Boston Tea Party" on 19 October 1774, when they forced Anthony Stewart to burn his brig, the *Peggy Stewart*, because he had paid the loathsome tax on a ton of tea with which the vessel was laden. Annapolis was a favorite resort of George Washington, who visited it to enjoy the social life and the horse racing at least eighteen times from 1751 on. Francis Scott Key was a resident during the time he was attending St. John's College. Lafayette with his colonial troops and Rochambeau with his French troops both made camp in Annapolis in 1781.

Annapolis became the temporary national capital in 1783 when the Congress of the Articles of Confederation decided to spend the winter here and to use the facilities of the State House, built in the 1770's (and now the oldest state capitol still in actual use). In this handsome building the Treaty of Paris, by which Great Britain recognized the independence of the United States, was ratified in 1784. Here too, a year earlier, General George Washington resigned his commission as Commander-in-Chief of the Continental Army. In the capitol also met the Annapolis Convention of 1786, whose deliberations led to the Constitutional Convention in Philadelphia the following year and the formulation of the Constitution of the United States.

During the Civil War, Annapolis became a highly important shipping depot and embarkation point for Union troops because of its strategic location as a gateway to the Confederacy and its proximity to the vital Washington area. Major expeditions into "Secessia" fitted out here, and over 70,000 troops were stationed here at one time or another. The Academy grounds, with the actual school moved to Newport, Rhode Island, became an Army post. Generals Grant, Burnside and Butler had headquarters here for brief periods.

The State Capitol and the mansions that remain from Annapolis' Golden Age are among the handsomest examples of Colonial Georgian architecture in the country. No visitor should miss the Hammond-Harwood, Chase-Lloyd, Paca, Carroll the Barrister, Brice, and Peggy Stewart Houses, among many others, or Reynolds' Tavern, or Ogle Hall, now the Alumni House of the Naval Academy Alumni Association.

The Naval Academy Grounds

Unhappily, perhaps, virtually nothing remains of the original Naval Academy, or of the "old" Academy prior to the turn of the century. Beginning in the year 1899, following an appropriation of $10,000,000 by Congress for the purpose, the Naval Academy was almost completely rebuilt in the French Renaissance style after the designs of the architect, Mr. Ernest Flagg, of New York. The grounds of the Academy proper now comprise about 290 acres along the west bank of the Severn River, on which are 219 major buildings.

The Naval Academy Grounds are grouped around a quadrangle called the Yard, bounded on the north by the academic group and on the south by the great granite dormitory, Bancroft Hall, named after President Polk's first Secretary of the Navy and founder of the Naval Academy, George Bancroft.

Starting at the Maryland Avenue Gate and turning right at Blake Road, one passes the ivy-covered Administration Building, then sees before him the Chapel with its huge dome. Within the Chapel, where services are non-denominational in character, and where over 2,000 midshipmen worship each Sunday, one's attention is drawn to the five great stained glass windows: Christ Walking on the Water, a memorial to David Dixon Porter; the Invisible Commission; the Sir Galahad Window; and the windows honoring our naval heroes, Admirals Farragut and Sampson. In the Crypt are contained the sarcophagus of John Paul Jones, and many historical relics and memorials. The Crypt is considered to be of especial interest to visitors. A guard is on duty there to answer questions. The anchors in front of the Chapel are from the armored cruiser *New York*, flagship of Admiral Sampson at the Battle of Santiago. The mortars near the Chapel, and nearly all the old Spanish bronze cannon around the Yard, are trophies of the Mexican War.

Next to the Chapel is the Superintendent's House, with its lovely lawns, where the annual garden party for the graduating class is held. Across the street from these quarters stands Dahlgren Hall. This building, named for the Civil War inventor of large calibre naval guns, houses the Weapons Department. Its great floor space is used for certain indoor athletics, as an auditorium, to accommodate brigade infantry formations, for other events driven indoors by bad weather, and for the "Farewell Ball" of June Week. West of this building is Ward Hall, a recitation building and Ordnance Laboratory.

All activity at the Naval Academy radiates from huge Bancroft Hall, the midshipmen's dormitory, which lies along the southeast side of the Yard. In its eight interconnected wings are housed all members of the brigade. Bancroft Hall is in itself a small city, with tailor, cobbler, and barber shops; a tremendous galley and mess hall capable of serving at one sitting the entire brigade; a store, a soda fountain, recreation rooms, post office, sick quarters, dental quarters, and all the miscellaneous facilities necessary to support such a large establishment. In Bancroft Hall visitors will see the Rotunda, decorated with murals depicting naval engagements, a sample midshipmen's room and Memorial Hall. In Memorial Hall is displayed Perry's battle flag at Lake Erie, with the memorable words, "Don't Give Up the Ship." From the windows of this Hall, one may view Farragut Field, Spa Creek, the harbor, and Chesapeake Bay beyond. Bancroft Hall is the largest single dormitory building in the world.

Directly in front of Bancroft Hall is the statue of "Tecumseh," a bronze replica of the figurehead of the old ship *Delaware*. The next building toward the Severn is the gymnasium, Macdonough Hall, named for the victor of Lake Champlain. Within are the athletic trophy room, handball and squash courts, instruction swimming pool, and facilities for basketball, wrestling, boxing, fencing and gymnastics. A section of this building, known as "Misery Hall," is occupied by the Athletic Medical Officer and his staff. The offices of the athletic coaches and physical training instructors, who plan and conduct the extensive intramural program, are located on the second floor of this building. Immediately adjacent is the Natatorium, which contains one of the largest indoor swimming pools in the country.

To seaward of the gymnasium is Luce Hall, named for an early Head of Department of Seamanship and writer of textbooks on that subject. This building houses the offices and activities of the Command Department.

The Academic Group stands across the Yard to the northwest. Maury Hall, named for the distinguished oceanographer, Matthew Fontaine Maury, is occupied by the English, History, and Government Department. Sampson Hall, named for the Commander-in-Chief at the Battle of Santiago, contains the classrooms and laboratories of the Science Department. The center building of the group, Mahan Hall, was named after the naval historian, Alfred Thayer Mahan, and houses the Library and the Auditorium.

Behind the Academic Group are Isherwood, Melville, and Griffin Hall, which contain the classrooms and laboratories of the Engineering Department as well as certain Electrical

Engineering laboratories. These are adjacent to the parade ground, Worden Field.

Still further to the northwest are Hubbard Hall (Boat House), Lawrence Field (baseball), and Halligan Hall (Public Works and Supply), with the Naval Hospital to the eastward overlooking the Severn River Bridge.

Completing the quadrangle of the Yard, near the Maryland Avenue Gate, are the buildings housing the Foreign Languages Department, the Museum, the Naval Academy Athletic Association, the U. S. Naval Institute, and the Commissioned Officers' Mess.

Administration

The faculty is composed of approximately 500 members. Of these, 200 are civilians, with the academic rank of instructor, assistant professor, associate professor, professor, and senior professor, who staff in large part the academic and scientific-engineering departments. Administration, and the professional departments, are staffed almost entirely by line officers of the Navy.

Events of Interest

The public is cordially invited to witness certain events indicated below, which are characteristic of life at the Naval Academy.

Outdoor infantry drills are held beginning in March and continuing until late November. During the Fall and Spring of the regular academic year, the entire Brigade drills at dress parades, Worden Field, on Wednesdays from 3:30 P.M. to 4:10 P.M., weather permitting. Brigade dress parades are also held during "June Week," usually the first week in June.

The Brigade marches to Chapel at 10:15 A.M. on Sundays.

Throughout the year, weather permitting, the Brigade forms on the terrace in front of Bancroft Hall for muster at 12:05 P.M. on week days, 12:10 P.M. on Saturdays, and 12:30 P.M. on Sundays and holidays, except on occasions when the weather is inclement.

Most athletic events are open to the public. On special occasions, tickets are required for admission.

Miscellaneous Information

Visitors are welcome to bring cameras into the Yard. There are no restrictions on the making of photographs out of doors, but visitors are expected to stand clear of all formations, drills, ceremonies, athletic events, etc. Usually civilian guards will be on hand to indicate acceptable limits of approach.

In general, photographs may be made indoors wherever visitors are normally permitted within the Academy. Photographs cannot be made in the Chapel in connection with any religious service without the prior approval of the Chaplain.

The ground rules for the guidance of the personal conduct of visitors are commendably few and brief; the do's and don'ts are reduced to the following minimum, which not even a misanthrope could view with alarm:

> Dogs must be on leash within the Naval Academy.
> Picknicking is not permitted.
> No smoking is permitted in buildings.
> Guides are not permitted to use megaphones.
> Automobiles are allowed in the grounds to an extent determined by existing traffic conditions.
> Motor coaches are not permitted in the grounds. They should be parked on King George Street, outside Gate No. 4.
> Speed limit within the Naval Academy grounds is twenty miles per hour except where lower limits are posted. Use horns in emergencies only.
> Stop at stop signs. Pedestrians have right of way.
> A red curb indicates no parking; yellow curb—loading zone or limited parking; green curb—preferential parking; no paint on curb—parking allowed.
> When passing on the walks and roads of the Naval Academy, visitors are requested to give the right-of-way to both large and small groups of midshipmen marching as a unit.

A former regulation against smoking in the Yard goes back so far into the past of the Naval Academy as to be a museum piece. There was a time when smoking was frowned upon as a major offense and was punished with unrelenting severity; many a naval career was nipped in the bud for an infraction of this rule. One of the sailors' yarns that has come down the years relates how on one occasion the midshipmen were drawn up in their white work uniforms for inspection by an officer whose diligence in enforcing the anti-smoking regulation had assumed fanatical proportions. Spotting a midshipman with the tell-tale tag of the familiar Bull Durham tobacco pouch hanging out of his blouse pocket, the officer strode up to his prey, under the eyes of the battalion, and with a conspicuous gesture yanked the tag from the offender's pocket. This is exactly what the offender had anticipated—for at the other end of the string had been carefully affixed a bright yellow lemon. In this enlightened day the midshipmen are permitted to smoke in their quarters, in Smoke Hall, in Smoke Park, and in the spaces reserved for smokers at the hops.

For June Week and other special occasions the visitor will find parking space on Farragut Field, Hospital Point, and other specially designated areas. Sometimes, when as many as 25,000 guests flock into the Yard, even these parking places are crowded.

The site of the now dismantled Thompson Stadium is marked by a bronze tablet that reads:

> Thompson Stadium. Dedicated May 30, 1931. To honor the memory of Robert Means Thompson, class of 1868, United States Naval Academy. His interest, encouragement and assistance were an inspiration to Naval Academy athletes and to the spirit of his alma mater.

The two uncovered grandstands, located on the east and west sides of the gridiron, accommodated 18,000 spectators; the southern end, flanked by low gunnery sheds on which the score boards were erected, looked out over the waters of Chesapeake Bay. The steelwork for the North Stand came from the men-of-war *Constitution*, *United States* and *Washington*, which were actually scrapped in 1922 under the terms of the Washington Arms Limitation Conference.

Those attractive evergreens growing in the Yard are holly trees, even though the skeptical visitor from the North may insist that holly grows only in the form of a Christmas wreath. They are of the American species, "ilex opaca."

Why do the midshipmen wear three brass buttons across the sleeves on their dress jackets? They are an inheritance from the days of Lord Nelson, who ordered them put there to discourage

*B*eginning in the spring, there
is a constant flow of visitors to the
Naval Academy.

*M*idshipmen enjoy
showing their friends around
the Navy Yard.

the midshipmen of his day from wiping their noses on their sleeves, because they had no pocket and could carry no handkerchiefs. Well, that's the story, anyway.

All the old guns that decorate the Yard are "spiked," meaning that the touch-holes have been permanently plugged up to make the discharge of the pieces impossible. This was done as the result of a prank by Midshipman Philo Norton McGiffin, of the class of 1882.

McGiffin became a legendary character early in his career. For rolling cannon balls down the stairs of the academic building in which he was quartered as a midshipman—tearing away the banisters, ripping through the stairway and crashing through the floors—young McGiffin was given punishment by being relegated in disgrace to the station ship *Santee*. There he became so chummy with one of his guardians that he wheedled enough gunpowder from him with which to load six old Mexican cannon in the Yard; before the guns were fired, however, McGiffin was apprehended and went back to the ship, in company with A. J. Jones, to whom the episode has also been attributed. The guns have been spiked ever since.

Irked at the slowness of promotion in the Navy, he resigned two years after graduating and shortly thereafter became an officer in the Chinese navy; his brilliant handling of a small number of Chinese war vessels against an incomparably greater fleet of Japanese warships at the Battle of the Yalu in 1894 attracted the admiration of the world. Grave injuries received in that action led directly to his suicide in 1897.

The 28 tennis courts between Stribling Walk and Dewey Basin are for the use of midshipmen. There are 8 more courts on the west side of Dahlgren Hall, where the intercollegiate matches are played. The courts near the Officers' Club are for the use of club members and guests only.

The building located between the Main Gate and the Chapel is the Administration Building, which serves as the headquarters of the Superintendent and his personal staff. It is here that the Academic Board assembles about its long conference table and gives a personal hearing to every midshipman whose academic standing or whose record of conduct threatens to sever his connection with the Naval Academy.

The approach to the Administration Building is flanked by

two 18-pounder smooth-bore cannon, cast in Peru in 1769 and captured by the United States Navy from the Mexicans in 1847. Here are mounted, also, two rare stone cannon balls, weighing 600 pounds or so each, of the type fired by the Turks from their great guns used at the conquest of Constantinople in 1453.

The children of naval officers are called "navy juniors." (The children of army officers are known less elegantly as "army brats.")

Visitors are not allowed to visit the mess hall except by special permission of the Commandant; this is ordinarily extended only to a midshipmen's male relatives, male guardians, male officers of the Armed Forces, civilian instructors, Congressmen, or "other male guests of distinction."

The house in which the original manuscript of the words of our national anthem was preserved for over a generation stood at the spot now marked by a granite slab on Chauvenet Walk, a few paces from the bandstand. It bears a bronze plate with this inscription:

ON THIS SPOT, WHERE THE INSPIRING STRAINS OF THE STAR-SPANGLED BANNER ARE HEARD EACH MORNING, FORMERLY STOOD THE HOME OF JUDGE JOSEPH HOPPER NICHOLSON, BROTHER-IN-LAW OF FRANCIS SCOTT KEY, TO WHOM KEY GAVE THE ORIGINAL MANUSCRIPT AND WHO SET THE WORDS TO A POPULAR TUNE OF THE TIME. HERE THE MANUSCRIPT REMAINED UNTIL THE NICHOL-SON HOUSE WAS TORN DOWN IN 1845.

The smaller radio towers across the Severn are located at Greenbury Point, Maryland, and are 500 feet high. The large tower to the left is 800 feet high. They are part of the equipment which transmits from the Cheltenham control and receiving center, and both are important links in the Naval Communications System, with headquarters at the Naval Communication Station in Washington, D. C. What looks like a huge reflector is the communication moon relay transmitter, the receiver for which is in Honolulu. This ingenius electronic device actually bounces radio waves off the moon to its distant receiver, thereby greatly extending the range of radio communication.

The two large benches that flank the Tecumseh monument are known as the First Class bench and the Second Class bench and are relics of the old Naval Academy; no midshipmen except members of those two classes are supposed to occupy them. (Neither do the First and Second classmen occupy them, for that matter.)

Phlox Landing was the name of the small floating dock at the foot of Maryland Avenue. Years ago it was the terminus of the steamboat *Phlox* that ran between Annapolis, Baltimore, and sometimes Washington. It was used by boats from visiting warships.

Five minutes before the bugler sounds "to the colors," near the flag pole in front of the Administration Building, he sounds the "first call." The ceremony of lowering the flag at sunset is called "retreat." Everyone within hearing, afoot and awheel, comes to a halt and faces the flag at salute. (The civilian salute consists of standing in silence with the hat held by the right hand, over the heart; if the civilian is hatless, he holds both hands at his side. Bringing the hand up in a military salute is required only of men in uniform.)

The flag that flies from the mast in front of the Administration Building is the station flag, and is officially designated as the "national ensign." The personal flag of the Rear Admiral, a dark blue field bearing two white stars, flies from the yardarm of this mast.

The foremast of the ill-fated battleship *Maine*, which was blown up in Havana Harbor at 9:45 on the evening of February 15, 1898, stands on new Farragut Field. It was recovered October 6, 1910, and first erected in the yard May 5, 1913. Its battered crow's nest and twisted plates give mute evidence of the force of the explosion. (The *Maine* is reported by the midshipmen to be the "longest ship in the Navy; her foremast is in Annapolis, Maryland, and her mainmast in Arlington Cemetery, Washington.")

Any marine you may see in the Yard on official duty, such as standing guard or directing traffic, is a member of the detachment of marines who are quartered at the Marine Barracks across the Severn River. This detachment also furnishes the marine who is on duty at the Superintendent's quarters. A marine always stands guard at the tomb of John Paul Jones, in the crypt below the Chapel when it is open to the public.

Members of visiting athletic teams eat at special tables in the mess hall, as the guests of the midshipmen. (Members of a visiting rifle team once left their guns in their motor car; when they emerged from the hall, they found themselves surrounded by the police—who had come prepared to capture a band of gangsters.)

The two 5-inch twin mounts on the floor of the armory are used for instruction purposes only. (The rumor that the roof is rolled back in order that projectiles may be shot through the opening is correct—except that the roof does not roll back and the guns are never fired.)

The grounds of the Naval Academy comprise exactly 290.61 acres. There are about 20 miles of roadways in the Yard. The total original cost of the land was $918,631.54 and of the buildings, $27,646,676.15. To this latter figure must be added the cost of all the new land acquisitions and the new construction. The current value of all this property cannot be reckoned, since, of course, it is not on the market. There are 219 major buildings in the Academy.

Visitors who damage flowers and shrubbery, annoy the birds and squirrels in the Yard, peddle souvenirs, solicit funds, distribute handbills of one kind or another and gamble in public are warned to quit—or get out.

Naval vessels of the United States and other countries frequently visit the Naval Academy and normally establish visiting hours when the public is welcome aboard. Submarines, landing craft, and other smaller ships moor along the docking areas; larger ships anchor in the roads. There is almost always a ship in port, on major National Holidays.

The Officers' Mess, designed by Ernest Flagg and built in 1905, cost Uncle Sam $149,636. The Mess is run by and for the benefit of the commissioned naval officers, the civilian instructors, and their families stationed in Annapolis. Guests may be introduced only by members, but the place is taboo for all midshipmen, except during June Week, and except for First classmen, who may now, under certain conditions, make use of various facilities.

That long stucco building with a red tile roof just north of Lawrence Field used to be occupied by the Post Graduate School. It was designed by Henry Ives Cobb, built in 1903, and cost $134,623. Its official name is Halligan Hall, after Rear

Admiral John Halligan, one of the founders of the school. It now houses Public Works, the Supply Department and other offices.

The official name of "Smoke Park," on the south side of Bancroft Hall, is Wilson Park; it is named in honor of Rear Admiral Henry B. Wilson, Superintendent from 1921 to 1925. The plebes use it during their first summer because the upper classmen are away; when the fleet comes home the usurpers are shooed out.

The barracks ships APL 31 and APL 32, moored at the end of Brownson Road, serve as the quarters for the mess attendants. They march proudly to and from Bancroft Hall; one of the most ignominious punishments meted out to delinquents by their boss is to be deprived of this coveted privilege.

The fact that the United States Naval Hospital immediately adjoins the cemetery is, of course, wholly without significance; it has, however, added to the cross borne by the medical officers who have had to meet with outward aspects of good nature the gibing to which they have been subjected ever since the first unit of the $332,657 building was erected in 1907. The hospital has one section reserved for the midshipmen and another for the enlisted men of the station; private rooms for officers are located on the second floor. Officers' and enlisted men's dependents as well as members of the armed service of our Allies are admitted as patients. Medical service at clinics is also provided for Navy families. The hospital is equipped with 270 beds, a daily average of about 50 midshipmen patients is regarded as normal; most of them are confined for short periods for minor ills. (The miraculous cures effected just before a vacation period or a football game constitute an impressive tribute either to the recuperative powers of the patients or to the Navy doctors' skill.)

The sites of the old Naval Academy buildings, which were torn down to make room for the present structures at the turn of the century, are indicated by stone markers; the oldest landmark thus memorialized was Fort Severn, built in 1808 and in its later days used as the gymnasium. The spot where it stood, on what is now the eastern corner of Bancroft Hall, is indicated by a block from the original Fort, set in the wall of Bancroft Hall, on North Arcade Road. It bears the words:

FORT SEVERN, 1808, 1909.

It has been referred to as the "cornerstone of the Naval Academy."

The classroom building in which Commander Buchanan, the first Superintendent, addressed the midshipmen on October 10, 1845, the day the Academy first opened, stood just in front of Bancroft Hall's main entrance.

Near the southern end of Stribling Walk lies embedded a plain stone tablet that bears the simple legend, "Old Chapel, Gunnery Building, Lyceum." To the midshipmen of today these names are but words; but if the ghosts of the old-timers come back to attend reunions, they cluster at this point, so laden with memories and charged with sentiment.

The old Chapel was built in 1850 in the architectural form of a basilica, with a portico supported by four pillars; in it were displayed several of the more famous of the captured battle flags and other trophies of war which are now exhibited elsewhere at the Naval Academy; among them was the famous blue burgee, "Don't Give Up the Ship." It was here that the first graduating exercises were held after the institution had changed its name from the Naval School to the United States Naval Academy; the six members of the class of 1854 merely assembled at noon, listened to prayers by the Chaplain and to a brief talk by the Superintendent, Commander Louis M. Goldsborough, and then stepped forward to receive their diplomas. The number one man in this small group was Midshipman Thomas O. Selfridge, who later became Rear Admiral; his original diploma was lost at sea on the sinking of the USS *Cumberland* on March 8, 1862, but a replica of it hangs in Smoke Hall today. In its later years the old Chapel was turned over to the midshipmen for use as a social and recreation center, under the name of the Lyceum.

The substantial faced-brick building on the south side of the Chapel is the official residence of the Superintendent. It was designed by Ernest Flagg and completed in 1906 at a cost of $77,539. Because of the many social duties that devolve upon its occupants, the building was laid out with the purpose of making the entertainment of guests as expeditious and painless as possible.

Among the more conspicuous of the class memorials presented to the Naval Academy is the large stone bench directly behind the Tecumseh monument and facing Bancroft Hall, the gift of the class of 1897; and the sundial beside Goldsborough Walk, just north of the Officers' Club, bearing the motto "Como la sombra hoye la hora," the gift of the class of 1925.

The Chapel Walk is a particularly consecrated area and is bordered by appropriate memorials of past glories that live in the present. On the way down from the Chapel to Dewey Field, the visitor should note the Hundredth Anniversary Stone, commemorating the founding of the Academy, the 1899 Bench, the 1911 Bench and Fountain, and the Rooks Fountain at the end of the walk. This last honors Captain A. H. Rooks, killed in action aboard the *Houston* in Sundra Strait in 1942.

A special section is provided at some of the athletic contests, for the exclusive use of the navy juniors. A very special, hand-picked Jimmylegs with a high aptitude rating in handling squirming, shifting and screaming masses of minors is placed in charge of them.

The excitement aroused at rallies just before the big games, by the appearance of weird-looking humans in the guise of tigers, bulldogs, Quakers, Indians and other living symbols of the teams of the Navy's opponents, is all a part of the stunt program devised by the Brigade Activities Committee to add to the gaiety of the occasion and work up a bit of steam for the coming contest.

Most of the roadways and walks in the Yard are named after former Superintendents of the Naval Academy, including Buchanan Road, Upshur Road, Stribling Walk, Goldsborough Walk, Blake Road, Porter Road, Parker Road, Balch Road, Ramsay Road, Phythian Road, Cooper Road, McNair Road, Sands Road, Badger Road, Bowyer Road, Fullam Road, and Eberle Road. Decatur Walk is named after Commodore Stephen Decatur, of the War of 1812 fame, and one walk is named after a civilian—the distinguished scientist and first Professor of Mathematics and Navigation at the Naval School, William Chauvenet.

Before what is now Farragut Field and Thompson Field was filled in as "made land," the shore line came close to the southern end of Dahlgren Hall; it was in this vicinity that the old drill field was located and where occurred the historic incident which was intended by the midshipmen to embarrass their instructor in military drill, Professor Henry Hayes Lockwood.

When Lockwood, who graduated in 1836 from the United States Military Academy, became the head of the Department of Natural Philosophy at the newly established Naval School in 1845, a link was forged between the two great service schools at West Point and Annapolis. The versatile Lockwood also became the head of the Department of Gunnery, the Department of Infantry Tactics and of Field Artillery Tactics; it was he who introduced the manual of arms and military drill to the institution, to the openly expressed opposition of the midshipmen. What have sailors to do with soldiering? was their attitude. "It is proposed to march officers of the Navy around like marines, sir, like marines!" angrily protested the outraged midshipmen.

But the views of the indefatigable Lockwood prevailed, although in the face of every obstacle that the midshipmen could place in the path of their instructor. Their big chance came on a hot day when they were being put through their paces in double time in a field artillery drill; as the head of the column approached the river bank, Lockwood undertook to give the command "halt," but his tendency to stutter under stress of excitement overcame him.

"Haw—haw—haw—" he shouted in his effort to get the word out.

Seizing the golden moment, the midshipmen accelerated their pace and gleefully plunged into the Severn, uniforms, field guns and all; when the belated command finally came, some of the lads were even going through the motions of preparing to swim on indefinitely out into the bay. The sequel came a few months later while Lockwood was drilling a battalion of infantry and refrained from giving a command as the midshipmen approached the bank. A wave of anticipation came over the ranks, which came to a hesitant stop at the water's edge.

"Well," queried Lockwood with a grin of reminiscence, "why d-d-didn't you do it?"

During the Civil War Lockwood served in the Army, in which he attained the rank of Brigadier General; he declined to accept a permanent commission, however, and returned to the Naval Academy to continue the work he had begun. He died in 1899, holding the rank of Brigadier General in the Army and of Commodore in the Navy.

Facing Mahan Hall is the wooden figurehead (now lead-sheathed) of the frigate *Macedonian*. The *Macedonian* was built at Woolwich, England, in 1810, for the Royal Navy and was put into service against the Americans in the War of 1812, in which it was unfortunate enough to run foul of the brilliant Stephen Decatur. What followed is told in a "bas relief" picture of a naval battle on the pedestal of the *Macedonian* monument, to which is appended the explanatory caption:

Capture of the *Macedonian*. The American frigate *United States*, commanded by Stephen Decatur, cruising between the Azores and Cape Verde Islands on October 25, 1812, was sighted by the British frigate *Macedonian*, Captain John S. Carden, and the two ships joined action. A sanguinary fight was maintained, when after two hours the *Macedonian*, losing her mizzenmast, became unmanageable, and with 104 casualties out of a total of 254, and many of her guns disabled, hauled down her colors.

The colors that were hauled down on that occasion are now preserved in a glass case in the main hallway of Mahan Hall, which may explain the figurehead's sour expression; his temper has not been noticeably improved by the fact that he is surrounded by four of the 18-pound guns that were captured at the same time he himself was taken prisoner.

The two glazed-brick buildings located on Badger Road, just north of Mahan Hall, contain machine shops and laboratories for use by the Science and Engineering Departments, and are not open to the public. One of them is Griffin Hall, built in 1918 at a cost of $201,087 and named in honor of Rear Admiral Robert S. Griffin (1857–1933), a distinguished engineer who from 1913 to 1921 was engineer-in-chief of the Navy. The other is Melville Hall, built in 1937 at a cost of $353,473 and named in honor of the last survivor of the *Jeannette* Expedition, George Wallace Melville (1841–1912), who was engineer-in-chief of the Navy from 1887 to 1903. Both buildings are practically annexes to Isherwood Hall.

The three large buildings at the northern extremity of Stribling Walk are known as the "Academic Group," designed as a unit by Ernest Flagg, and all erected in 1907. The largest is Mahan Hall, from which the clock tower rises and which houses the Library and Auditorium. On the seaward side, nearest the Severn, stands Maury Hall, built in 1907 at a cost of $418,882 and named in honor of the great oceanographer, Matthew Fontaine Maury (1806–1873); it houses the English, History and Government Department. On the opposite side stands Sampson Hall, built at the same time and costing a like amount, named after Rear Admiral William T. Sampson (1840–1902), where chemistry, physics and electricity are taught.

It is an old Navy custom to send plebes out on the terrace to locate the one brick out of the million or so which bears the initials "C.I.R." (Confidential note to plebes; it may be found just thirteen paces in front of the ancient cannon at the right of the main entrance of Bancroft Hall, as you face it.)

The Prayer of a Midshipman was written by Chaplain William N. Thomas, and was introduced at the graduation service in the Chapel ("Sob Sunday") in June, 1938.

The average number of demerits awarded each midshipman during the years 1920 to 1933 was 54.137.

Midshipman M. T. Wordell, of the class of 1935, completed his four-year course without receiving any demerits.

For over fifty years every First classman has been presented with a Bible; until the funds gave out, the Seaman's Institute of New York was the donor; now the Maryland Bible Society gives each First classman a Testament, and the American Bible Society each a Bible.

Perhaps the highest percentage mark ever attained for the four-year course in the history of the Naval Academy was 95.65—a record made by Midshipman D. W. Taylor, of the class of 1885. His aggregate multiple was 727.07 out of a maximum of 760. Taylor retired in 1923 as Chief Constructor, with the rank of Rear Admiral, rated as one of the foremost naval architects of the world.

Bancroft Hall contains 1873 midshipmen's rooms and has something like five miles of corridors. Estimates of the "floor space" vary with the definitions of the term, but it is probably in the neighborhood of forty acres or so. The mess hall is the largest dining area in the world—some 65,000 square feet.

Midshipmen are by law "officers in a qualified sense." They are classed as being of the line. Warrant officers take precedence next after midshipmen; a chief warrant officer is commissioned, and ranks above a midshipman but below an ensign.

A midshipman is obligated to remain in the service after graduation for periods which have varied from three to six years.

The laundry handles 4 million pounds of wash a year, and employs 145 workers. So well does it make minor repairs that a midshipman once sent only a button to the laundry with the note, "Please repair this shirt."

So that the folks back home may see Junior in all his glory when he comes home for Christmas, the midshipmen officers of the First Group (whose term expires) are permitted to wear their stripes, as well as the midshipman officers of the Second Group who have just put their stripes on.

Old Carvel Hall, an historic hotel in Annapolis, was built in 1763 and for many years was the home of William Paca, signer of the Declaration of Independence and Governor of Maryland from 1782 to 1786.

The milk served in the mess hall comes from the U. S. Naval Academy Dairy, located ten miles out at Gambrills, Maryland. Its herd of pure-bred Holsteins produce 1,300 gallons daily, and it is all pasteurized. The bacteria count allowed by law is as high as 10,000; the milk produced at the dairy is so pure that it is far below that figure. The excess cream produced during the summer when most of the midshipmen are away is frozen and used in ice cream later.

How would you like the job of feeding the midshipmen? Each day they consume 4,800 quarts of milk and 1,500 loaves of bread. Each week they put away 12,000 pounds of beef, 1,260 gallons of ice cream, 8,000 pounds of sugar, 18,000 pounds of potatoes, 10,500 pounds of fresh and frozen vegetables, and 7,500 pounds of fresh and frozen fruits. When iced tea is served, 450 gallons disappear. Midshipmen can punish 700 pies at a sitting. All this costs about $38,500 a week.

There are two rotary ovens in the galley in Bancroft Hall with a capacity of 3,000 pounds of meat each.

The U. S. Post Office in Bancroft Hall is a branch of the Annapolis Post Office. With a "postal population" of about 9,000, it handles about 10,000 outgoing and 12,000 incoming pieces of mail a day, and makes deliveries on Sundays and holidays to midshipmen. Its annual receipts amount to $50,000.

The importance of air power in the modern Navy is emphasized by the aircraft exhibited at the corners of Thompson Field. They are both Douglas carrier-based planes of high speed and intense striking power. The smaller A-4B (A4D) Skyhawk is of modified delta-wing design and is capable of transonic speeds. It carries two 20 mm. cannon as well as bombs, rockets and nuclear weapons. The A-3A (A3D-1) Skywarrior is a high-altitude, high-speed heavy attack plane specifically designed to carry nuclear weapons in a range up to 1,500 miles.

At the junction of McNair and Decatur Roads will be found two interesting prizes captured in recent wars. The vehicle which looks like a miniature tank is a German reconnaissance car captured by American forces at the Rhine near the close of World War II. The field piece is a 76 mm. gun of Russian make fired by the North Koreans on United States destroyers during the Marine invasion of Inchon in 1950.

In the spring of 1956 Admiral Smedberg, the new Superintendent, eliminated compulsory reveille and breakfast formation on Sundays. Midshipmen may now enjoy the rich luxury of a long sleep on Sunday mornings if they have no conflicting commitments.

The Naval Academy Library contains about 165,000 volumes, including the Park Benjamin collection of 1,200 rare books dealing with the history of electricity; some of them date back to the fifteenth century. The main reading room of the library is 130 feet long and 33 feet wide. It is open from 8:30 A.M. to 6:15 P.M. on week days, and from 2:00 P.M. to 6:00 P.M. on Sundays. The library owns probably the best collection of books on naval history and biography in the world.

It was here that a woman visitor asked the librarian to suggest a good work of fiction to read over the week-end. He proposed James Lane Allen's classic *A Kentucky Cardinal*.

"No, I don't want anything theological," she replied.

"But, madame," protested the librarian, "this cardinal was a bird."

"Well," she answered, "I don't care anything about his private life, either."

The collection of relics in front of Dahlgren Hall includes guns used or captured during the Mexican War, the Civil War, the Boxer Rebellion in China in 1900, the Spanish-American

War and World War II, as well as two Japanese torpedoes. Many items in this once extensive collection were scrapped for their metal during World War II. Among the exhibits within the building is the stadimeter used by Yeoman Ellis, of the USS *Brooklyn*, who deliberately exposed himself to a devastating fire at the battle of Santiago in order to obtain the exact range of the enemy vessel *Viscaya*. He had no sooner called "1,100 yards, sir!" than the *Brooklyn* delivered a broadside that sent her adversary reeling to destruction; at the same time Ellis paid with his life for his superb act of heroism—with this instrument still in his hands.

In addition to the relics on view in Dahlgren Hall, the walls are hung with memorial plaques to graduates who met death in line of duty—in turret explosions, airplane crashes and submarine accidents. "Lost at sea" is the requiem of many of them. Typical of the tributes paid to lost comrades is that to Harlow M. Pino, of the class of 1921, who died on the submarine S-51, September 25, 1925:

> Death found him in the dark, sudden and unheralded, not in the fever of war nor in the sight of men. His was a man's fate, for he died at his post, carrying on the Navy's work.

The tribute to Thomas E. Zellers, of the class of 1920, who was killed June 12, 1924, in a turret explosion on the USS *Mississippi* reads:

> His hand was found grasping the flood valve which extinguished a burning powder train and saved his ship. Flaming death was not as swift as his sense of duty and his will to save his comrades at any cost to himself. His was the spirit that makes the service live.

Chapter 16

Extracurricular

A midshipman's life is not all prescribed routine, though it may seem so to the free-wheeling civilian. Though he has relatively little leisure time compared with the average college student, he makes a virtue of necessity, and extracts from his precious moments of free time the full measure of accomplishment. As a matter of fact, it is little short of miraculous how much activity the midshipmen can engage in outside of their long working hours. There are more than forty extracurricular activities (exclusive of athletics) in which hundreds of midshipmen participate with great enthusiasm and success. Like all endeavor at the Naval Academy the activities are designed to produce better officers, as well as to furnish recreation, and participants are awarded certificates at a special ceremony which honors them during June Week.

In the group designated Class Activities are the Class Organization, the Class Crest and Class Ring Committee, the *Lucky Bag*, the Class Hop Committee, and the Ring Dance and Farewell Ball Committee. Each of the three upper classes has its class organization, the purpose of which is "to enable each class to function as a unit through duly elected representatives, to foster good will among the classes, and to cooperate in maintaining morale in the brigade." It is impossible to define the objectives further, since these groups consider almost anything of interest to the class, even to the prevailing prices of automobiles among the dealers out in town. The functions of the other committees are obvious.

On the brigade level there is a wide variety of organizations, one of which, the Brigade and Class Honor Committee, is significant enough to be, actually, almost out of the realm of what we normally associate with the term "extracurricular activities." The Brigade Honor Committee consists of the

President of the First Class, The Brigade Commander, the Secretary of the First Class, six elected First class battalion representatives, and the Presidents of the Second and Third Classes (these latter two being present only when matters pertinent to their own or lower classes are considered). This committee is the guardian of the personal honor of the Brigade; it investigates all offenses involving moral turpitude by First classmen submitted to it by the Commandant or from within the Brigade, and forwards its findings, when guilt is indicated, to the Commandant. The Second, Third and Fourth Class Honor Committees, consisting of the respective class president, secretary, and six elected class battalion representatives, perform the same functions for the underclasses. (Since the Fourth class has no organization, the president and secretary of the First class serve as components of the Fourth Class Honor Committee.) These committees are, of course, advisory only, and have no powers to discipline.

The pride of the marching brigade is the midshipmen's Drum and Bugle Corps, sometimes known as the "Hellcats." Expert in music and smart in military precision, they play the brigade into the mess hall at noon and evening meal formations, and with elegant flourish of drumsticks and twirl of cymbals participate in all brigade parades. Members of the corps wear on the sleeves of their blue uniforms the distinguishing insignia of a gold bugle.

In support of the Academy's athletic program are three very useful groups: the Brigade Activities Committee, the Public Relations Committee, and the Reception Committee. The Brigade Activities Committee is the official pep committee, and it is their job to keep brigade spirit at a high pitch and to arrange pep rallies and team send-offs. The Public Relations Committee are the press men for Academy events and make themselves generally useful to visiting newsmen, photographers and radio and television announcers as spotters and informants. It is their job to stand by the announcers and to "spot" the Navy plays and identify the Navy players; they perform this task silently by pointing to the names of the athletes on a large chart —a system which explains the broadcasters' instant and miraculous skill in announcing who is running with the football and who are tackling him even before the play is completed. The Reception Committee sees to it that visiting teams and other guests are hospitably entertained during their stay at the Academy.

Religious activities include the Naval Academy Christian Association and the Newman Club. Every midshipman is required to attend divine service, but he is free to attend a church of his own choosing. The Chapel of the Naval Academy is strictly non-sectarian, though for the sake of uniformity the Episcopal Prayer Book is used so that future captains of Navy ships will be familiar with a form of service should they ever have to conduct divine service in the absence of a chaplain on shipboard, as Navy Regulations require.

About 2,000 Protestant midshipmen attend Sunday service in the Chapel at 10:30. Many of these also attend Holy Communion at 9:00 on a voluntary basis. Some 1,000 Catholic midshipmen go to Mass at the Chapel at 8:00. Those of the Jewish and Greek Orthodox faiths attend synagogue and church in town. Other smaller groups of midshipmen attend some twelve churches of other denominations out in town. The parade of the midshipmen from Bancroft Hall to the Chapel, headed by the Brigade Staff and received at the Chapel door by the Superintendent and the Commandant, with their aides, constitutes one of the most impressive ceremonies at the institution.

A major religious activity at the Academy is the singing of the choirs, of which there are three, the Chapel Choir, the Antiphonal Choir, and the Catholic Choir. In addition to singing at the services, the Chapel Choir each year presents at Christmastime an excellent performance of Handel's great oratorio, *The Messiah*, in conjunction with the women's choir of Hood College, Frederick, Maryland. The choir has also sung in the Washington Cathedral, the National Gallery of Art, and the White House.

There have been in the Academy a number of very popular professional clubs—the Sailing Squadron, the Foreign Languages Club, the Radio Club, the Engineering Club, Radio Station WRNV, the Foreign Relations Club, and the Mathematics Club—and hobby clubs—the Chess Club, the Model Club, the Stage Gang and Juice Gang, and the Stamp Club. Inter-

*E*xtracurricular activities include the "No More Rivers" ceremony, an intercollegiate student conference, and sailing on the Severn.

PHILIP B.
FULLER
U. S. M. A

GE. | HAR | NANCY SEIBER | CARO PATL U. OF DEL | MICHAEL T. CORGAN U.S.N.A | ROBERT A. BILDERSEE COL | MICHAEL SPRINGE BOSTON U.

*Relaxing after a hard
day is good for any young man.*

collegiate and intramural debating is conducted by the Forensic Activity under the supervision of the English, History and Government Department.

The Sailing Squadron, which holds high prestige as a social and recreational activity, also serves the purpose of making the midshipmen's professional training enjoyable. Its serious aim, as expressed in official language, is "To advance professional knowledge by providing additional training facilities for midshipmen in boat-handling; repair and operation of power plants; the operation, sailing, handling and racing of small craft; in piloting and general seamanship; and to provide recreation and encourage interest in water-borne craft." In attaining this objective it is aided by the yachts *Norderney*, *Highland Light*, *Royono* and *Freedom*, twelve yawls and thirty small sloops called "knockabouts." The midshipman officers of the club bear the titles of Commodore, Vice Commodore and Rear Commodore. The midshipmen work on the boats themselves and put in many hours keeping them in top sailing condition.

Under the aegis of the Naval Academy Sailing Squadron the Academy enters its boats in many races on Chesapeake Bay as well as in the Newport-Annapolis and Newport-Bermuda races. There is also interbattalion racing for the DuBoise Trophy.

The most famous of the Academy's "water-borne craft" in recent years has been its varsity eight-oared shell, which with the other crews operates out of Hubbard Hall, named in honor of Rear Admiral John Hubbard, of the class of 1870, who as a midshipman stroked the first Navy crew to victory. At Helsinki, Finland, in 1952, the Navy crew won the Olympic Championship, and Navy varsity crews were undefeated from 1952 to 1955, winning 31 straight races to set an all-time intercollegiate record.

The midshipmen operate a licensed "ham" radio shortwave station, W3ADO, which can maintain far-ranging contact with other such stations the world over. The members of the Brigade also have their own radio station, WRNV, which can be received by sets in Bancroft Hall, and which broadcasts programs of all sorts for the pleasure of the Brigade and the profit of the operators who learn radio programing and engineering by the do-it-yourself method.

Those who enjoy the complexities of social activity find outlet for their enthusiasms on the Brigade and Class Hop Committees. The Brigade Hop Committee is an august body composed of the Brigade Commander, the Senior Regimental Commander and the Deputy Brigade Commander, as well as two First classmen, one Second classman and one Third classman from each battalion. They plan and conduct the big hops including the Christmas and Thanksgiving Hops. It is the custom that the wife of the Superintendent receives at the Christmas Hop and the Farewell Ball and the wife of the Commandant at the Thanksgiving Hop and the Ring Dance. Members of the Brigade Hop Committee wear aiguillettes when they attend hops as insignia of office. As formal dances of some kind are held almost every weekend, to say nothing of uncounted informals, these committees play conspicuous parts in the social life within the Yard.

To the budding Horace Greeleys with journalistic impulses is offered useful and practical experience in reporting, editing and publishing on the biweekly periodical, *The Log*. The professional magazine, *Trident*, opens the door of opportunity to the midshipmen whose bent is creative writing. In *The Lucky Bag*, the ponderous year-book published by the First class, and in that pocket-sized compendium of useful information, *Reef Points*, the amateur writer, photographer, editor, historian and statistician finds his chance to show what he can do. The only credential he needs is proof of his capacity to be useful.

Every fall the editors of *The Log*, who were appointed by their predecessors the preceding spring, send out a call for candidates to report at the editorial sanctum in Bancroft Hall. Members of all four of the classes respond. Assignments are given out to cover news, sports, features, humor, literary and musical criticism and other subjects in accordance with each candidate's preference. On the evidence of their work, the more capable of the candidates are appointed to the staff or are made "associates." Only two offices are elective, those of editor-in-chief and business manager. The duties are all performed on the personal time of the staff, during their liberty hours on Wednesday afternoons and Sunday evenings. As practically every midshipman in the regiment subscribes for himself and usually also for the folks back home or for his O.A.O., the circulation runs about 7000 copies. Despite its success, however, the editors get neither remuneration nor special privileges; they labor for love and glory alone. The money received from subscriptions and from advertising is all put back into the magazine itself.

While the bulk of the editorial content deals with news and sporting events, schedules of coming occasions and changes in the organization and policies of the Navy Department, the most popular features of *The Log* are found in the departments and in the comments in lighter vein on the foibles of midshipman life. When, in the throes of examination hysteria, for example, a midshipman gravely writes: "Luther died by being excommunicated by a bull," that happy conception is perpetuated in type. And how many of us could improve upon this distinction between a bolt and a nut?

"A bolt is a thing like a stick of hard metal such as iron with a square bunch on one end and a lot of scratching wound around the other. A nut is similar to a bolt only just the opposite, being a hole in a chunk of iron sawed off short with wrinkles around the inside of the hole."

The courses in the professional subjects offer a rich field for humor.

"I don't think that I should get swabo in this recitation," complained a Second classman to his instructor in ordnance.

"Neither do I," concurred the instructor, "but it's the lowest we have."

When an instructor queries of a First classman: "Mr. Gish, after reading your Naval Regulations, what do you think an officer must be to rate a full naval burial?" and Mr. Gish replies, "Dead, sir," the plausible contention is duly recorded in *The Log*.

The repartee in the mess hall furnishes an endless flow of merriment. Here are some representative items from this source of copy:

> *First classman*—"What signal do they use when a man falls overboard?"
> *Fourth classman*—"A gun shot, sir."
> *First classman*—"Anything else?"

Fourth classman—(after much thinking)—"I guess they run up the absentee pennant, sir."

Third classman—"What do the new destroyers displace?"
Fourth classman—"The old ones, sir."

Published in alternate weeks with *The Log* is *The Log Splinter,* a pint-size (5¼ by 7¼ inches) magazine not unlike the parent *Log* in type, except that there is more emphasis on news and sports. *The Log* outfit also prepares each year an indispensable little booklet especially for the ladies, *The Drag's Handbook,* a good-natured but highly useful guide to the special aspects of midshipman social life, designed to be helpful especially to the uninitiated drag and calculated to put at her ease any jittery female who is worried about the novelty of visiting Annapolis and a military institution.

Because the Naval Academy is a national institution its publications assume a quasi-official status; for that reason all the material that appears in the undergraduate periodicals is submitted for visé by a commissioned officer before it is released. The purpose of this censorship is neither to curtail the self-expression of contributors nor to protect the morals of the midshipmen; its primary object is to guard against commitments in partisan politics and comments that might bring political repercussions, involve the Navy Department or the State Department in international complications, or subject the Naval Academy to unjust criticism.

Most of the Naval Academy's widespread activities in the arts and letters are conducted and coordinated by the *Trident Society,* founded in 1923. This society publishes the Academy's literary magazine, the *Trident Magazine,* issued every six weeks and presenting the original literary and artistic work of the brigade, as well as professional articles by naval officers. It also produces the *Trident Calendar,* an interesting and useful amalgamation of engagement book, schedule of events, notebook, and photograph and cartoon album. *The Book of Navy Songs* is another notable *Trident Society* project. Each year the Christmas Card Committee designs, sells and distributes an appropriate Brigade card, available to officers and civilian instructors as well as midshipmen, to convey the special holiday greetings of the

Academy. *Reef Points*, "The Annual Handbook of the Brigade of Midshipmen," is also the work of the Society. This volume contains a vast fund of lore about the Naval Academy and the Navy and is a particularly valuable source of information for each incoming class of plebes, who must soon know almost everything in it. The Society sponsors the House Library Committee, which has charge of the issue of books from the two Regimental Libraries, and it also directs the work of the Photo Club and the Art Club, which handle the pictorial work required in Academy publications and exhibits. The Photo Club maintains three darkrooms and complete equipment for processing films. It is the Art Club, by the way, which has the cherished job of giving Tecumseh his splendid coat of pre-Army game war paint.

The Lucky Bag is the huge *de luxe* year-book that is published each year by the graduating class; while its profusion of photographic illustrations and drawings and its record of undergraduate activities give this work a permanent value as a historical reference volume, it is largely devoted to the four-year record of the First class, and a portrait and biographical sketch of each member of the class is included in it. Both the editor and the business manager are elected by the class as far in advance as March of their Youngster year, and these two appoint their own assistants.

Before the introduction of radio made the living quarters of the midshipmen hideous with a varied assortment of conflicting programs, Orpheus laid direct hands upon the aspirants to musical accomplishment. Enduring evidence of the effect of the homemade efforts of one midshipman to woo the muse may be found in the Naval Academy Museum in the shape of an informal warning dated October 25, 1867, written in longhand and signed by David D. Porter, Superintendent of the Naval Academy. It reads:

"Midshipman Thompson (1st class), who plays so abominably on a fish horn, will oblige me by going outside the limits when he wants to practise, or he will find himself 'coming out of the little end of the horn'."

It was addressed to Robert Means Thompson, whose name was given to Thompson Stadium and among whose many benefactions to the Naval Academy are the massive bronze doors of the Chapel.

Today the number of undergraduate activities devoted to music are so many and varied in character that they have been coordinated under the name of the "Combined Musical Clubs." Membership is open to all from plebes to First classmen who can sing, play a musical instrument, dance, act, write librettos or compose scores. For one of the major purposes of the Musical Clubs is to produce a musical show every year, usually an original creation with book, music and lyrics by the midshipmen themselves. This annual show always reveals an amazing amount of top-flight talent in both composition and performance.

Those who contribute their bit by installing and manipulating the stage electrical effects are designated as the "Juice Gang." The manipulators of the curtain, the scene shifters, property men and creators of off-stage noises are known as the "Stage Gang" and "Property Gang." The dispensers of harmony are divided into several groups; the aggregation in most active demand is the modern dispenser of dance rhythms known as the "N.A.-10," although it actually consists of about twenty. The Glee Club of about one hundred and fifty voices confines itself to vocal numbers; its members are heavily drawn upon for roles in the musical productions. Altogether over two hundred midshipmen participate in this annual production.

The more serious dramatic productions are staged by the "Masqueraders." Usually a play that has had a successful New York run is chosen for performance, particularly one that features an all or predominantly male cast. These productions are made under the general supervision of the authorities of the Naval Academy, whose efforts are rewarded by invariably sold-out houses; so popular have these performances been indeed, that no provision is made for deficits—which puts the Masqueraders one up on the Broadway impresarios. The proceeds are used for defraying the expenses of having the scenery made and of hiring the costumes. Four performances are given during the season. Plebes have been permitted to drag a guest to one performance—always, of course, "at discretion of the Commandant."

First Girl—"I'll have you know that I'm going to marry an officer and a gentleman."

Second Girl—"You can't. That's bigamy."

Thus does the midshipman paraphrase the ancient jest about that traditional duo, the officer and the gentleman. Like so many of the midshipmen's jokes, it relies for its humor upon a variation from the standard and consequently expected norm. When the wife of one of the officers gave an "At Home" to a number of plebes who were advised that tea would be served from four to six and two unsophisticated lads who were unfamiliar with the social conventions showed up precisely at four and left precisely at six on the assumption that this literal interpretation of the hours of the function was *de rigueur*, the incident caused as much merriment to the regiment as the standard story of the old lady who was told by her doctor to drink hot water "one hour before each meal" but who reported that she could not drink even as long as three minutes without bursting.

Education in the social conventions is undertaken at the Naval Academy not alone because it is a cultural accomplishment of a gentleman but because it is an essential part of a naval officer's equipment. Unless he is trained in the niceties of social intercourse he is not wholly qualified for his duties. Everywhere he goes he is thrown into contact with the best people throughout the world—with officers of our own and of foreign navies, with diplomats, statesmen, men in official positions, leaders in society, representatives of the arts, the tycoons of industry. A part of his job is specified in *Customs of the Service*, a condensed version of Emily Post's classic work on etiquette that has been adapted to apply to the duties of a naval officer. This is a miniature guide-book to naval and social usages. A copy is given to every plebe upon his entrance and he is expected to familiarize himself with it—a task which he is anxious to undertake in order to avoid embarrassments when he makes his prescribed calls upon the officers at the station. During the season the Superintendent gives several formal receptions which are attended by the entire First class in installments. The midshipman learns how to make social calls by making social calls. The do's and don'ts of his behavior are comprised in the book

Service Etiquette which treats of salutes, official relations among officers, social behavior, deportment, speech, and correspondence. It provides the answer to many problems. Here is an example:

> SITUATION. While you are hurrying through the Yard to keep an engagement you overtake an officer.

The proper procedure is presented thus:

> SOLUTION. As you draw abreast of the officer, pass to his left or inboard side, come to a walk (if running) and salute. As you salute say, "By your leave, sir." When well past the officer you may go at the double time again.

A knowledge of the customs of the service extends considerably beyond the confines of the academic in Midshipman Gish's curriculum.

The costs to the midshipmen of keeping up with the Joneses are all so modest as to require no occasion for seeking financial help from home; besides, the Joneses are not keeping up much of a pace themselves. Receiving funds from any outside source is definitely frowned upon. "Money in their possession may lead to irregularities," states the Superintendent in his annual Letter to Parents and Guardians; "those who do receive extra funds will make expenditures that others cannot afford. This inequality reacts against the best interests of the brigade and often tempts a midshipman to go into debt."

The regular pay of a midshipman is sufficient to meet all of his needs. Only when Midshipman Gish is granted leave and makes a long journey home, and when he starts out on a practice cruise, is financial help smiled upon. A check of $25 from Aunt Minnie to spend on his summer practice cruise abroad will carry Midshipman Gish farther and to better advantage than that sum will ever carry him again. But even without that check, the midshipman will fare adequately, as he is commonly allowed to draw from his pay $125 while on his travels.

Midshipman Gish goes on Uncle Sam's payroll at the moment he is sworn in. At that time he is required to deposit $300 as the first payment on a total of $900. This sum represents the costs of his initial outfit of clothing, gear and books. The balance of $600 (in case he does not pay it at the same time) is deducted in monthly installments from his monthly pay of $111.15, plus $1.35 a day for ration allowance. He is normally out of debt by the beginning of second class year.

To keep his financial account straight and constantly before his attention, the midshipman receives a statement of his account at monthly intervals. For spending money he may draw in cash from his pay each month—if he wants to—in the following amounts:

> First classman, $15.00
> Second classman, $11.00
> Third classman, $9.00
> Fourth classman, $5.00

In addition, the midshipman may draw against his account for articles purchased over his signature upon sales slips at the midshipmen's store and at the Steerage (where light refreshments are obtainable during recreation hours at a minimum price); in the same manner he may enter his subscriptions to the Athletic Association, to the special class functions, to the midshipman periodicals, as well as pay his dues to such undergraduate organizations as he may choose to join. Some of the midshipmen organizations require no dues at all, while a few, such as the Radio Club, soar as high as one dollar annually. All activities authorized to engage in financial transactions must submit statements monthly; these are audited by a board of midshipmen which always includes the Officer Representative supervising that particular undergraduate activity. Even if Midshipman Gish paid dues in every midshipman organization, his gesture of prodigality would scarcely equal the cost to Father of a round of cocktails at the club.

In rare emergencies—as serious illness or death in the family—funds from the Navy Relief Society may be borrowed through the Chaplain, or from the midshipman's welfare fund maintained in Bancroft Hall.

To guard against extravagance after he graduates, Midshipman Gish is fortified against his coming grapple with the sordid world of commerce by a series of about twelve talks that are given under the formal title of "Personal Finance" but that might more aptly be termed "Gullible's Travels." He is shown what the living expenses of an ensign are. He is warned against the various forms of rackets, against subsidized "financial news sheets" that promise fortunes overnight, against the wiles of high-pressure salesmen, against stock-market speculations and other sources of worry that "distract interest and attention from the prime job of being a naval officer."

"Are there any questions?" asked the instructor before dismissing a class. A midshipman who had been industriously doing some figuring raised his hand.

"Please, sir, how far is it from San Diego to the Santa Anita race track?"

Chapter 17

Trails of Glory

Memorial Hall does not belong only to the Naval Academy. It is the Hall of Fame of the entire United States Navy.

As the visitor ascends the noble stairway that leads to Bancroft Hall (in which Memorial Hall is located), pausing for a moment to glance upward at the two stubby but decorative granite ships riding on permanently marcelled granite waves atop the cornice, and proceeds through the stately doorway into the imposing corridor, his eyes are led up the palatial marble staircase confronting him and into the great hall beyond. Against the far wall, at just the right height to be visible and framed within the marble doorway itself, hangs the most treasured of all the priceless relics of the Naval Academy—a faded blue flag, crudely inscribed with letters dim with age, that spell the words:

"DONT GIVE UP THE SHIP"

This immortal phrase was uttered by Captain James Lawrence as he lay dying on board the American frigate *Chesapeake* during its ill-fated action with the British frigate *Shannon* on June 1, 1813. A bare hundred days later, on September 10, 1813, Lawrence's friend Commodore Oliver Hazard Perry wrought vengeance. Aboard the brig *Lawrence*—named in honor of his dead compatriot—flagship of a squadron of nine small American vessels mounting 54 guns manned by 490 officers and men, he met the British squadron of six vessels mounting 63 guns and manned by 502 officers and men, in an action that has gone down in history as the "Battle of Lake Erie." What happened is thus described by a participant, Usher Parsons, assistant surgeon on the *Lawrence:*

> Just before the American fleet moved to attack the enemy, distant at 10 o'clock about four or five miles, Commodore Perry

produced the burgee or fighting flag hitherto concealed in the ship. It was inscribed with large white letters on a blue ground, that could be read through the fleet, "Don't Give Up the Ship," the last words of the inspiring Lawrence, and now to be hoisted at the masthead of the ship bearing his name. A spirited appeal was made to the crews assembled on the quarterdeck, who returned three hearty cheers that were repeated along the whole line of our vessels, and up went the flag to the top of the fore-royal. When Perry was rowed from his sinking ship to the *Niagara*, making his way through the hail of broadsides of the British vessels, he flung this flag over his arm, and under it, on the *Niagara*, he entered again into the battle and in short order vanquished the British fleet.

Since that turning point in history, Lawrence's dying words have become the slogan of the United States Navy. Beneath this ten-by-eight-foot flag, now enclosed in glass, the visitors stand close to the source of tradition which has made the Navy great and victorious. The phrase has become a byword throughout the service. To such supreme heights of determination and heroism did it raise the fighting men at Lake Erie that it led directly to the coining of another immortal phrase. When Commander Perry saw that his victory was secure, he seized an old letter, rested it on his navy cap, and in pencil wrote on the back this dispatch to Major General William Henry Harrison, to whose aid he was hurrying in defense of the northwest frontier:

> We have met the enemy and they are ours—two ships, two brigs, one schooner and one sloop.

Directly beneath the Perry flag is the huge plaque which is the dedication of the Naval Academy's roll of honor, which lies in a large case under the plaque. The impressive inscription reads:

DEDICATED TO THE HONOR OF THOSE ALUMNI
WHO HAVE BEEN KILLED IN ACTION DEFENDING
THE IDEALS OF THEIR COUNTRY

* *

WITH IMMORTAL VALOR AND THE PRICE OF THEIR
LIVES THESE PROVED THEIR LOVE OF COUNTRY

AND THEIR LOYALTY TO THE HIGH TRADITIONS
OF THEIR ALMA MATER BY INSCRIBING WITH
THEIR OWN BLOOD THE NARRATIVE OF THEIR DEEDS
ABOVE, ON, AND UNDERNEATH THE SEVEN SEAS.
THEY HAVE SET THE COURSE. THEY SILENTLY
STAND WATCH WHEREVER NAVY SHIPS PLY
THE WATERS OF THE GLOBE

There is nothing more that can be, or need be, said.

If there is a Valhalla where the spirits of the heroic dead of the Navy congregate to hold wassail and to relive the great exploits that brought them immortality in the annals of the sea, their gathering place must surely be Memorial Hall. The portraits that look down from its walls upon the gay merrymakings of their young successors, as well as the bronze tablets erected to perpetuate their names and fame, have been placed there to do honor to men who both created and maintained the finest ideals of the Navy. To be eligible for inclusion in this hall of fame, a man must do more than merely die in line of duty; he must die "in the gallant performance of duty in action" or in performing an act of exceptional bravery that "maintained a cherished naval tradition." Places are reserved, too, for those who have rendered such distinguished service in time of war as to receive special recognition by the Navy Department or higher authority, or who by their attainments have acquired public recognition. Within this category come young and old alike, from seaman to admiral. Here they meet on a plane of equality, unaged and ageless. Captain Death knows no rank or title.

Over there, in the east wing of the hall, hangs a plaque that tells in a sentence of the sacrifice of a mere boy, Naval Cadet William Henry Boardman, of the class of 1900, who met a gallant death during the Spanish-American War at San Juan, Puerto Rico, while a "volunteer member of a party landed from the USS *Amphitrite* for the defense of women and children." Almost adjoining is the tablet to Lieut. Commander Henry Barlow Rumsey, graduated in the emergency class of 1861, who, "safely escaping from a burning hotel, heard the cry of a child and returned to save her. He brought her out, but at the cost of his life." Near by is the brief epitaph to Lieut. (junior

grade) Stanton Frederick Kalk, of the class of 1916, who within
a year and a half of his graduation paid with his life for up-
holding one of the proudest traditions of the sea. It reads
simply that:

> HE SACRIFICED HIMSELF BY GIVING UP HIS PLACE ON A RAFT TO
> OTHERS, AFTER THE TORPEDOING OF THE USS *Jacob Jones* BY A
> GERMAN SUBMARINE. DISTINGUISHED SERVICE MEDAL FOR EX-
> TRAORDINARY HEROISM.

When Lieut. John Melton Hudgins, of the class of 1894,
plunged into a blazing inferno on board the USS *Kearsarge* on
April 13, 1906, in a superhuman effort to save the lives of his
men, one of the dying victims cried out the warning, "You are
killing yourself trying to save us." Undaunted, he went to his
death, his tablet tells, "in the endeavor to shield the crew of the
turret of which he had command from flames caused by the accidental ignition of powder during target practice."

Drama, self-sacrifice, devotion to duty, death—all the elements from which are compounded the great sagas of the sea—
find brief but poignant echoes in these inscriptions. What a
heart-stopping picture is evoked by the simple paragraph:

> CHARLES FLINT PUTNAM, MASTER U.S.N., WHO VOLUNTEERED
> FOR DUTY ON USS *Rodgers*, A VESSEL DISPATCHED TO THE ARCTIC
> OCEAN FOR THE RELIEF OF THE *Jeannette* EXPLORING EXPEDITION.
> AFTER HAVING GALLANTLY SUCCORED HIS SHIPWRECKED COM-
> PANIONS, WHILE RETURNING TO HIS STATION AT CAPE SERDZE
> KAMEN, SIBERIA, HE DRIFTED OUT TO SEA AND PERISHED ALONE
> ON THE ICE IN SAINT LAWRENCE BAY, BEHRING STRAITS, ABOUT
> JAN. 1, 1883.

Stories that arouse the imagination and stir the pulses lie behind single sentences that epitomize a life. A lad who had not
yet been commissioned ensign, Naval Cadet Loveman Noa, of
the class of 1900, found the end of the road of adventure:

> FIGHTING SINGLE-HANDED, AMBUSHED BY THE NATIVES OF THE
> ISLAND OF SAMAR, WHILE IN COMMAND OF AN EXPEDITION DURING
> THE PHILIPPINE INSURRECTION, OCT. 26, 1901.

Into the ranks of the Navy's immortals entered Lieut. Commander William Merrill Corry, Jr., of the class of 1910, when:

HE HEROICALLY GAVE HIS LIFE IN AN ATTEMPT TO RESCUE A
BROTHER OFFICER FROM A FLAME-ENVELOPED AIRPLANE, OCT. 7,
1920.

Dim, far-away echoes of one of the epic tragedies of the sea
come down the years to him who reads the tribute to Walter
Seba French, of the class of 1871:

THE LAST OFFICER ON THE *Huron*, WRECKED NOV. 24, 1877,
CHEERING AND SAVING HIS MEN. HE GAVE HIS LIFE TO DUTY.

Memories of the Spanish-American War surge backward
through time as one contemplates the plaque to Commander
Edward Parker Wood, of the class of 1867. He sent his name
down the centuries when he received orders to "Go inside,
destroy shipping," and forthwith took his little vessel, the
Petrel, into the harbor of Cavite and alone and single-handed
sunk every enemy ship. No wonder the entire fleet cheered
when the *Petrel* came out! Not by accident did Commander
Wood win his terse accolade, now graven in bronze:

FAITHFUL AND FEARLESS

It was on the same vessel and at the same place that another
graduate, Lieut. Commander Jesse M. Roper, of the class of
1872, found the end of the trail to glory when he "sacrificed
his life in attempting to save one of his crew at a fire on board
the USS *Petrel*, at Cavite, P. I., Mar. 31, 1901," A young
graduate, barely two years out of the Naval Academy, Edward
Canfield Fuller, of the class of 1916, Captain of Marines, up-
held the traditions of his branch of the service when he was:

KILLED IN ACTION WHILE ENDEAVORING TO PROTECT HIS MEN,
BOIS DE BELLEAU, JUNE 13, 1918. DISTINGUISHED SERVICE CROSS.
NAVY CROSS.

"Both sure and steadfast" is the citation on the plaque to
Ensign Joseph Cabell Breckinridge, class of 1895, proto-martyr
of the war with Spain, who was washed overboard from the
torpedo boat *Cushing* on February 11, 1898, while carrying dispatches to the USS *Maine*, which was blown up just four days
later. Two tablets commemorate the heroic deaths of two
graduates who perished on that vessel on the fateful night of
February 15, 1898—Lieut. Friend William Jenkins, of the class

of 1886, and Assistant Engineer Darwin Robert Merritt, of the class of 1895. The "first naval aviator to meet death in the performance of duty," Ensign William De Votie Billingsley, of the class of 1909, crashed to immortality on June 20, 1913.

But not all of those in this proud galaxy died in the performance of the act that brought them recognition in this hall of fame. Some won their laurels and survived to render other services; others entered by virtue of their outstanding accomplishments.

Here is Commander John Rodgers, of the class of 1903, for instance—one of a long line of the fighting Rodgers clan. A pioneer in naval aeronautics, he met his fate in a crash in August, 1926, but before that he had won international acclaim. His epitaph reads:

> HIS COURAGE, FORTITUDE AND LEADERSHIP DURING THE FIRST FLIGHT ATTEMPTED ACROSS THE PACIFIC TO THE HAWAIIAN ISLANDS MADE HIM A HERO IN THE EYES OF THE WORLD AND REFLECTED GLORY UPON THE NAVAL SERVICE.

Over there hangs the portrait plaque of a commander, class of 1870, whose death did not occur until five years after the feat-of-arms that is perpetuated in the annals thus:

> IN COMPLIANCE WITH ADMIRAL DEWEY'S ORDER "BURN AND DESTROY THE ENEMY'S SHIPS," AFTER THE BATTLE OF MANILA BAY, MAY 1, 1898, LIEUTENANT EDWARD MERRITT HUGHES, IN A SMALL BOAT WITH SEVEN MEN BOARDED AND SET FIRE TO THE SPANISH VESSELS DON JUAN DE AUSTRIA, ISLA DE CUBA, ISLA DE LUZON, GENERAL LEZA AND MARQUES DEL DUERO, IN THE FACE OF A WELL-ARMED BUT DEMORALIZED FORCE.

Here stand the tributes in imperishable bronze to the discoverer and explorer of Wilkes Land, Lieut. Charles Wilkes, who in 1840 cruised 1500 miles along the unknown coast of East Antarctica and announced to the world the existence of the Antarctic Continent; to Captain Charles Vernon Gridley, of the class of 1863, who commanded the flagship *Olympia* at the battle of Manila, and to whom Admiral Dewey gave his historic command, "You may fire when ready, Gridley"; and to Rear Admiral John Woodward Philip, "whose immortal words to his crew of the *Texas* at the battle of Santiago, July 3, 1898,

'Don't cheer, the poor devils are dying,' will live with him in history."

The first officer to receive a diploma of graduation from the United States Naval Academy, Thomas Oliver Selfridge, joins the legion of the valiant not merely by virtue of standing first in his class, but for being "unanimously recommended by the Board of Admirals to be advanced 30 numbers for conspicuous gallantry in battle." Rear Admiral Aaron Ward, of the class of 1871, began a long series of heroic feats by jumping overboard as a young officer and saving the life of a seaman, and ended up by being highly commended by the Commander-in-Chief for gallant conduct while in command of the USS *Wasp* in 1898, and by being advanced in rank by authority of Congress "for eminent and conspicuous conduct in battle." The outstanding value of the services rendered by the brilliant Vice Admiral Joel Robert Poinsett Pringle, of the class of 1892, who during World War I served as Chief of Staff to Sir Lewis Bayly, won the tribute:

TO TREAD THE PATH OF DEATH, HE STOOD PREPARED,
AND WHAT HE GREATLY THOUGHT, HE NOBLY DARED.

It is but a brief step from the bronze plaque to the bronze portrait bust. Four such memorials now stand in the hall of fame. One is that of John Paul Jones, "the father of the American Navy"; it is a replica of the original made by Jean Antoine Houdon, the French sculptor. Another is a portrait of Rear Admiral Robley D. Evans, better known as "Fighting Bob Evans," of the class of 1863. The third is that of Rear Admiral William Adger Moffett, of the class of 1890, the first Chief of the Bureau of Aeronautics, "an outstanding leader in the development of naval aviation who gallantly gave his life in that cause on April 4, 1933, upon the occasion of the loss at sea of the USS *Akron*." The fourth is a bust of Admiral William Sowden Sims, of the class of 1880, the famous naval gunnery expert and Commander of the United States Naval Forces in Europe in World War I.

The list of portraits in Memorial Hall reads like a roll-call of the heroes of the United States Navy; it is indeed just exactly that. Here hang the likenesses of many, but not yet all, of the outstanding officers whose exploits have made history, around whom legends grow and about whose very names glamour clings—John Paul Jones, Perry, Farragut, Porter, Sampson, Dewey—names that reach back into the dim past and evoke visions of white sails against blue seas, of clouds of smoke pierced by flashes of flame to the obbligato of ghostly guns. Slowly, one by one, as the desired portraits are obtained by gift or are purchased with donated funds, this gallery of the Navy's great is growing.

The list of portraits now hanging in Memorial Hall, with the names of the artists when known, follows:

BAINBRIDGE, COMMODORE WILLIAM (1774–1833); painted by J. W. Jarvis.

BARRY, JOHN (1745–1803); painted by Robert Hinckley.

BOLTON, CAPTAIN WILLIAM COMPTON (date of birth unknown-1849); painted by J. W. Jarvis.

CHAUNCEY, COMMODORE ISAAC (1772–1840); painted by Gilbert Stuart.

DEWEY, ADMIRAL GEORGE, class of 1858 (1837–1917); painted by N. M. Miller.

DUPONT, REAR ADMIRAL S. F. (1803–1865); painted by Robert Hinckley after D. Huntington.

FARRAGUT, ADMIRAL DAVID GLASGOW (1801–1870); painted by N. M. Miller.

GODON, REAR ADMIRAL SYLVANUS W. (1809–1879); artist unknown.

HOBSON, REAR ADMIRAL RICHMOND P. (1870–1937); painted by Olive Bigelow.

JONES, COMMODORE JOHN PAUL (1747–1792); painted by Cecilia Beaux.

LAWRENCE, CAPTAIN JAMES (1781–1813); painted by J. Herring after Gilbert Stuart.

LEVY, COMMODORE URIAH P. (1792–1862); painted by an unknown artist.

MCDOUGAL, REAR ADMIRAL DAVID STOCKTON (1809–1882); painted by an unknown artist.

NICOLSON, COMMODORE JOHN B. (1783–1846); painted by J. W. Jarvis.

PERCIVAL, CAPTAIN JOHN (1779–1862); painted by Ethan Allen Greenwood.

PERRY, COMMODORE OLIVER HAZARD (1785–1819); painted by J. W. Jarvis.

PORTER, COMMODORE DAVID (1780–1843); painted by J. W. Jarvis.

PORTER, ADMIRAL DAVID DIXON (1813–1891); painted by Carl Becker.

SAMPSON, ADMIRAL WILLIAM T., class of 1861 (1840–1902); painted by N. M. Miller.

SHAW, CAPTAIN JOHN (1773–1823); artist unknown.

WHIPPLE, ABRAHAM (1733–1819); painted by Edward Savage.

These heroes, whose likenesses hold honored place in Memorial Hall, exemplify the highest traditions of the service career, which has been brilliantly defined in our day by former Secretary of State Dean Acheson and also by former Secretary of the Navy Thomas S. Gates, Jr.

Mr. Acheson put it this way:

Why should men of quality go into government service?— not to gain a halo, or because of a duty to sacrifice their lives, but because there is no better or fuller life for a man of spirit. The Greek concept of happiness is relevant: "The exercise of vital powers along lines of excellence, in a life affording them scope."

The prize of the general is not a bigger tent, but command. The managers of industry and finance have the bigger tents; but command—supreme leadership—rests with government service; and it demands and gives scope to every vital power a man has, along lines of excellence.

The Secretary restated the service tradition in these terms:

The Naval profession is an honorable one, which has traditionally commanded the respect and affection of our country. To maintain the support and respect of society, as well as to meet the requirements of his own conscience, every Naval leader must be in himself an example of our military ideals.

The United States Navy has long been distinguished for the high quality of its officers and men. By Naval leadership is meant the aim of accomplishing the Navy's mission through people. It is the sum of those qualities of intellect, of human understanding and of moral character that enable a man to inspire and to manage a group of people successfully. Effective leadership, therefore, is based on personal example, good management practices, and moral responsibility.

During the years 1950 and 1951, Vice Admiral Harry W. Hill, then Superintendent, instituted a splendid new method of honoring Academy heroes, that of dedicating rooms in Bancroft Hall to alumni Medal of Honor winners in World War II and the Korean action. The rooms were dedicated, if possible, on the anniversary of the honored deed. Each room so dedicated is indicated by a nameplate, the "Callaghan Room," for example, and by plaques on which the citation is inscribed, and each honor room is one of those occupied by the Medal of Honor winner during his career as a midshipman.

The one shrine to which the largest number of visitors flock is the sarcophagus which contains the casket in which rests all that is mortal of Admiral John Paul Jones. It is located in the crypt under the Chapel.

It is a curious chance of fate that the "Father of the American Navy" should have come from Scotland, where he was born July 6, 1747. He first came to America as a boy of thirteen. In the Revolutionary War he received a commission in the American Navy; after many gallant exploits in the early stages of the war, he attained on September 23, 1779, supreme distinction when in command of the *Bonhomme Richard*, off Flamborough Head, he engaged and captured HMS *Serapis*. This action, fought by moonlight, was the most brilliant sea battle of the war, and one of the most remarkable in history. When his own ship was sinking and he was called upon to surrender by the British Commander, he replied:

"I have not yet begun to fight."

This answer has become one of the famous slogans of the American Navy. The victorious ship sank, and Jones transferred his prisoners of war and his much depleted crew to the captured *Serapis*. In 1781 he was appointed to command a ship of the line, then building, the *America*. He lost the opportunity to command this ship when Congress gave the *America* to France. As the war was now practically over, he was no longer needed at sea, and was sent on a mission to Paris. He succeeded in this task, but was never rewarded. While in Paris he received a flattering invitation from Empress Catherine II of Russia, then engaged in war with Turkey, to enter her service; in his desire for active duty, he accepted the invitation. The Empress appointed him a rear admiral and gave him a squadron in the Black Sea. He defeated the Turks repeatedly, but jealousy and intrigue forced him to leave Russia. Returning to Paris much broken in health, he died on July 18, 1792.

Through the generous act of a foreign admirer, his body was preserved by being placed in a lead casket filled with alcohol, and was buried in a cemetery in the outskirts of Paris, and for more than a hundred years his burial place remained unknown. In 1899, General Horace Porter, our Ambassador to France, began a diligent search, which in 1905, aided by the French Government, came to a successful ending. The body had been so well preserved that positive identification was possible. A squadron of American warships was sent to bring the hero to America, and on July 6, 1905, John Paul Jones passed once again in triumph through the streets of Paris with a French and an American military escort. On April 24, 1906, commemorative services were held at the United States Naval Academy, participated in by President Theodore Roosevelt, the French Ambassador, and other high civil and military representatives.

Surrounding the sarcophagus stand eight monolithic columns of white "grand antique des Pyrenees" marble in which nature has traced weird black designs; to them imaginative minds have given strange interpretations. On the pillar at the right of the entrance may be seen the silhouette profile of George Washington; on another the head of a clown; on the sarcophagus itself appears the semblance of a butterfly.

In a circle in the marble floor are inlaid the names of the six ships commanded by Jones during the Revolution. The surrounding rope is made of gold braid, which is reputed to have cost $17,000. A large book is available to visitors who may wish to write their names in it; this ceremony serves no known purpose except as an outlet to the impulses of those who might otherwise inscribe their names on the walls. The massive black garlands that drape the walls are made of natural magnolia leaves. Within a lighted compartment built within the wall is exhibited the sword of the Admiral. The inscription in the marble floor in front of the sarcophagus reads:

HE GAVE OUR NAVY ITS EARLIEST TRADITIONS OF HEROISM
AND VICTORY

The Chapel in itself is a treasure-house of memorials. So deep is the sentiment in which it is held that graduates have returned to it from halfway round the world in order to be married in it. Rebuilt in 1939–40 in the form of a Christian cross, with a dome 192 feet high, it is the most conspicuous landmark within the Yard. The cornerstone was laid June 3, 1904, by Admiral George Dewey; since that day the Chapel has been steadily drawing to itself those associations, those traditions and those little human touches from which spiritual values stem. Even before the visitor enters the doorway he is greeted with yew and lavender bushes that came from the rectory garden at Burnham Thorpe, England, the birthplace of Lord Nelson; they are just around the corner at the right. Does the romanticist see in them symbols of that comradeship which holds together the seafarers of the globe? Within the doorway hangs a small glass case containing the much-thumbed prayer book of Admiral Farragut, opened to that page in the Book of Psalms containing favorite passages marked by him while he was in command of the *Hartford* during the Civil War. Trifles though these be, they are the kind of trifles from which reverence springs.

Pretty much everything in the Chapel—altar pieces, doors, windows, baptismal fonts, colors, marble tablets, bronze plaques—pay tribute to naval officers who have lived greatly and died greatly. The keynote is struck in the typical message on the gold cross on the altar itself. On the reverse is engraved a tribute to Lieut. Commander J. M. Roper of the class of 1872, who lost his life in a heroic attempt to save others in a fire aboard ship in 1901; warned of his peril as he started down the hatch, he replied simply, "My men are down there and it is my duty to get them out." On the face of the cross is emblazoned that one phrase which perhaps more than any other expresses the spirit of the service:

FAITHFUL UNTO DEATH

The three large stained-glass windows are memorials to as many great admirals. The chancel window, behind the altar, honors Admiral David Dixon Porter; it is the gift of the class of 1869. The period of his administration as Superintendent exactly coincides with the undergraduate life of the class itself —1865 to 1869. The design shows Christ walking on the Sea of Galilee. The large window at the north honors the Navy's first four-star admiral, David Glasgow Farragut; he is represented at the dramatic moment of his career, lashed to the rigging of his ship in Mobile Bay, August 5, 1864, with his binoculars in hand and surrounded by the smoke of battle. The third large window, to the south, honors the victor at the battle of Santiago, Rear Admiral William Thomas Sampson; it is the gift of the officers and men who served in the fleet under him. It shows an angel poised on an ark, holding a lowered sword and bearing aloft a dove of peace.

Flanking the altar are two smaller windows. The one at the left (as one faces the altar) is quite the finest in design and workmanship in the Chapel; it represents a knight in armor, Sir Galahad, as the symbol of the ideals of the Navy. This window was originally installed in the old chapel at a cost of $20,000, as the gift of the widow of Lieut. Commander Theodorus Bailey Myers Mason, of the class of 1868; by the time the present Chapel was completed, new regulations had been promulgated to govern the memorials; consequently the transfer required a special Act of Congress—and $6,000 more for remodeling and installation in its present position. The small window at the right of the Farragut window is noble in its inception. It is called "The Invisible Commission" with reference to the duty the officer depicted has to God as well as to country. The gift of the class of 1927, it sets forth the spirit of the Naval Academy in its inscription, which reads:

IN REVERENT TRIBUTE TO ALL THE SONS OF THEIR ALMA MATER WHO, IN WAR AND PEACE, HAVE REALIZED HER IDEALS OF HONOR, COURAGE, LOYALTY AND DUTY IN THE SERVICE OF GOD AND COUNTRY.

The most ornate tablet in the Chapel is hewn in marble; it pictures in deep relief the scene of the death in battle with naked savages in Formosa, June 13, 1867, of Lieut. Commander Alexander Slidell Mackenzie, of the class of 1859. Another marble tablet memorializes Lieut. Hugh W. McKee, of the class of 1866, who met death in Korea while heroically leading the assault over the parapet of the Citadel, Kanghoa Island, June 11, 1871. Ensign Jonathan M. Wainwright, of the class of 1867, is honored with a marble memorial that records his death in Mazatlán, Mexico, while fighting pirates on June 19, 1870.

Here hang the bronze records, too, of Welborn C. Wood, class of 1899, who met his fate as the youthful commander of the gunboat *Urdaneta* on the Orani River, Luzon, in an action against insurgent natives on September 25, 1899; of Lieut. Clarence C. Thomas, class of 1908, "the first American naval officer to give his life in the War with Germany, while in command of the armed guard on the USS *Vacuum*, which was sunk by a German submarine," April 28, 1917, and to Ensign Worth Bagley, class of 1895, "the first American naval officer who fell in the Spanish-American War," killed on board the torpedo boat *Winslow* during the bombardment at Cardenas, May 11, 1898. To this tribute is appended that noble epitaph so often inscribed on the tombs of the knights in the days of chivalry:

> I HAVE FOUGHT A GOOD FIGHT, I HAVE FINISHED THE COURSE, I HAVE KEPT THE FAITH.
>
> —II Timothy, 4: 7.

The most unusual and perhaps most appropriate memorial in the Chapel is the Votive Ship, a twelve-foot model of a fifteenth-century Flemish carrack, which hangs from the ceiling high up in the back of the nave. The idea of exhibiting a ship model in a church is a very old one and symbolizes the dedication of seafaring men to their God. The model in the Naval Academy Chapel was presented in 1941 by alumni who had served in the Construction Corps, which no longer exists as a separate corps.

A nineteen-year-old girl designed the massive bronze doors of the Chapel. Her name was then Evelyn Beatrice Longman (she has added the name of Batchelder to it since), and she won the contract in open competition conducted under the auspices of the National Sculpture Society in 1902. The doors were donated as a memorial to the class of 1868 by one of its members, Robert Means Thompson, whose many benefactions won him the title of the "best friend the Academy ever had." When he was told that the youthful designer lacked the technical knowledge needed to prepare a working mold for the casting, he replied: "Then I will send her abroad for a year of study." And he did.

The two doors, heavily decorated with symbolic figures and surmounted by a panel bearing the motto "Non Sibi Sed Patriae," are 10 feet wide and 15½ feet high; with the transom the total height of the doorway is 22 feet. At the dedication ceremonies on June 2, 1909, the members of the class of 1868, appropriately enough, were the first to pass through it.

One of the most exciting and inspiring relics of Naval glory is no longer at the Naval Academy, but its story is still well worth telling. It is the story of the small ship's boat, or gig, belonging to the ill-fated *Saginaw*.

The gig of the *Saginaw* is only 24 feet 8 inches long and a bare 6 feet 4 inches wide. Even within the walls of Macdonough Hall it seemed small; many an American boy sports a pleasure craft of larger proportions. But it was big enough to carry a cargo of adventure, tragedy and heroism such as the sea has seldom known.

The USS *Saginaw* sailed from the Midway Islands—on an ill-omened Friday, it may be noted—October 28, 1870. On October 29 it was wrecked on tiny Ocean Island, three miles long and three quarters of a mile wide, in the North Pacific. The problem of bare existence for the survivors became acute at once, as the only food available was an occasional albatross, gannet or seal, which the officers had to kill with their swords at night; firearms would have scared all life away and removed even this source of supply. A few fish were obtainable, but many were poisonous and caused illness.

In a forlorn but magnificent effort to save their comrades, a crew of five, headed by Lieut. John G. Talbot, U.S.N., volunteered to seek help in the ship's cockleshell of a gig. The nearest help was 1500 miles away. Setting forth on their hazardous voyage with the most meager of equipment and supplies, the men ran into a violent storm when only five days out, and lost all their lights and their tin oil stove. The boat was hove to with the sea anchor, which was soon lost. A drag was then constructed with three oars; the storm swept it away. Another drag was made with the two remaining oars rigged to support a square sail; this too was torn away, and it was this loss that proved fatal. When, after 31 days of incredible hardship, the little gig reached Kauai Island, of the Hawaiian group, on December 19, 1870, it was capsized in the surf, and with victory and life ironically within grasp, all of the crew were drowned—except one. The sole survivor was Seaman (later Lieutenant) William Halford. Through him the call for help was sounded. The only ship owned by the Hawaiian government, the *Kilauea*, set forth at once and reached the 100 or more marooned men on January 4, 1871.

The memory of these valiant souls is kept alive on a tablet in Memorial Hall; it was erected by the shipmates whose lives were saved through their sacrifice. It bears the tribute:

GREATER LOVE HATH NO MAN THAN THIS, THAT A MAN LAY DOWN HIS LIFE FOR HIS FRIENDS.

Even to list the relics of battle and trophies of war preserved in the Naval Academy Museum would require a volume. Furthermore, the Museum is more than the relatively small building located in the Yard at the corner of Maryland Avenue and Decatur Road, for its treasures are exhibited all over the Academy grounds in almost every major building. It is difficult to call attention to or single out any particular exhibits because there are so many of them and because they are frequently changed and moved about.

The exhibits cover the range from priceless manuscripts to famous battle flags, from bits of shot and shell that have changed the course of history to the personal effects of great naval leaders; from nautical instruments that have figured in epic adventures to figureheads of historic vessels. Here is a list selected at random of the exhibits that attract most interest:

The bullet that killed Stephen Decatur, Jr., in his duel with James Barron, March 22, 1820.

The log book of the frigate *Constitution*, opened at the page showing the entry of August 1, 1805, when Commodore John Rodgers dictated the terms of peace to be accepted by the piratical ruler of Tunis.

The kedge anchor, or drag, of the *Constitution*, by means of which its commander, Captain Isaac Hull, was enabled to escape from a pursuing British squadron after a sixty-mile chase, July 16, 1812.

The famous collection of 1200 naval medals, collected by Dr. Malcolm Storer.

The cuirasse worn by John Paul Jones during his fight on the *Bonhomme Richard* against the British frigate *Serapis*, September 23, 1779.

Battle flags flown by the *Monitor* in her fight with the *Merrimac*, and by many more of the important American warships, together with the flags of many of the captured vessels.

The 128-word cable message from Rear Admiral Sampson to the Secretary of the Navy, announcing the naval victory at Santiago "as a Fourth of July present" to the American people, July 4, 1898.

A section of the stern post of the USS *Kearsarge*, containing a 55-pound British-made shot fired at her on June 19, 1864, from the Confederate ship *Alabama*, commanded by Captain Raphael Semmes.

The table presented by the Emperor of Japan to Commodore M. C. Perry on his momentous visit to that country.

The ornate saddle presented to Admiral Halsey by the Chamber of Commerce of Reno, Nevada, to enable him to ride the Emperor of Japan's favorite white horse into Tokyo (had not the war ended before that triumphant entry became a possibility).

The mess table at which the Japanese officials signed the instruments of surrender aboard the *Missouri* in Tokyo Bay, September 2, 1945.

One of the most poignant of the relics is a small socket wrench used by young Lieut. Graham Newell Fitch, class of 1923, for tapping out messages on the hull of the submarine S-4, which had been rammed and sunk off Provincetown December 17, 1927, in a tragedy that for days held the world spellbound. For three days the divers communicated with Fitch in the Morse code; the final conversation on December 20, with not a hint of either suffering or defeat, ended in silence within the doomed vessel. The rescuers listened all night but could hear nothing further. The S-4 was not brought to the surface until March 17, 1928. Five officers and 34 men lost their lives.

The Naval Academy Museum is the frequent and fortunate recipient of priceless and hallowed treasures donated or given in custody by those who wish to see their collections well cared for and displayed.

The armada of 108 ship models, known to collectors and connoisseurs the world over as the Rogers Collection, constitutes in itself a museum; in fact, it was housed in a building of its own at Southampton, Long Island, by its former owner, Col. Henry H. Rogers, who bequeathed the fleet to the Naval Academy upon his death in 1935. It is by far the finest collection of its kind in this country; it takes rank with the only two collections with which it is comparable—that in the British Museum in London and the collection at the Marine Museum of the Louvre in Paris.

Many of the models have historic associations and are irreplaceable at any price; consequently no real money valuation can be placed upon them. Several of them are British and French Admiralty models, built with watchlike precision; because these served the purpose of blueprints and working drawings, they are made on exact scale, usually 1:48, even to such minute details as the panelings. Members of the Admiralty Board in England used to retain the models as their perquisites of office; from such sources some of these specimens have come. Samuel Pepys, the diarist, was a Commissioner of the Board from 1660 to 1685; it is possible that some of these models once belonged to him.

Two of the most elaborate of the models—that of H.M.S. *Royal George*, built in 1756, and the *St. George*, built in 1701—are valued at $18,000 each. The model of the New Bedford whaling ship *Niger* cost $5000 to make; it is complete from the cutting stage erected for slicing up the catches to tiny blubber hooks and buckets for bailing the head oil. The smallest model includes not only the French ship *Le Caton* on its ways but the entire fence-enclosed shipyard as well, with minute guns, anchors, masts and cross-trees spread out on the ground; the entire scene measures only 12 by 14 inches. Included in the exhibit are numerous British ships-of-the-line; American clipper ships (including an especially fine model of the *Great Republic*, built by Donald McKay in 1853); private yachts of British kings; "fire-ships," designed to invade enemy ports as innocent merchantmen only to be exploded to the destruction of enemy vessels; old English revenue cutters, the fastest small boats afloat, used for running down smugglers; and royal barges. Here too may be found models of ships that have figured largely in history; among these are the *Shannon*, which fought the 'American ship *Chesapeake;* and the ship-of-war *Duke*, which called at the Island of Juan Fernandez for water in 1709 and there discovered and brought home Alexander Selkirk, better known as Robinson Crusoe. Seven of the models were made at Dartmoor by French prisoners-of-war who were originally carvers of ivory in Brittany; their jewel-like reproductions of the ship on which they served in 1813 are made of beef bones. Even the cases in which the models are exhibited are valued as high as $2000 each, while the two Queen Anne cupboards are valued at $4000 apiece.

No single exhibit anywhere in the country and perhaps in the world can give such a picture of the pageantry and the romance and the glory of the sea as does this priceless fleet of ship models.

Among the Museum's invaluable possessions are certain collections worthy of special mention: some 400 paintings, including the thirteen items of the Historical Marine Paintings Collection by Edward Moran (1829–1901); the superb Beverley R. Robinson Collection of Naval Battle Prints, an incredible assemblage of 1044 prints depicting virtually all single ship and fleet engagements from 1218 up to and including the American Civil War (1861–1865); the David C. Hanrahan Collection of Naval Battle Scenes; and the Rosenbach Collection of Memorable Documents, including such items as the original contracts for building of the frigates *John Hancock* and *Boston* in 1776, various letters of John Paul Jones, and the log of the *Monitor*.

The Academy also possesses many historic flags of every description; carefully mounted behind glass in specially built airtight compartments, are preserved the captured battle flags of enemy ships, flags seized by American landing forces around the globe, and flags rescued from historic American vessels. The stories behind these emblems are the story of the nation. Beneath them men have fought and suffered and died; battles have been lost and won, nations have risen and fallen. No one with a trace of imagination can view these priceless relics, many of them torn to mere shreds, without a stir of the emotions.

There is the jack of the British frigate *Guerrière*, sunk by the U. S. frigate *Constitution* in 1812; there is the ensign of the British frigate *Macedonian*, captured by the *United States*, and the ensign of the *Java*, captured by the *Constitution* later in the same year. Over yonder is the ensign of the French frigate *l'Insurgent*, captured by the *Constellation* in 1799. The cases are filled with scores of trophies won in history-making naval battles that won and maintained American freedom—ensigns, jacks and pennants that are the tokens of victory bought at the cost of lives of men to whom the principles of American liberty meant more than life itself. Here are the flags of such famous British ships as the *Cyane*, the *Levant*, the *Confiance*. In a prominent case of its own hangs in solitary dignity the rarest item of all the collection—the "only British Royal Standard in captivity." It was captured at York, Ontario, April 27, 1813, by a squadron under command of Commodore Isaac Chauncey, aided by a body of American troops under General Pike.

Case after case is filled with flags captured during the Spanish-American War. Some of them are scarred with shot and shell; others are as unblemished and as rich in heavy embroidery as the day they were made. Among them is the proud battle flag flown from the main of the valiant cruiser *Don Antonio de Ulloa* at Manila in 1898, a ship that "refused to surrender and was sunk with all flags flying and guns blazing." In that case yonder hangs a curious flag captured during the Boxer Rebellion in China in 1900, and a strange standard of the Korean Generalissimo, captured in 1871 in personal, hand-to-hand encounters that were rewarded with Uncle Sam's highest distinction, the Medal of Honor.

The collection of historic American flags includes, among others:

> The ensign of the *Maine*—the very flag lowered at sunset on the evening of February 15, 1898, shortly before the explosion; also the jack, which was found rolled up at the foot of the jack staff, ready to be hoisted on the morning that never dawned.
>
> The ensign of the *Huron*, wrecked in 1877.
>
> The Admiral's flag flown by Farragut on the USS *Tallapoosa* in 1870, the last ship on which he put to sea.

The ensign of the Confederate ship *Albemarle*, sunk by Cushing, 1864.

The tiny flag of the gig of the *Saginaw*, wrecked in 1870.

The first U. S. ensign hoisted in Japan by Commodore Matthew C. Perry, 1853.

The ensign of the U. S. sloop-of-war *Kearsarge*, hoisted in her action with the Confederate cruiser *Alabama*, 1864.

The first American flag hoisted on Spanish soil at Cavite, P. I., May 3, 1898.

The method of mounting and preserving the more tattered and moth-eaten flags is unique. The undertaking cost $30,000. Forty women were employed to mount 172 flags, covering a total of 15,000 square yards. The technique is thus described:

> The process consisted of spreading the tattered remnants of each flag upon a backing of heavy Irish linen of neutral color. The reconstruction work was guided by the original measurements of the flag and a knowledge of its design, and by placing in vertical and horizontal lines the warp and woof threads in the fragment of the bunting. What remained of the original flag was then sewn firmly to the linen backing by needlewomen. The stitches of silk or linen thread cover the entire surface of the flag and its backing, with a very strong yet hardly visible network of circular meshes about ½ inch in diameter. The thread is carefully dyed to match the colors of the old flag. Where there are gaps or missing parts in the original, the stitches, dyed to match the adjacent edges of the old bunting, complete the design of the flag and tell graphically the story of the pieces that are gone.

Around the wall of the main reading room of the library hang lithographic, crayon and photographic likenesses of all the Superintendents of the Naval Academy, up to the present incumbent.

A famous vessel, which once rode proudly at her moorings in the Yard beside a dock named in her honor, no longer exists. Badly in need of repairs and in danger of sinking at her moorings, she was hauled out of the water for reconditioning. But before the rebuilding could be accomplished, she collapsed beyond all hope of repair under the weight of a heavy snowfall on Palm Sunday in 1942.

Lying at her dock in Dewey Basin, near the cutter shed, she was a slim, black vessel with yellow trim, that had probably figured in as many stirring adventures as any ship of her size afloat in the country. It was the yacht *America*, the original winner of the international race around the Isle of Wight in 1851, from which the *America's* Cup derives its name. Queen Victoria and the aristocracy of England trod her decks in the golden days when the ship was the toast of the world of sport. Then came the Civil War in 1861. The *America* was purchased by the Confederates, renamed the *Memphis*, and put to work as a dispatch boat and blockade runner. To avoid capture, she was scuttled in the St. Johns River, Florida, in 1862; there she was discovered and raised by the crew of the USS *Ottawa*, who patriotically waived their claims to prize money, provided she was given to the Naval Academy. This was done, and the vessel reported at Newport, R. I., for use as a training ship. But as she was technically considered a prize of war, the prize court sold her to the U. S. Navy for $700, which in turn reassigned her to the Naval Academy. She was used as a training ship and sailed on the midshipmen's cruise, summer of 1863. Uncle Sam sold her in 1873 to General Benjamin F. Butler, and in his family she remained until 1917. After a series of vicissitudes, she was purchased with funds raised by a committee headed by Charles Francis Adams (later Secretary of the Navy) and sold to the Naval Academy October 1, 1921, for one dollar.

What was once the largest museum piece in the yard, the old Spanish cruiser *Reina Mercedes*, no longer exists, and there is no longer a real station ship. Sunk at the battle of Santiago by the *Massachusetts* and the *Texas*—after discharging two torpedoes and a broadside at Lieut. Hobson and his men when they scuttled the *Merrimac* to blockade the harbor, and missing on all counts, with a score of 0.0 hits—she was salvaged and sent to the Naval Academy in 1912 to replace the old *Hartford* as the station ship. Here, in addition to her other duties, she then became something of a marine museum on her own account. Not the least of her exhibits was a plate from the side of the *Reina* herself, showing 13 shot holes grouped within a small area, made by American guns on the night of July 5, 1898.

There is ample opportunity for the visitor to the Naval Academy (if he has unlimited time at his disposal!) to trace for himself the trails of glory of the United States Navy.

*V*isitors to the Naval Academy always enjoy seeing
the midshipmen on parade. Here, the Color Guard passes in
review. On the following pages, we see the Color Girl
being escorted by the Admiral.

Chapter 18

June Week

For six days in the early summer the Yard of the Naval Academy is converted into a Pleasure Ship. For six triumphant days youth rides into the quaint old community of Annapolis to participate in a pageant of celebration and romance. For six days the Yard is filled with starry-eyed lovelies, with ecstatic young sisters and brothers and proud fathers and mothers from back home. For six days the schedule is replete with athletic events, with parades and ceremonies, with exhibition boat drills and air shows, with the sounds of martial music by day and of dance music by night, with the thunder of gun salutes, with garden parties under the glow of colored lanterns and with all the delights ever dear to the hearts of men and maids. It is "June Week."

June Week marks the alpha and the omega in the year of the midshipmen; the ending of the old, the beginning of the new. Lowly plebes are miraculously metamorphosed into Youngsters; Youngsters rise to the proud estate of Second classmen; Second classmen step forward to take command of the brigade as the graduating class passes out of the Naval Academy into that world of service, of adventure and of glory that is the Navy. The sands of the midshipman year have run their course; once again the hourglass is turned.

By automobile, by bus and by taxi the families, friends and sweethearts of the midshipmen pour into town. Every available room within a radius of miles of Annapolis has been spoken for, usually months earlier; enterprising Annapolitans, mindful of the substantial profits they can realize, leave town on early vacations, renting their homes to June Week visitors; folks who venture without reservations may have to seek lodgings as far away as Baltimore or Washington. To enable the First classmen to visit their guests, many of whom have found accommodations at a distance, the ban against midshipmen riding in automobiles is removed. Even the ban on smoking in the Yard is overlooked in deference to the wishes of the visitors. For everyone who comes to June Week comes to rejoice; the spirit of excitement, of anticipation and of happiness permeates the very air. Midshipmen stroll about artlessly hand-in-hand with their One-And-Only girls and sit in the shadows with their arms about them, after the manner of sailormen the world over. There is an endless movement of people in and out of the gates and up and down the yard. Physical stamina is a prime requisite.

So much has to be concentrated into the precious six days of June Week that a more or less standardized schedule of events has been evolved over a period of years; variations and changes occur from time to time, of course, but in general the program conforms to a formula. It culminates in the one unchangeable event: Graduation Day.

The festivities that precede this climactic occasion start, so far as the midshipmen and their friends are concerned, on the Friday afternoon preceding Graduation Day; it is usually the last Friday of May. That first day starts out with a bang. It offers the visitor such a bewildering choice of entertainment that in order to cover them all he would be on the move from nine o'clock in the morning to midnight.

The festivities begin with a Dress Parade on Worden Field in the afternoon. An honored guest takes the review of the midshipmen resplendent in their nattiest uniforms: white caps, blue, gold-buttoned waist-length jackets and white trousers. On Saturday there are athletic contests with the ancient and honored rivals of the midshipmen, the cadets of the United States Military Academy at West Point. These events, though held each year on the same day, are split between the two locations, Annapolis and West Point; thus the visitor may find he has a choice among baseball, track and golf, the other games being played that day at the Point. Another year lacrosse and tennis might be on tap for the June Weekers. Sometimes (as in 1954) the results of the long afternoon of athletic activities look like this—

Lacrosse: Navy 9—Army 3
Baseball: Navy 8—Army 4
Track: Navy 81 7/12—Army 49 5/12
Tennis: Navy 8—Army 1
Golf: Navy 4—Army 3 (*A clean sweep!*)

—and then there is jubilee in the Yard, and the *Enterprise* bell clangs victoriously far into the night.

During the day, too, a number of special ceremonies may be scheduled. Does one of the alumni classes present a painting or a statue or a tablet or a bench to its alma mater, as a memorial? Does some benefactor donate a historic relic to the Naval Academy for safekeeping? If so, a formal ceremony may be staged.

The visitors can easily find entertainment in various parts of the Yard; among the interim forms of amusement provided are band concerts and motion pictures in the auditorium of Mahan Hall. At the end of the day comes a hop in the huge armory, Dahlgren Hall, attended by the midshipmen of the First, Third and Fourth classes, together with their guests. The plebes formerly rated only the grand and glorious Farewell Ball on the eve of Graduation Day. Until the Farewell Ball on Thursday they had to be content with what the Program of Events for June Week scheduled for them each night with grim regularity: "8:00 P.M. Motion Pictures, Fourth Class, Mahan Hall."

With the temporarily insignificant thus happily provided for and out of the way, the Second classmen in the meantime are holding the most intimate and certainly the most romantic and cherished of all the social events of the entire undergraduate course—the traditional Ring Dance, described on page 137. The dance itself is held generally in Memorial Hall, but the real romance of the Ring Dance, the unique feature that sets it apart from all other hops and gives it a symbolism and a significance all its own, finds expression not on the dance floor but in the traditional ritual, so charged with sentiment for each midshipman, not only of receiving his coveted class ring but of receiving it from the hands of his One-And-Only as they pass together through the replica of the ring, pausing in the center of it to memorialize the moment with the transfer. For hours the line of couples moves toward the dais on which the gold replica stands, each awaiting turn to perform this ancient rite, perhaps only to return later and reenact the scene. Certain it is that more couples pass through the ring than there are couples— which is one phenomenon that does not require an Einstein to fathom.

The next day used to be known as "Sob Sunday," not because the midshipmen actually shed tears over the pending departure of the First classmen but because, in the dim past, the simulation of uncontrollable grief on the part of the plebes rose in such a crescendo over a period of years that on one never-to-be-forgotten occasion it culminated in a travesty. Since that "faux pas" no trace of the former goings-on during divine service now remains except the name. The midshipmen liked the term "Sob Sunday" and it has stuck.

On Sunday morning the midshipmen worship in the Chapel according to the regular routine, but the services are, of course, charged with a special feeling because for all the First classmen this will be the last time they attend church together as midshipmen, and for some it will be the last time they attend service in the Chapel. The events of the afternoon and evening are essentially musical in character and blissfully restful for the guests: a popular music concert with a dance orchestra and singers high on the list of favorites at the moment; a program by the Midshipmen's Concert Band from the bandstand in the early evening; a subsequent concert by the Glee Club in Mahan Hall.

The Baccalaureate occurs on Monday morning in the Field House. This brief but impressive service begins with a prelude of anthems sung by the choir from the distant balcony in this huge structure, and then the band begins the Processional as the dignitaries of the occasion enter and the civilian faculty in their traditional robes parade to their seats in stately measure. In a solemn ritual the colors are marched briskly up the aisle to the platform where they are slowly dipped before the altar in token of presentation to the Eternal Father. After the invocation and the offering of The Prayer of a Midshipman, a distinguished officer or civilian official of high rank gives the Baccalaureate Address. The service concludes with the singing of "Navy Blue and Gold" and the Navy Hymn, and the Retreat of Colors. The "pledge to the Blue and Gold" and the prayer to the "Eternal Father, strong to save" have had a special significance on this occasion.

And then the wonderful frenzy of holiday activity begins again, with parades and award ceremonies and concerts and demonstrations almost every day, and dances in the evening. Third classmen celebrate on Monday evening the end of their second year at the Academy with the Youngster Hop, a special affair all their own in Macdonough Hall, while the First, Second and Fourth Classes get along without them at another hop in Dahlgren.

Tuesday morning finds the crowd of well-wishers wending their way toward the Field House for the presentation at eleven o'clock of the athletic, academic and military awards. Visitors settle themselves where they will in the spacious auditorium as the band makes the rafters ring with the ever-inspiring strains of "Anchors Aweigh," approved by the brigade in their summer uniforms. At the Dress Parade on the previous afternoon, the Superintendent has already presented his Letters of Commendation to a highly select list of those First classmen whose officer-like qualities and exemplary leadership have substantially benefited the Brigade and established models of military excellence.

Over the amplifiers the names of the activities and sports are called out with the names of the representatives who are to receive the awards for their groups. As each representative arrives at the platform before the brigade, he receives the awards or letters for his group, as well as a hearty handshake and some smiling words of congratulation from the Superintendent or the Commandant, which he acknowledges with a smart salute. In June Week all are honored—the class committees, the boards of the midshipman publications, the choirs, the Drum and Bugle Corps, the religious associations, the hobby clubs, and many more—and each sport is acclaimed—cross country, football, soccer, basketball, fencing, gymnastics, pistol, rifle, squash, swimming, wrestling, baseball, crew, golf, lacrosse, sailing, tennis, track. At the end individual awards go to the special heroes whose athletic prowess has been outstanding. Thus each receives his accolade, his reward of service and the plaudits of the crowd. When the last man has resumed his place in line, the brigade pays tribute to its representatives on the fields of sport by giving them the brigade's most honored yell, the "Touchdown 4-N," and all join in singing "Navy Blue and Gold."

On one evening there is the garden party given by the Superintendent and his wife to the members of the graduating class, their families and their young women guests. The spacious garden adjoining the Admiral's residence is transformed into what the society reporters delight to term a "veritable fairyland." Colored lights glow from a myriad of Chinese lanterns, fountains play and music fills the air as ladies with gleaming shoulders emerging from diaphanous gowns mingle with the gold, blue and white of the naval uniforms. Across the roadway in Dahlgren Hall arrangements have been made for dancing as part of the mammoth party.

Monday is one of the busiest days in June Week. Right after breakfast the visitors wander over to the parade ground, Worden Field, and settle themselves in the grandstands to watch the brigade rehearse the "Presentation of the Colors" ceremony that is formally held the following day. Except for the small army of cameramen, for whose benefit the proceedings are halted at intervals to provide ample opportunity to get good photographic records for the newspapers and motion-picture screens of the country, the affair is conducted precisely the same as on the following day. One of the main purposes of this rehearsal is to give the photographers a real field day of their own, and thus avoid marring the ceremony when it is held officially.

"Would you please go through that again?" ask the cameramen when the midshipman commander of the prize-winning color company reaches the point where he kisses the color girl. Doing it again is apparently one of the easiest jobs the midshipman commander is called upon to perform; batteries of cameras close in upon the young couple as they render this traditional—but non-regulation—salute as often as demanded. No midshipman commander has been known to refuse.

Simultaneously the prize winners practice in the Field House for the Presentation of Prizes ceremony to take place at the ceremony the following day. At nine o'clock also there is a band concert as there is almost every day. At various hours of the day on Monday and Tuesday there are demonstrations of maneuvers in YP boats, the sturdy, diesel-propelled, 80-foot craft in which the midshipmen have practiced ship handling and practical navigation throughout their four-year course. (YP stands for "yard patrol.") Guests who wish to view the maneuvers may embark at Santee Pier and incidentally get a taste of the salty life which their ensigns-to-be have adopted as their careers. The long happy day concludes with no less than four dances in the evening: the "N" Dance for athletes who have won their "N's" in varsity competition, in Hubbard Hall; the "E" Dance for extracurricular activity award winners, in Memorial and Smoke Halls; the Youngster Hop in Macdonough Hall; and a hop for everybody else in Dahlgren Hall.

The Tuesday morning ceremony in the Field House for the presentation of prizes and athletic awards clearly demonstrates that the alumni and friends of the Naval Academy are eager to foster achievement and commend accomplishment among the midshipmen. There are some fifty-five academic and twenty athletic prizes awarded at this time. They are, for the most part, the gift of patriotic societies, industrial firms, Naval Academy classes and individual benefactors, and range from items of professional military gear to extensive subscriptions to appropriate magazines. The prize table is characteristically heaped with a valuable assortment of certificates, swords, clocks, watches, cups, sextants, cameras, binoculars, pistols, trays, and other awards which are to be bestowed. Many of the donors are present in person, or their representatives are, and it is their pleasant duty to add the special, in some instances very personal, touch to the presentation. Many prizes have been given in donor of some individual or group very near and dear to the presenter. It is equally true that many of the recipients will be remembered throughout their lives as the winner of the prize which they now so happily accept.

The most colorful and altogether the most spectacular of the outdoor ceremonies during June Week is the Presentation of the Colors Parade held at 5:30 on Tuesday afternoon. For an hour or more before the scheduled ceremony the more knowing of the friends and relatives of the midshipmen have been gradually strolling to the grandstands on Worden Field, the parade ground. Holders of tickets are entitled to admission to the reserved chairs grouped about the pavilion of the Superintendent and his staff and can therefore enjoy the luxury of arriving on the scene at their leisure. Exactly on the minute the rhythmic throb of distant drums rises above the babble of voices, and the strident notes of brasses strike the ears. All eyes turn toward the south; a murmur of expectancy sweeps the stands. As the martial music approaches, the inevitable dog contributes his mite by rushing rapturously out to clear the field of birds; the crowd breaks into laughter.

"Here they come!" the cry rises. It might more accurately be "Here they are," for suddenly the brigade staff, followed by the band, bursts into view as they turn from Badger Road onto the parade ground; the brigade is practically unseen until it emerges from under the trees and swings onto the field in a column of companies. Four thousand white caps bob in unison; four thousand pairs of white trousers move in cadence across the panorama of green trees and the blue waters of the Severn; the afternoon sun glitters on the steel bayonets. Within a few minutes the brigade is formed in line of battalions and the music ceases. Commands are barked up and down the line; the brigade comes to parade rest.

"Sound off!" the adjutant commands.

The band bursts into a fanfare which is followed by "retreat." The brigade is brought to present arms, and to the strains of the national anthem the crowd rises to its feet; the brigade colors dip in salute. The brigade commander next puts the midshipmen through a few movements of the manual of arms; then he directs the adjutant to receive the reports of the two regiments.

At this point occurs the traditional Naval Academy variation of the standard military formula. The sword of the commander of the First Regiment flashes in salute as he proclaims:

"Nineteen men absent, sir!"

The commander of the Second Regiment reports:

"Fifty-seven men absent, sir!"

A roar of approbation goes up from the crowd. Thus are the numerals of the date of the next graduating class, in this case the class of 1957, woven into the fabric of the Naval Academy ceremonial. (The number of absentees is a matter of record, so that the standard report on the parade ground is a mere matter of form anyway.) This is the brigade's farewell hail to its members who will never march with it again; it is the traditional manner in which the graduating class say, in effect, "1957, take over!"

After this comes the high spot of the parade—the formal presentation of the colors to that company which, by virtue of its excellence in athletic and professional accomplishments, demonstrated during an entire year of competition, has won the honor of being designated as the "color company."

The old color guard is called out to take its position at the right of the brigade staff. Then the new color company is called out, to form three sides of a square in front of the brigade; with it come the five midshipmen selected from the prize-winning company, who will constitute the new color guard. The old and the new color guards stand face to face. The stage is set for the entrance of the leading lady.

The "Color Girl," on the right arm of the Superintendent, steps forward onto the field carrying a huge bouquet and followed by a plebe orderly chosen from the winning company. She is selected each year by the midshipman commander of the new color company; not the least of his prerogatives is that of bringing to his lady the honor of appearing in person—as well upon the motion-picture screens and in the newspapers of the country—to convey the national flag, the brigade flag, and the Navy flag into the keeping of the company whose efficiency has brought this proud privilege upon it. When this act has been completed, the midshipman company commander steps forward, removes his cap and kisses her right out in public before the entire brigade. Nor does he appear reluctant in so doing—quite the contrary.

"Is that kiss specified in the order for the parade?" queries the stickler for the technical formalities.

"No, ma'am," replies the bluejacket with an SP (shore patrol) brassard on his arm. "But every midshipman knows the custom and does his duty. He's a sailor, isn't he?"

As soon as the colors have actually changed hands, the blue guidon flag with the company numeral in gold is rolled up, and the coveted gold guidon with the numeral in blue is unfurled to take its place. The first act of the new color company is to salute the Color Girl with three cheers; the midshipmen raise their white caps into the air with each outburst. Then the brigade commander calls upon the twenty-three unsuccessful company contestants to give three cheers for their successful rival; three roars resound as the caps are raised in salute.

The color company resumes its place in the line. The Superintendent, with the Color Girl on his arm, takes a position in front of the pavilion.

"Pass in review!" the order rings across the field.

As the band breaks into the music of "Anchors Aweigh," the head of the column swings into line and parades down the field in columns of companies. Past the grandstands. Past the reviewing officers. Back under the screen of trees whence the brigade emerged a bare half-hour before.

The parade is over.

The review is the last of the academic year, the last military ceremony in which those who graduate on the morrow will wear the dress uniform. Within a few hours all but a small detail of the brigade will be scattering to the far ends of the earth, some never to return. It is a ceremony that burns itself deep into the memory and into the heart of every man who takes part in it.

In the evening comes the most imposing single social function of the year, the Farewell Ball. This is a huge affair, with guests so numerous that it is held in two buildings, Dahlgren Hall and Macdonough Hall most usually. All classes attend, including the long-suffering plebes! The armory is hung with blue and gold bunting; even the huge balcony is decorated, for that too is used as a promenade by couples who cannot find room to dance on the floor; as an overflow, the south doors of the armory are thrown open and the adjoining Thompson Field, flooded with lights, becomes dotted with couples who cast long, arabesque shadows as they stroll about the athletic field and find more or less secluded vantage points where they can. As this Farewell Ball is given to the graduating class, it is attended not only by the officers of the Naval Academy but also by all four classes; consequently it marks the début of the plebes into the social life of the community. The hostess of the occasion is always the ranking lady of the station, the wife of the Superintendent.

Wednesday furnishes the big climax—Graduation Day at last! The momentous event is actually at hand. If the visitor consults his program he will find that the only ceremony scheduled for the day is the graduation exercises in the Field House at 11:00 o'clock. But for many years there has been a bit more to it than that.

For many years custom decreed that during the hours between the close of the Farewell Ball and the breakfast formation on Graduation Day the Youngsters "rated brooms." In layman's language, that meant that the Youngsters were permitted to use brooms upon the plebes as a stimulant to duty, and perhaps, too, as a robust reminder of their own humble estate before they passed into the security of Youngsterhood. For many years it was the custom to require such plebes as could be located to spend their last plebe night huddled on top of their lockers "in order to train them to sleep in hammocks" (so the implausible explanations ran), preparatory to the experience that confronted them on the practice cruise just ahead.

The breakfast formation on the terrace—the last formation of the academic year—is a distinctly informal affair. The underclasses appear in normal uniform, but the First classmen appear in anything and everything. On one occasion, an imaginative First classman, clad in pajamas, had himself carried to formation in his bed. After the brigade has reported, everybody just straggles into the mess hall, often accompanied by a jam session by the Drum and Bugle Corps.

Long before the scheduled hour the spectators assemble in the Field House for the graduation exercises. Each guest is furnished with a ticket that entitles the holder to a seat in one of the designated sections. Have Mr. and Mrs. Gish come to see their son Joe get his degree of Bachelor of Science? They rate seats in the choice section reserved for and plainly marked for "Parents of the Graduating Class." Joe's sisters and his cousins and his aunts are accommodated in the seats labeled "Relatives of the Graduating Class." In like manner sections are set aside for Captains and Commanders and their guests, and for the guests of the Superintendent, and for other groups. The solid block of seats in the center of the hall and directly facing the platform is, of course, for the graduating class.

The tension is kept under control and the appropriate atmosphere is created by the Naval Academy Band, which plays for about half an hour before the exercises begin. The guests are required to be in their seats well in advance so that there will be no distractions when the great hour commences. The photographers on the staging come to life and start to check over their cameras; the sound technicians and the cameramen down on the floor under the speaker's stand adjust the microphones and test their equipment Through a door behind the platform the Superintendent makes his entrance, accompanied by the Commandant, the speaker of the day, and the admirals, generals and public officials, all of whom are escorted by gold-braided naval aides to seats on the platform, all arranged beforehand in order of official precedence.

Through the doorway opposite have entered the white-clad members of the graduating class; a roar of welcome greets them. Quickly and with military precision (it has all been rehearsed beforehand) each man goes directly and in formation to his designated seat. The "star men" of the class, the men who rank at the top in their academic course, sit in the first rows, in order of their standing; these are the men who will receive their diplomas first; each midshipman graduating with distinction will get his individually. All the other men of the class are seated by companies so as to make the distribution of diplomas as simple and expeditious as possible.

At this point, the members of the civilian faculty, resplendent in their academic costumes, with hoods and facings of many colors (all symbolic of the degree the wearer holds, and the university that awarded it), file past the platform to their seats.

A prayer by the Chaplain, a brief introduction by the Superintendent, the address by the speaker of the day, are followed by a presentation of the diplomas. In former years when the graduating classes were smaller the diplomas were presented one by one as the recipients walked up on the platform. As each man's name was announced he was greeted with applause as the esteem in which he was held by his fellow midshipmen dictated. Noted athletes, brilliant students, popular midshipmen officers, and men who had fought their way doggedly through the course in the face of illness, setbacks, tragedy and other handicaps that would have daunted the less stout of heart, came in for the loudest acclaim. As the graduating classes became larger, this made for a long-drawn-out and slightly tedious ceremony. The midshipmen are now graduated by companies, the diplomas for each company being presented to the man with the highest academic standing in the company, each company standing while the representative goes forward to secure the diplomas of his company. And they do say, too, that if the visitor watches closely he may observe that the plebes are "sitting on infinity" until their company gets their diplomas.

A comic break in the solemn tension of the graduation ceremony occurs when the company to which the anchor man belongs is called out. This necessarily good-natured midshipman, who has been singled out because he stands last in his class academically, is hoisted aloft on the shoulders of his classmates, brandishing a blue and gold anchor, symbolic of his honor, to the deafening cheers of the brigade. There is no sting to this designation, however; many an anchor man has gone on to become a very useful officer to the Navy.

When the last diploma has been given out, Navy Blue and Gold is sung. Joe Gish has now won the right to add B.S. to his name, but he is not yet an officer; that distinction comes only when he has received his commission and been sworn in. The oath of office is administered separately to those to be commissioned in the Marine Corps, the Navy, the Air Force, or even the Army, by a high-ranking officer from each service.

The fledgling officer does not need to pause to read the document that is the outward symbol of his new rank; he already knows its old-fashioned phraseology and its sonorous but ever-stirring words that constitute his accolade:

> Know ye, that reposing special Trust and Confidence in the Patriotism, Valour, Fidelity and Abilities of *Joseph Gish*, I have nominated him and by and with the advice and consent of the Senate do appoint him an *Ensign in the Navy*. . . .
>
> > *By the President.*

After the commissions are given out, the band plays "The Star-Spangled Banner." There is then a call for "three cheers for those who are about to leave us." The compliment is immediately returned when the honored President of the class, exercising his time-honored prerogative, calls:

"Three cheers for those we leave behind!"

The class then gives three cheers; with the final "hooray" they let forth a cry of triumph and hurl their caps wildly into the air, creating the impression of a white cloud of Gargantuan snowflakes. No, they never get them back. While the caps appear to the layman to be perfectly good, they are in reality worn out, despite their immaculate cleanliness; they are "throwing away hats," so to speak. Even if they were valuable, the graduates would still throw them away, if for no other purpose than to carry on the old custom.

As soon as the captains and the kings have departed, a mad rush is made for the doors by the plebes—pardon—by the Third classmen. The plebes officially ceased to exist the moment the First classmen graduated, and every lower class automatically moved up a peg. This happy circumstance serves as the theme for the traditional song, "T'ain't No More Plebes," in celebration of this epoch-making transformation. The Third classmen prepare for the joyous ordeal of celebrating their promotion by boosting one of their classmates to the top of the grease-smeared Herndon monolith; at the same time, for some reason not so patent, they don their caps backward too and proceed to invade the precincts heretofore denied them by executing a wild rush through Lovers' Lane and the Youngster Cut-Off, and about the Herndon monument. For the most of them this is the first time they have "felt the touch of grass or gravel under their feet" in the Yard. But they aren't really out of plebe year until they hoist one of their number to the top of the monument to place his cap there—tradition has it that the one so elevated has a good chance to make admiral some day.

The last act of all is as unofficial as it is personal. Ensign Gish rejoins his mother, if the fates have been kind enough to preserve her for him, and his One-And-Only, if they have been gracious enough to grant him one. Within the shadow of Bancroft Hall, where his years of test and trial have at last been crowned with victory, and within a few paces of the Japanese Bell, where tradition decrees this last ceremonial of all shall be enacted, the two women nearest to his heart adjust upon his two sturdy shoulders the insignia of his rank as an officer and a gentleman. So did the knights of old receive their gages from the hands of their beloved in the golden days of chivalry.

Chapter 19

A Proteus[1] Chapter

Plus ça change, plus c'est la même chose.[2]
—J. B. A. KARR

Any institution worth its salt is constantly changing. Ways of doing things are revised, abandoned and, not infrequently, restored again. Physical objects are moved around, done away with or replaced, and new ones are added. A book like *Annapolis Today* needs a Proteus chapter to accommodate this phenomenon —a chapter to indicate certain details of Academy life that are new or revised, though the core of its existence remains essentially the same. Here, then, are some items of that sort.

The scope of the exchange weekends has now been broadened to include the Air Force and Coast Guard Academies, as well as West Point. Midshipmen and cadets of the Second class exchange long weekends from Thursday to Saturday at West Point and Annapolis as they have since 1946; but, in addition, midshipmen of the Third class exchange with their counterparts at New London, Connecticut and Colorado Springs.

Two yawls have been added to the Naval Academy Sailing Squadron. Both are fifty footers, slightly larger than the Academy's basic fleet of Luders yawls. The *Windfall*, renamed the *Annie D.*, was the gift of Mr. Francis T. Nichols; and the *Blue Water*, renamed the *Gypsy*, was donated by Mr. Alexander White.

The Office of the Hostess was established in a friendly and homey room in Bancroft Hall in 1959. Here presides, with her

[1] A Greek god of the sea, who, while retaining his identity, could change his shape at will.
[2] "The more anything changes, the more it stays the same."

three assistants, the Social Director "to aid and nurture the social growth of the members of the Brigade," but her activities far exceed the strict letter of this precise assignment and extend over a thousand and one responsibilities from aiding the Hop Committee to answering the plaintive inquiries of bewildered drags. The charm, energy and transcendent wisdom of the original incumbent, Mrs. J. G. Marshall, have added immeasurably to the grace and poise of Academy life and solved many a sticky problem.

Of late the Ring Dance Committee has shown considerable ingenuity and inventiveness in staging this most famous of all Academy hops. In 1960 they hired an excursion boat, supplied its decks with a variety of orchestras and combos, and for the first time ran a real sea-going dance with all the added delights of a moonlight cruise on Chesapeake Bay. The waters from the seven seas, into which the girls dip the class rings before presenting them to their midshipmen, were gathered from twenty-two places in the world's oceans by the nuclear submarine *Triton* on its submerged cruise round the world. The 1962 Ring Dance was held on ballroom flooring installed on either side of the Reflecting Pool in front of the new wings of Bancroft Hall.

Luce Hall, the headquarters of the Command Department, contains, appropriately enough, an ever-increasing number of significant historical reminders. Of special interest are the steering wheels of the Spanish cruiser *Reina Mercedes* and of Farragut's flagship at Mobile Bay, the *Hartford*, both former Academy station ships. It was on the deck of the latter ship that Farragut issued his famous order: "Damn the torpedoes; four bells, Captain Drayton. Go ahead, Jouett—Full speed." Luce Hall also has the plaque which marked on the deck of the *Missouri* the location where the Japanese surrendered on board that ship in Tokyo Bay, 2 September 1945.

The annual Naval Academy Foreign Affairs Conference, known as "NAFAC," was organized by the Foreign Relations Club and the English, History and Government Department in 1961. Undergraduate representatives from colleges all over the country attend the four-day meeting, which features addresses by distinguished statesmen, executives, and military and naval officers, as well as round-table discussion groups, presided over

*B*rigade staff
watching colors pass in review.

*F*irst classman giving
his plebe a preinspection check.

by authorities in world affairs and embassy staff members from the areas under consideration. Each conference has a topical theme, such as "Problems of U. S. Foreign Policy in Latin America" or "Southeast Asia."

Midshipmen and cadets competed against each other in the "General Electric College Bowl" television quiz program in 1959, 1960 and 1961 on the day after the Army-Navy football game, thereby compounding the battle of brawn with the battle of wits. The Naval Academy won twice and West Point once.

The Naval Academy Museum was doubled in size by a skillful expansion-addition completed in 1962. Actually, it would take something like a ten-acre lot to display completely and do full justice to all of the historical treasures in the Museum's care.

David K. Bishop, of the Class of 1959, graduated with a perfect conduct record. He did not receive a single demerit during his entire four years at the Academy, nor did he ever walk off a single foot of extra duty. Other members of his class had averaged something like 180 demerits each, which is about par for the course. Even more fantastic, perhaps, is the fact that no fewer than eight previous midshipmen have also had a 4.0 conduct score, the last in 1953.

Each year about one hundred midshipmen depart on Christmas Leave a day or two early, bound on an important mission known as Operation Information. Armed with films about the Academy and other display materials, they undertake the pleasant task of telling the country about their school and its aims and aspirations. They address home-town organizations, attend banquets, and appear on radio and television programs. The venture has done much to win friends and candidates for the Academy and the Naval Service.

Midshipmen used to change to blue cap covers on the day of the Army football game, and back again to white for Easter. Since 1956 they have worn white covers all year round. The new covers are of durable plastic material, water repellent and dirt resistant.

Since 1957 midshipmen have been allowed to use certain facilities of the Commissioned Officers' Mess (exclusive of the bar) on occasion during the academic year, as further training in the social graces and to introduce them to the benefits of membership.

The large bronze figure of the rampant Navy Goat in front of Macdonough Hall was dedicated, in 1957, by the Class of 1915 as a symbol of the fighting spirit of the Brigade and the Navy.

Plebes toss First classmen into the reflecting pool between the new wings of Bancroft Hall at the slightest excuse—when First classmen become engaged, celebrate their birthday, etc.

A new midshipman entering the Naval Service has to learn his *A B C*'s all over again. The trouble is that in voice communication, especially when other noises interfere, too many of our letters sound alike and are easily confused or misunderstood: *B, C, D, E, G, P, T, V,* and *Z,* for example—or the classic sound-alikes, *M* and *N.* Therefore, all the allied navies have agreed to a standard set of distinguishing names for the letters, whose designations often sound strange and playful to the civilian ear:

A Alpha	H Hotel	O Oscar	U Uniform
B Bravo	I India	P Papa	V Victor
C Charlie	J Juliett	Q Quebec	W Whiskey
D Delta	K Kilo	R Romeo	X Xray
E Echo	L Lima	S Sierra	Y Yankee
F Foxtrot	M Mike	T Tango	Z Zulu
G Golf	N November		

Visitors to the Academy will be able to identify the rank of commissioned officers, midshipmen, and enlisted men by using the charts found on the facing page.

The oldest weapon in the Naval Academy is the thousand-year-old Viking sword, found in a grave north of Oslo, Norway, and presented to the United States by the commanding officer and the midshipmen of the Norwegian schoolship *Christian Radich.* It was given to the Academy in 1957 by President Eisenhower for display in Memorial Hall.

For administrative purposes, and to insure efficient, centralized military control in time of war, the Naval Academy is associated with the other Naval shore activities around the mouth of the Severn River in a special Naval District known

MIDSHIPMAN SLEEVE RANK AND INSIGNIA

CAPT   CDR   LCDR   LT   LTJG

ENS   1st Class   2nd Class   3rd Class   4th Class

Brigade Regimental Batt. Company Mustering 1st Class 2nd Class
C. P. O.   C. P. O.   C. P. O.   C. P. O.   C. P. O.   P. O.   P. O.

Color
Company

E

Drum
and
Bugle Corps

				ENLISTED				
E-1	E-2	E-3	E-4	E-5	E-6	E-7	E-8	E-9
SEAMAN RECRUIT	SEAMAN APPRENTICE	SEAMAN	PETTY OFFICER THIRD CLASS	PETTY OFFICER SECOND CLASS	PETTY OFFICER FIRST CLASS	CHIEF PETTY OFFICER	SENIOR CHIEF PETTY OFFICER	MASTER CHIEF PETTY OFFICER

				COMMISSIONED					
O-1	O-2	O-3	O-4	O-5	O-6	O-7 O-8	O-9	O-10	
GOLD	SILVER		GOLD	SILVER					
ENSIGN	LIEUTENANT JUNIOR GRADE	LIEUTENANT	LIEUTENANT COMMANDER	COMMANDER	CAPTAIN	REAR ADMIRAL	VICE ADMIRAL	ADMIRAL	FLEET ADMIRAL

251

as the Severn River Naval Command. The Superintendent of the Naval Academy is also the Commandant of SRNC. Among the other components of the Command are the Engineering Experiment Station, the Naval Hospital, the Naval Radio Station, and the Naval Station, which includes the Naval and the Marine Barracks.

The Naval Air Facility, formerly located across the river in the "North Severn" area, was disestablished in 1962. The days of the "Yellow Peril" training planes and later amphibious types are no more. The midshipmen's practical indoctrination in Naval aviation is accomplished chiefly during Second Class Summer at Jacksonville and Pensacola, Florida.

The age of sail is by no means a mere historical sentiment at the Naval Academy. In addition to their fleet of ocean-sailing yachts and the training knockabouts, the midshipmen have their flotilla of fourteen-foot dinghies, in which they are active participants in a full schedule of intercollegiate sailing races. The boats are International 14 Mark VII Fiberglas hulls, with Tempest dinghy rigs.

Two evening meals in the mess hall are very special occasions each year: Thanksgiving Dinner and the last evening meal before Christmas Leave. Appropriate holiday fare is served, and the smoking lamp is lit (although it never is on any other occasions). Male guests may be invited to enjoy the festivities with the midshipmen.

The inhabitants of every plebe room must conceive and execute a poster for every game on the football schedule and exhibit it on their door. Ingenuity and wit are desired commodities, and the best posters are accorded a special showing in the Rotunda of Bancroft Hall. Before the Army game the plebes of each company are in charge of decorating their respective company areas, and the creators of the best decoration are treated to some special chow by the Commissary Department.

Midshipmen on summer practice cruise unexpectedly took part in an actual Naval operation on 15–16 July 1958 during the Lebanon crisis when a task force from the Sixth Fleet landed Marines on the Lebanon beaches. No shots were fired, but the Marines took control of the Beirut airport and remained until 29 September, by which time the situation had greatly improved. The commander of the U. S. Forces in Lebanon, Admiral James L. Holloway, Jr., had been Superintendent of the Naval Academy from 1947 to 1950.

One of the most interesting and substantial activities through which the Naval Academy educates its midshipmen for the modern world of science and technology is the Advanced Science and Mathematics Seminar. Midshipmen eligible for the electives program attend a series of lectures, usually five each term, given by distinguished authorities inside the Academy and out. The program is designed to lead to a science research project in which a midshipman undertakes an original investigation and prepares a useful paper, as any professional scientist would do. He receives full course credit for the successful completion of his work.

The long-established midshipmen's dance orchestra, the NA-10, has in recent years had a very popular rival in a rock-and-roll outfit which rejoices in the rather dubious name of "The Spiffies." These worthies evoke rhythm and pep from an assortment of instruments which usually include piano, drums, trumpet, trombone, saxes, and the indispensable guitar.

Visitors to Memorial Hall should lift their sights high enough to view the splendid and inspiring new murals in the lunettes above the seaward and inboard bulkheads. The three which depict the ships *Constellation*, *Monongahela*, and *Delaware* were painted by Charles R. Patterson, and are the gift of Mrs. Louis McCoy Nulton in memory of her husband, Admiral Nulton, of the Class of 1889, who served in the *Monongahela*, the Academy training ship when he was a midshipman. The *Constellation*, still very much in existence, is on exhibition in her home port of Baltimore, Maryland, where she was built. The other three murals represent the Battle of Lake Erie, the *Hartford* and the yacht *America*, and the First Foreign Salute to the Stars and Stripes, 14 February 1778. These were presented by Admiral and Mrs. Thomas C. Hart in memory of their son, Lieutenant Commander Thomas Comins Hart, and are the work of Howard B. French.

Chapter 20

A Brief History
of the Naval Academy

From the establishment of a permanent United States Navy in 1794 to the opening of the Naval School at Annapolis on 10 October 1845, no carefully planned, fully organized, efficient national system of education was in existence in the United States for the training of prospective officers of the fleet ashore. Nevertheless, despite a continuing prejudice against training seafaring men anywhere but at sea, responsible and foresighted men from the days of John Paul Jones had perceived the need for the systematic and intensive education of the young naval officer. The comment of Secretary of the Navy A. P. Upshur, in his report on the condition of the Navy in 1842, is typical:

> Little or no attention has hitherto been paid to the proper education of naval officers. Through a long course of years, the young midshipmen were left to educate themselves and one another; . . . their schools are kept in receiving ships and cruising vessels, in the midst of a thousand interruptions and impediments, which render the whole system of little or no value.

The education of the midshipmen had indeed been a hit-or-miss affair. Naval regulations issued by the President in 1802 directed that the chaplain aboard ship should "perform the duty of a schoolmaster" and "instruct the midshipmen and volunteers in writing, arithmetic, and navigation, and in whatsoever may contribute to render them proficients." In 1813, Congress authorized one schoolmaster for each twenty midshipmen aboard the seventy-four gun ships (of which there were only three) but no teachers for smaller vessels. Since these school-masters received but $25.00 a month, paid only when they were actually at sea, the quality of instructor could not have been high. This condition was improved when in 1835 Congress provided a salary of $1200 a year for professors of mathematics, but teaching conditions, as Matthew Fontaine Maury pointed out, were still intolerable:

> The teacher has no authority whatever over the pupil, nor can he claim the attendance or attention of the latter in the school-room, or to any particular study. The whole plan is without order . . . the duties of the school-room, when one is to be found aboard of a man of war, are subordinate to every other duty in the ship. There the Midshipman is practically taught to consider his attendance at school as the matter of least importance in his routine of duties. He is interrupted at his lessons to go on shore for the Captain's pig; or he is called from recitation, to count the duck-frocks and trousers contained in the wardrobe of Tom Brown, the sailor. I have known a Captain, who forbade the Midshipmen to work out longitude, on the ground that it was a secret of the Captain and the Master; . . .

In the 1820's three informal schools for the casual instruction of midshipmen on waiting orders between cruises had been cobbled up at Norfolk, New York and Boston, but attendance was in fact voluntary and discipline was nonexistent.

In addition to this general state of inadequacy and ineptitude, several other factors were conducive to the actual founding of the Naval School in 1845. The notorious *Somers* affair in 1842, which resulted in Midshipman Philip Spencer's being convicted of mutiny and hanged from the yardarm at sea, seemed to confirm public opinion that something had to be done to elevate the standards of the Navy, and particularly of its young officer candidates. The introduction of steam propulsion and the screw propeller brought the Navy into the age of technological complexity and made engineering knowledge a necessity, especially when the first appropriations for steam warships were made in 1839. A fourth naval school established at the Naval Asylum in Philadelphia in 1839 had had the good fortune to prosper under the talented leadership and dedicated enthusiasm of Professor William Chauvenet, and had thus demonstrated the feasibility of a naval school ashore. Perhaps most important of all, George Bancroft, experienced educator and distinguished scholar, and a resourceful and energetic man as well, became Secretary of the Navy on 11 March 1845.

Bancroft set to work immediately to make the long desired naval school a reality. On 1 May he requested four professors of the successful Philadelphia Asylum school to make a report of the instruction and procedures there as a basis for the planning of the new school. In August he accomplished the transfer from the Army to the Navy of Fort Severn, an old Army fortification located on a point of land at the confluence of Spa Creek and the Severn River, in the harbor of Annapolis, Maryland. In this critical transaction, which gave him a site and nine buildings for the school, he was no doubt aided by the influence of a promising young instructor at the Philadelphia school, Passed Midshipman Samuel Marcy, whose father, William L. Marcy, was Secretary of War. On 7 August, Bancroft appointed Commander Franklin Buchanan Superintendent of the school and directed him to draw up a plan for its operation.

The original faculty had as its nucleus four of the best men from the Philadelphia school: Lieutenant James Harmon Ward, U. S. Navy, who became Executive Officer and Instructor in Gunnery and Steam; Professor William Chauvenet, Instructor in Mathematics and Navigation; Professor Henry Hayes Lockwood, Instructor in Natural Philosophy; and Passed Midshipman Samuel Marcy, U. S. Navy, Assistant Instructor in Mathematics. To these were added Professor Arsene Girault, Instructor in French; Chaplain George Jones, U. S. Navy, Instructor in English; and Surgeon John Alexander Lockwood, U. S. Navy (elder brother of H. H. Lockwood), Instructor in Chemistry.

Commander Buchanan, as Superintendent, took charge at Fort Severn on 15 August 1845, faced with the immediate problems of converting an old Army post into a naval college and sorting out a highly miscellaneous group of prospective students (their ages ranged from thirteen to twenty-eight) into practicable groupings for instruction. The former bakehouse, the hospital, the married enlisted men's barracks, and two other small buildings were utilized as quarters for midshipmen. The two-story barracks for unmarried enlisted men became the midshipmen's mess hall, kitchen and recitation building. The Superintendent took over the former Post Commandant's quarters. The first four faculty members were accommodated in former officers' quarters. The Academy was formally opened on 10 October 1945.

The problem of academic organization was a complicated one. The "student body" was made up of midshipmen who had entered the Navy in 1840, 1841, and 1842 (there were no midshipmen appointments in 1843 and 1844) and a new class of "acting midshipmen" of date of 1845. It was decided to establish two classes, Senior and Junior. All midshipmen of the 1840 date were in the Senior Class; all acting midshipmen were in the Junior Class; the intermediate groups were assigned either to the Senior or Junior Classes, depending upon their previous education, some indeed being assigned to recitations with both classes.

As far as status in the Navy was concerned, there were actually three classifications. Midshipmen of 1840 date, with five years of sea duty, had as their chief interest preparation for the examinations for promotion to passed midshipman, for which rank they would be eligible after a year at the school. Midshipmen of the 1841 and 1842 dates were those who were sent to the school because they were not needed at sea, though they were subject to detachment for sea duty at any time, an unsatisfactory arrangement which was soon eliminated. The eleven acting midshipmen of the 1845 class were the first real "midshipmen" in the modern sense, in that their training for officer qualification was to begin at the Naval School. On 30 January 1846 there were in all eighty midshipmen at the school.

Basic funds for the establishment of the Naval School in the amount of $10,000 came from an annual Congressional allotment of $28,200, used primarily for the pay of the professors of mathematics and the language teachers. By placing half of these instructors on waiting orders without pay, Bancroft made available for the new school the money thus "saved." Equipment and apparatus for instruction were garnered wherever they could be found: chronometers, sextants and other materials from the Naval Asylum School in Philadelphia; a telescope and six sextants from the Naval Observatory in Washington; a bell, four gun carriages, and a frame built like a ship's deck for mounting a practice battery from the Washington Navy Yard; thirty muskets and four 24-pounders from the Bureau of Ordnance—Secretary Bancroft had requested the Army to "leave the powder behind" when it vacated Fort Severn. The basic plan of organization for the school derived from the system in operation at West Point as described to Superintendent Buchanan by Passed Midshipman Marcy and Professor H. H. Lockwood, who was a West Point alumnus and who, with Marcy, went to West Point in July 1845 to study the organization in detail.

A candidate for admission to the new Naval School had to be between the ages of thirteen and sixteen inclusive, of good moral character, and free from any physical defects that "would disqualify him performing the active and arduous duties of a sea life." He also had to pass examinations in "Reading, Orthography, and the elements of Geography, English Grammar, and Arithmetic." The original plan was that the students should remain at the school for one year and then be sent to sea for three. After six months at sea they could, with the approval of their commanding officers, be warranted midshipmen. At the end of their three years at sea they were to be ordered back to the school to prepare for their promotion examinations.

The original curriculum provided that the Junior Class should study "arithmetic, elements of algebra and geometry, navigation as far as the sailings and the use of the quadrant, geography, English grammar and composition, and the French or Spanish language." The Senior Class studies were "algebra, geometry, plane and spherical trigonometry, nautical astronomy, navigation, descriptive astronomy, mechanics, optics, magnetism, electricity, ordnance, gunnery, the use of steam, history, composition, the French and Spanish language," as well as lectures on natural philosophy, chemistry, ordnance, gunnery, and steam. Practical drills in infantry and ordnance and in the use of astronomical instruments soon became part of the training.

The Naval School had been in existence only about six months when war with Mexico was declared on 13 May 1846. The ensuing confusion in matters of attendance, admission and detachment for active war duty at sea might well have proved fatal to the fledgling school had not an orderly system of advancing the date of commissioning been established, so that ninety officers were furnished to the Navy before the end of the war. As things turned out, the school's successful adjustment to the war needs may well have been the proof of its value to the Navy needed to justify its existence and silence skeptical opposition.

With the war crisis over and the validity of the school demonstrated, a process of reorganization, designed chiefly to avoid interruption of and fragmentation in the education of the midshipmen, was undertaken in 1850. The school was placed under the Chief of the Bureau of Ordnance and Hydrography and renamed the Naval Academy. The post of Commandant of Midshipmen was created with the incumbent serving as executive officer and instructor in tactics and seamanship. A uniform was designed for acting midshipmen. The course was extended to two two-year periods, with a three-year cruise intervening between them; but before this arrangement was ever put into practice, the assignment of the USS *Preble* to the Academy as a practice ship for annual summer cruises made possible the establishment of an uninterrupted four-year course, approved by Secretary of the Navy Graham on 15 November 1851.

The midshipmen's practice cruise in the *Preble* in 1851 inaugurated a major feature of Academy training which has never been relinquished except in wartime emergency. After the Civil War it became common practice to include steam vessels among the practice ships, although sailing practice cruises lasted until 1909. Usually the first and third classmen cruised together on a sailing ship with the second classmen on a steamer. In the period 1871–1882 the cadet engineers made special cruises of their own on steam vessels. Two vessels, the *Bancroft*, used from 1894 to 1896, and the *Chesapeake* (renamed the *Severn* in 1905), used from 1900 to 1907, were specially built and equipped as midshipmen training ships, but because of their relatively small size, crowded quarters and atypical arrangements, they proved unsuccessful. In 1904 the coast squadron of the North Atlantic Fleet, comprising two battleships, four monitors and seven destroyers, embarked part of the midshipmen, thereby setting the pattern for the standard midshipman cruise in ships of the fleet which actually began in 1912. In 1958 midshipmen were distributed for summer training among ships of the active fleets rather than in "cruise ships," whereby some of them, aboard ships of the Sixth Fleet in the Mediterranean, participated in the landing of U. S. Marines in Lebanon in July. Since 1925, when summer aviation training for second classmen began, midshipmen of this class have specialized in air and carrier cruises and in flight indoctrination, in recent years at Pensacola. Since 1946, the second class has also received two weeks of training in amphibious operations which conclude with a ship-to-shore assault in landing craft and helicopters.

In general, the Naval Academy prospered in the thirteen years from the close of the Mexican War to the outbreak of the Civil War. Experience showed the way to improvement of the courses, athletic and social activities were organized, the Academy grew in respect and repute, and some fifteen to twenty officers were normally furnished to the fleet each year.

The Civil War occasioned the only major disruption in the history of the steady growth and development of the Naval Academy—the physical transfer of the whole establishment to Newport, Rhode Island, for the duration of the war. There were several compelling reasons for this unique transfer, which followed close upon the bombardment of Fort Sumter, 11–13 April 1861. Annapolis was predominantly Southern in sympathy, and there were strong and dangerous secessionist activities in Maryland. The Academy would be in obvious jeopardy if Maryland seceded. With rail lines into Washington in danger of being cut at any moment, Annapolis took on great strategic significance as a distribution center for troops and supplies coming down the Chesapeake from the North, and the space occupied by the Academy was badly needed. A valuable vessel, the historic frigate *Constitution*, was stationed at the Academy, and there were fears that Southern forces might try to capture her and that the debacle of the evacuation of the Norfolk Navy Yard, on 20 April, might be repeated. The arms and ammunition and other supplies at the Academy might also be a temptation.

The Superintendent, Captain George S. Blake, recommended

to the Navy Department that the Academy be removed to Fort Adams at Newport and was officially ordered to make the move on 27 April 1861. All books and other portable equipment were loaded aboard the steamer *Baltic*, on which Academy officials and their families also embarked on 5 May. The *Baltic* arrived in Newport on the evening of 9 May, just two hours after the *Constitution* with the midshipmen on board. By 13 May the Academy in exile was in full operation again.

Before the move from Annapolis, ten midshipmen of the First Class had been ordered to active duty. Soon after the arrival in Newport, the rest of the First Class and all of the Second and Third Classes were ordered to active service. To compensate for these depletions, each Congressman was allowed an increase to two appointments, which provided a new class of about two hundred midshipmen and kept the enrollment at Newport around the four hundred mark for the duration of the war. To accommodate this expansion, the Atlantic House in Newport was leased by the government to augment the space provided by Fort Adams and the *Constitution*.

An act of Congress, on 21 May 1864, provided that the Naval Academy should be returned to Annapolis. The midshipmen left Newport on their summer cruise on 22 June 1865 in the *Macedonian*, *Marion*, *Marblehead* and *Winnipec*, these ships returned them to Annapolis on 11 September 1865. The Academy had provided nearly two hundred officers to the Federal Navy during the war years.

In July 1862, the Naval Academy was placed under the supervision of the Bureau of Navigation, and in March 1867, came under the direct charge of the Navy Department. The student officers at the Academy, designated "acting midshipmen on probation" from the founding of the Academy, became known as "midshipmen" in 1862, with the title subsequently changed to "cadet midshipmen" in 1870, and "naval cadets" in 1882, and back to "midshipmen" in 1902.

A major task of the post-war Superintendent, Admiral David Dixon Porter, was the rehabilitation and expansion of the buildings and grounds at Annapolis, which, having been utilized for about sixteen months as an Army post and thereafter as an Army hospital, were in wretched shape. Admiral Porter obtained appropriations to repair and renovate the old establishment, to buy additional land, and to construct new buildings including a chapel, an armory, a hospital, a steam-engineering building, marine barracks, and new quarters for midshipmen and officers.

In the twenty years of naval decline following the Civil War the Academy administration had to wrestle with various problems, chief among them an oversupply of line officers for a greatly reduced number of billets, and the need for attracting to the naval service candidates for engineering-officer training as the Navy transformed from sail to steam. Meanwhile the work of making the Academy more efficient and attractive went on: organized athletics were introduced, mature social activities were developed, military organization and smartness were stressed, and practical drills were put on a firmer basis.

The problem of inadequate billets and stagnation in promotion was never satisfactorily solved and created the frustrating situation that the Academy's supply of trained officer material was being wasted. In 1873, Congress attempted to relieve the congestion by adding two years of sea duty to the four-year course, thus creating a six-year course and delaying the appointment of any new ensigns for two years. In 1882, Congress also limited the number of graduates who could be taken into the Navy. But these were desperate measures which, when the inevitable period of naval expansion began, resulted only in serious shortages of officers.

To acquire a corps of officers trained in steam engineering, Congress passed a bill, approved 4 July 1864, providing for the training of engineers at the Naval Academy. Sixteen candidates, known as Acting Third Assistant Engineers, were admitted on 10 October 1866, the Department of Steam Enginery having been established the previous year under Chief Engineer W. W. W. Wood. The results were at first disappointing; more than half of the sixteen resigned within five years of their graduation in 1868. In 1871, Chief Engineer King devised a new plan of appointing young men to the Academy as cadet engineers who would specialize in marine engineering, particularly in the last year of the course, and have a status comparable to that of the cadet midshipmen, particularly after 1874, when the engineers course was extended from two to four years. This system worked well and accomplished its purpose. Some 135 cadet engineers were furnished the fleet up to 1882, when the distinction between cadet engineers and naval cadets was abolished in both name and training.

The Spanish-American War was of such short duration (April–August 1898) that it had but little impact on the Naval Academy. However, the thirty-nine naval cadets of the class of 1898 were graduated two months ahead of schedule and ordered to the fleet on 2 April. Members of the class of 1899 were ordered to sea at their own request a month later, followed in June by forty-six men from the class of 1900, and twenty-nine from 1901. Following the American naval victory at Santiago, on 3 July, Admiral Cervera and other officers of the Spanish Navy were quartered in Academy buildings as "prisoners of war," though they were soon paroled and spent the summer enjoying the hospitality of the Academy personnel and Annapolis society more as guests than prisoners.

The turn into the new century was also a turning point in the history of the Naval Academy, which entered upon its greatest period of growth and development as an immediate consequence of the revival of interest in and concern for adequate naval strength, and the growth of the United States as a world power with worldwide commitments. Congressional investigations in the early 1870's revealed the disgraceful and dangerous inadequacies of the American naval forces and led to building programs designed to create a fleet of modern ships. The studies of Captain Alfred Thayer Mahan, U. S. Navy, in the 1890's emphasized the importance of sea power in history. The energy and enthusiasm of Theodore Roosevelt, as Assistant Secretary of the Navy and as President, enhanced naval development, culminating in the epoch-making, round-the-world cruise of the Great White Fleet in 1907–1909. The Spanish-American War, essentially a naval war, demonstrated the importance of the Navy as an instrument of national power.

Symbolic, as it were, of this vast naval renaissance, the Naval Academy was completely rebuilt in the opening years of the twentieth century; only two small buildings (the guard houses on either side of Number 3 Gate) remain today from the previous century, and nothing at all from the original establishment. The Board of Visitors in 1895 recommended new buildings to replace those erected during the administration of Admiral Porter, and the architect Ernest Flagg was engaged to design the comprehensive plan of new construction. An appropriation of $10,000,000 by Congress made possible the development of the Academy plant much as it stands today; Bancroft Hall, Dahlgren Hall, Macdonough Hall, the Chapel, Isherwood Hall, the Commissioned Officers' Mess, the Superintendent's Quarters, and the Administration Building all date from this era. Old Fort Severn, built in 1808 and the principal landmark of the old Naval School, was demolished in 1909.

Meanwhile, the battalion (later regiment and brigade) of midshipmen grew steadily in size. U. S. Senators were authorized to appoint midshipmen to the Academy in 1902, and the number increased to 2 the next year. In 1916 the number of appointees for each Senator, Representative and Delegate was increased to 3; in 1917, to 4; and, subsequently, to 5 (the present quota). As a result of this expansion, the Academy was able to graduate classes of about 200 to duty in the fleet in World War I, and classes of from 500 to 1,000 in World War II. In October 1916 there were 1,231 midshipmen at the Academy, and over 3,100 in October 1941.

As in previous national emergencies, the Academy responded to the United States' entry into World War I by speeding up its readying of officers for sea duty. The class of 1917 graduated in March of that year, 2 months early, and the class of 1918 in June, 1 year in advance. In April 1917, it was decided to decrease the 4-year course to 3 years and graduate the class of 1919 1 year early. The Academy also undertook the indoctrination of 2,569 men for commissioning in the U. S. Naval Reserve Force.

The interim between the two great wars was spent largely in modernizing the curriculum and the training equipment to keep pace with the rapid advances in naval technology. The textbooks in ordnance were brought up to date, and the latest model fire-control and gun-director equipment was installed for drill purposes in Dahlgren Hall. A course in flight tactics was incorporated in the Seamanship Department, and a course in

An officer and a midshipman at the turn of the century.

*T*he Naval Academy has changed
greatly since the 1860's: The Main Gate
from 1866–1932; midshipmen resting
on a mortar, 1869; and the United States
Naval Academy racing crew of 1868.

*R*ecitation rooms on the
wharf, and the U.S.S. Santee, 1869.

aeronautical engineering in the Engineering Department; in 1925, Second Class summer was devoted to aviation indoctrination; the Department of Aviation was established in 1945.

The Naval Academy was accredited by the Association of American Universities on 25 October 1930, and an act of Congress, of 25 May 1933, authorized the Superintendent to confer the degree of bachelor of science on all graduates from the date of accreditation, an honor extended to all living graduates by Congress on 8 July 1937. By the end of the year 1958, the total number of graduates of the Naval Academy stood at 28,229.

Significant physical expansion of the Academy grounds and buildings was begun in 1941 when 22 acres were added at the foot of the slope in front of the Naval Hospital by pumping silt from the Severn River into a steel-bulkheaded area along the shore. Seven and one-half acres more (the site of the present Field House) were also added at this time by purchase, and work on the new ordnance building, Ward Hall, was begun. A subsequent landfill operation, begun in February 1957, added a total of 53 acres by filling in Dewey Basin and extending Farragut Field, to bring the yard area to approximately 290 acres. Since the establishment of the Naval School, some 120 acres have been added, by purchase and reclamation, to the original Fort Severn site. The Field House was completed in 1957. The new, 29,000 seat Navy-Marine Corps Memorial Stadium in West Annapolis was completed in August 1959.

In World War II the course was again shortened to three years, though by instituting a schedule of summer academics, a substantial amount of the original course was retained. Reserve officers were again trained at the Academy. The class of 1942 was graduated in December 1941, and the classes of 1943 through 1948A (upper half of the original class of 1948) all graduated one year in advance.

On 10 October 1945 the Naval Academy celebrated its Centennial. Three special platoons of midshipmen paraded in uniforms of 1845, 1870 and 1900. On the previous Sunday, 7 October, a memorial Chapel service honored the 729 graduates who died in line of duty in the Academy's first hundred years of existence.

Though the changes and adjustments in the work and appearance of the Naval Academy dictated by growth, progress and technological advancement have been many in its 114-year history, the fundamental mission has remained steadfast: to prepare for the Naval Service the very best junior officers possible, capable of professional growth and the assumption of high responsibility. Though the present statement of that mission has been codified only in recent years, the job of the Naval Academy was explicitly stated at the very beginning by the first Superintendent, Commander Franklin Buchanan, in his original order to the first Academic Board, 4 October 1845:

> The course of instruction will be comprised under the following heads—Mathematics, Natural Philosophy, Chemistry, Gunnery, the use of Steam, Geography, English Grammar, Arithmetic, History, the French and Spanish languages and such other branches desirable to the accomplishment of a Naval officer as your judgment may dictate.

The "accomplishment of a Naval officer" remains the sole objective of the United States Naval Academy.

The Naval Academy Seal, or Coat of Arms, was designed by Park Benjamin of the class of 1868, and officially adopted by the Navy Department on 25 January 1899. The shield pictures a Roman war galley "coming bows on into action," under which is an open book. The shield is affixed to the trident of

Neptune, god of the sea, this trident held aloft by a hand. On either side are flaming torches, and on the unrolled scrolls are the designation, *U. S. Naval Academy*, and the motto, *Ex Scientia Tridens*, also the creation of Park Benjamin. The motto is translated, as its author specified, as "From Knowledge, Sea Power." *Tridens* is, of course, the Latin word for trident; literally, but, by metonymy, it signifies sea power, which the trident, since Neptune's days, has always stood for. The galley represents active naval strength arising from the open book, or active learning, and the torches symbolize the ardent aspiration to that learning. Oddly enough, this well-nigh perfect representation of the purpose of the Naval Academy, with its handsome and appropriate design and apt motto, was received by some old grads with indifference, and even some open hostility, when it was first displayed, because it did not seem sufficiently home-grown, belligerent, and patriotic—and because the motto was in Latin!

Epilogue

Looking Ahead

Although enormously proud of its long established traditions and its century-old historical past, the Naval Academy by no means has its eyes riveted exclusively on that past. On the contrary, it is constantly going through the process of evolutionary change, and constantly planning improvements and developments for the future. These changes involve not only the expansion and modernization of the Academy's physical equipment but also the deepening and widening of the midshipmen's professional, intellectual and social capacities.

Visitors to the Academy in the next few years will see unrolling before their eyes an exciting drama of the expansion and improvement of the physical plant. Act one of this drama, which began in 1955, has just about reached its climax. The most obvious change is the striking alteration of the whole topographical profile of the Academy land area brought about by the new land fills, which have added approximately 54.5 acres to the grounds. In a vast and miraculous undertaking in hydraulic engineering, about 3,900,000 cubic yards of river bottom were pumped up from the mouth of the Severn and deposited behind bulkheads on either side of the Academy peninsula. On the Severn side was thus created the 26.5 acres of Dewey Field; and on the Spa Creek side, the 28 acres of the new Farragut Field. (The new wings of Bancroft Hall were built on the original Farragut Field.) These new areas, graded and sodded, added much needed athletic and drill areas to a cramped Academy which has always been pinched for land. (Such an unusual method of acquiring elbow room for the Academy is nothing new at Annapolis: about one third of the Academy's current acreage is "made" land resulting from some five previous land fills.) On Dewey Field and Farragut Field has been planted the "Iron Forest," nearly one hundred light poles, eighty feet high. The illumination from the powerful flood lights atop these poles makes athletics on the field possible almost two hours into the fall and winter twilight.

In a gracious little park on the tip of the new Farragut Field nearest to Chesapeake Bay stands one of the most appropriate and meaningful monuments in the yard, the Triton Light, the first navigational light on the Academy grounds. It emits a sequence of four and then five flashes to signify the Class of 1945, who dedicated it, on 14 November 1959, not only as a class memorial, but as an invocation for "the safe return of all those who go down to the sea in ships." Its three sides symbolize the three faiths of the Naval Officer—Faith in God, Faith in Country, Faith in One's Ship. Nearby, a saluting battery is mounted. In this park also has been erected the foremast of the battleship *Maine*.

Just inside Gate One is one of the most imposing new structures in the yard, the Field House. Work on this building, the first ever erected on Academy grounds exclusively for purposes of physical education, began on 20 April 1955. It is divided into three sections: a southern wing containing dormitories, dressing rooms and a lounge for visiting teams; a northern wing containing physical education areas, locker rooms, offices and lecture rooms; and a great central field area, 200 by 370 feet, where almost any sport may be played, and almost any other activity accommodated, notably the Graduation ceremonies. The arched roof over this area is seventy feet high, and 12,000 people can be seated under it for Graduation.

The new Seventh and Eighth Wings of Bancroft Hall were first occupied in 1962. Externally, they are exact copies in structure and materials of the older wings, but internally, the 550 new rooms with their built-in closets, stowage lockers, bunks and gun racks, and their marble shower stalls, are far more lavish, efficient and practical than their older counterparts. Meanwhile, the new space will allow two of the old wings to be vacated each year for thorough renovation, until, by 1964, all of Bancroft Hall will be completely modernized.

The structure between the two new wings houses two of the most attractive interiors in the Academy, the Brigade Library and the Assembly Hall. The former fills a long-felt need for a place where midshipmen may practice and enjoy the art of reading in comfortable informality. It was not designed as a mere extension to the Main Library in Mahan Hall; its collections were specially selected to offer a solid body of good literature and supplementary reading for the academic courses. A special feature of the library is an audio room with a substantial library of records and tapes to train midshipmen in the important art of good listening. The adjacent 700-seat Assembly Hall with its spacious stage and well-equipped projection booth serves for meetings, lectures and entertainment, and has the special advantage of being much more conveniently located than the distant Mahan Hall auditorium.

In front of these new buildings is the beautiful new Reflecting Pool, surrounded by pleasant terraces and benches and approached by a broad flight of steps. This area is so attractive a setting that it was chosen as the site of the 1962 Ring Dance, and the choice proved most successful.

Outside the grounds proper, but efficiently located on the access road to U. S. Route 50 in West Annapolis, stands the magnificent Navy-Marine Corps Memorial Stadium, dedicated 26 September 1959. It seats over 28,000, nearly twice as many as the now demolished Thompson Stadium in the yard did. The stadium consists of twin structures on either side of the field of an unusual but highly efficient design: Each stand is double-decked, the upper deck cantilevered over the lower so as to combine maximum seating capacity with maximum visibility and proximity to the field. On the façades of the upper decks the great battles fought by the Navy and the Marine Corps in World Wars I and II and the Korean action are memorialized in bold letters. Funds for the construction were contributed by the crews of ships and stations, alumni, industrial companies, and friends of the Navy and the Academy, many of the contributions being designated as memorials, including 5,800 chair seats, each marked with a plate honoring the member of the Navy or Marine Corps in whose name the chair was donated. The dedicatory plaque of the stadium indicates its noble purpose and intent:

> This stadium is dedicated to those who have served and will serve—upholders of the traditions and renown of the Navy and Marine Corps of the United States. May it be a perpetual re-

minder of the Navy and Marine Corps as organizations of men trained to work hard and to play hard; in war, defenders of our freedom; in peace, molders of our youth.

These new additions and constructions, however, are only the beginnings of the new building program designed to accommodate the midshipmen with the very best and the very latest in educational and training facilities and to insure that the Academy keeps pace with the rapid march of events in science, technology, world affairs and human aspiration. On 10 June 1961, the Chief of Naval Personnel, Vice Admiral William R. Smedberg III, constituted a Special Advisory Commission on Future Development of Academic Facilities to "determine the required modern physical plant best suited to fulfill the mission of the Naval Academy for a Brigade strength of four thousand midshipmen." The report of this commission, known as the "Moreell Plan" from its chairman, Admiral Ben Moreell, Civil Engineer Corps, U. S. Navy (Retired), recommends the most extensive series of acquisitions, new constructions, modernizations, rehabilitations and demolitions since the Academy was virtually rebuilt at the turn of the century.

Paramount objectives are:

An atomic-age Science Building with generous space for lectures, demonstrations and laboratory experiments as well as research facilities with computer systems. This building is considered "the essential key to the entire Facilities Program," and it is to become "the center of scientific activity for faculty and students."

A greatly expanded and modernized Library with adequate space and equipment for study, research and writing.

An Auditorium with a seating capacity to accommodate the entire Brigade of 4,000 and with modern staging, lighting and projection facilities to make possible almost any kind of presentation, demonstration or cultural program.

A renovated Dahlgren Hall with a complete new Weapons System Facility for up-to-date instruction and drill for this most fundamental of all aspects of the military profession.

The filling-in of Santee Basin and the development of a modern, fully equipped boat basin, with look-out station and signal tower, at the northeast corner of Farragut Field.

When these and many other improvements are accomplished, the Naval Academy will be able to fulfill its mission and maintain its high standards for many years to come.

But "Bricks and Mortar" improvements, however significant, are, of course, only a part of growth and progress. Since 1958, admission of candidates has been by means of the tests designed and administered by the College Entrance Examination Board and the Educational Testing Service. By participating in this system the Academy has gained access to the principal source of the best prospects for college-level work in the country, and therefore has its pick of more and better candidates. Coupled with this testing procedure is an evaluation program designed to seek out the "Whole Man." Panels of officers and professors go through all the entrance credentials of the candidates who have passed the examinations to determine which of the prospective midshipmen have, in addition to their demonstrated mental abilities, the best additional backgrounds in athletics, extracurricular activities, and all other enterprises which reveal character, energy and leadership. In this way, the Academy strives to select men who are not exclusively scholars, athletes or campus leaders, but happy combinations of all three who will make the best officers. There is more than an echo here of the ancient ideal of the sound mind in the sound body.

To recognize and encourage achievement in academics and leadership there is promulgated periodically the Superintendent's List, similar to the Dean's List in in most colleges. The former, however, requires that those midshipmen so honored stand high in aptitude and conduct as well as scholarship. Certain attractive privileges go with the distinction, including extra leave.

The Naval Academy has its military, professional and academic programs under constant and vigilant scrutiny to insure that it satisfies its responsibility to the nation in the most effective manner possible. In March 1959, for example, a Curriculum Review Board under the chairmanship of Dr. Richard G. Folsom, president of Rensselaer Polytechnic Institute, undertook a thorough appraisal of the Academy's work. The criticisms, suggestions, and approval of such boards, along with the annual recommendations of the Board of Visitors and the progressive enthusiasm of the Academy's own faculty, enable the Academy to keep in the forefront of higher education in America and provide the most productive opportunities for the midshipmen's growth in body, mind and spirit. The instructional departments are constantly developing and instituting new educational materials and techniques, and the administration is constantly striving to improve the methods of training and supervision.

An excellent example of this academic progress is the Advanced Placement and Elective Program begun in 1959. Under this new program qualified midshipmen may greatly enhance their education by transcending the limits of the basic curriculum and seeking the level of academic and professional maturity that their particular aptitudes and stages of development entitle them to. Upon entrance the new Fourth classman may "validate" (that is, receive credit for and not have to take) courses in the basic curriculum that are essentially the same as courses he has already taken in college; in some instances, he may also validate work in which he demonstrates a high native proficiency, as in English and foreign languages. Special examinations, high school records, college transcripts, and personal interviews determine who will be allowed to undertake advanced work. The classroom time thus made available is utilized for elective courses which enable the qualified midshipman not only to advance more rapidly, in accord with his demonstrated competence, but also to concentrate in a field in which he is especially gifted and interested, even to the point of majoring in a certain subject. For example, if a midshipman with special talents in French successfully validates the two-year course in the basic curriculum, he can begin his study of the language where the base course leaves off and go on to major in French and thus acquire a well-developed language skill which will be of special value in his professional career.

Midshipmen of high academic standing, even if they have not validated, may take elective courses after the first term of Fourth class year in addition to the regular curriculum. By concentrating in a particular discipline, they may attain the benefit and distinction of having majored in a subject. Majors are offered in all the principal academic subjects. Midshipmen are enthusiastic about these offerings and quick to take advantage of them. The program has developed rapidly since its inception, and it has notably enriched the substance and texture of the curriculum. In 1961, which was only the third year of its operation, 24% of the entering class validated one or more subjects; and, of the 2,782 men of the three upper classes, 705 enrolled in electives.

Further academic advance is evidenced by the announcement by the Secretary of the Navy, Fred Korth, on 24 May 1962, that a civilian dean of academics would be appointed and that there would be a gradual replacement of officer instructors, in all departments except those in the Division of Naval Science, by civilian professors. The purpose of these innovations was described as "the need for accelerated improvement, particularly in the fields of mathematics, science and engineering, in order that the Navy keep pace with present rapid technological advancements." The Academy, of course, already had a substantial core of professional civilian instructors as the permanent component of most of the academic work.

The strictly professional training of the midshipmen likewise is constantly improved and extended with ever-increasing opportunities to practice the science of ships and the sea at first hand. The famous training fleet of "YP's" (Yard Patrol boats) was augmented and improved in 1958 by the addition of ten of the new 600-series of boats which are considerably advanced in design and instructional efficiency over the older 500-series boats. The new craft have a length of 80 feet 5 inches, a beam of 17 feet 9 inches, and a draft of 64 inches, and displace 64.3 tons. They have a cruising speed of 12 knots, and are powered by four 165 HP diesels which drive twin 36-inch, three-bladed screws. They are maneuvered by twin rudders, and equipped with advanced navigational gear, including radar, Loran, fathometers, and DRT (Dead Reckoning Tracers). The midshipmen are frequently "at sea" in these miniature ships, larger, faster, more maneuverable, and better fitted out than any previous training craft, and they thus come to know and appreciate from the start the naval vessels they will navigate and fight as officers.

To expand this practical shipboard training further, the YP

Squadron was organized in 1958. A new YP is assigned to each of the six battalions for extended cruises during weekends and Spring Leave to various Chesapeake Bay ports and even to the Philadelphia Naval Base. Under way, there is opportunity for invaluable practice in shiphandling, navigation, tactical operations, and marine engineering. Competitions, which include operational readiness inspections, enliven the activity in the fall and spring, and the battalion with the highest aggregate score is awarded the Battle Efficiency Pennant at the end of the academic year.

New technological developments are under constant surveillance by the midshipmen, and the laboratories are well furnished to give them a first-hand acquaintance with the latest scientific achievements. They may consider the marvels of atomic energy through experiments with the Science Department's subcritical nuclear reactor, activated by 5,500 pounds of uranium fuel. (The department offers elective courses in Atomic and Nuclear Physics and Neutron Physics.) The Weapons Department has installed a Computer Laboratory and teaches a course in Analog and Digital Computer Fundamentals. The Engineering Department can illustrate its courses in hydrostatics and hydrodynamics in its own tow tank, where the actual behavior of ships in the water may be demonstrated by models, and can teach aerodynamics in its own wind tunnel. Missile warfare and space flight are also prime considerations in the curriculum, as the guided missile mounts and the model of the Polaris in front of Dahlgren Hall indicate to every visitor.

The most realistic of all phases of midshipman training, the summer cruise, has been made even more authentic than the long-established "Practice Cruises" were. Instead of cruising aboard ships of a special fleet set aside for the purpose, the midshipmen are now integrated with the officers and crews of ships which are actually components of existing U. S. Fleets and even the fleets of other navies. As far as is practicable, midshipmen may choose the type of ship in which they wish to sail. Some join the Second Fleet out of Atlantic Ports; others may learn aboard ships of the Sixth Fleet in the Mediterranean. Volunteers with high aptitude, good grades, and the requisite language proficiency may be selected to train with the navies of Latin-

American and NATO countries, and, in turn, midshipmen of these nations become exchange guests of our Navy. The Cruise Coordination Center of the Executive Department has, in recent years, implemented exchanges with the navies of Great Britain, France, Italy, West Germany, Denmark, Greece, Turkey, Canada, Brazil, Ecuador, Chile, Peru, and several other countries.

Midshipmen may sample life and work aboard aircraft carriers, cruisers, destroyers, and submarines in the Atlantic, the Pacific, the Mediterranean, or even the Arctic. Some have made the training cruise in the Coast Guard Academy's 1,800-ton, three-masted auxiliary bark *Eagle*. Midshipmen on cruise participate in the work of both enlisted men and officers: in general, the Third class concentrate on the work of the crew and even take the rating examinations for Seaman and Fireman. The First class assume the responsibilities of junior officers.

In Second Class Summer, where the emphasis is on amphibious and air operations, Second classmen are integrated with regular Marine Corps units and participate in a full-scale mock assault on the beaches at Little Creek, Virginia. Realism is the keynote of these maneuvers. The beaches are "softened up" by simulated aerial bombardment. Frogmen are dropped by parachute or disembarked from speedboats to blast out under-water obstacles. Offshore destroyers act out a bombardment of the beach. Troops and mechanized equipment make the landing and join forces with airborne units which have landed from helicopters behind "enemy" lines.

The acceleration and expansion of the Naval Academy's comprehensive program of education and training has the sole fundamental objective of preparing the midshipmen for the new concepts of career service that the twentieth century has created. Essentially, the fundamentals remain the same, of course; but the new officers of our day will be called to duties and responsibilities unimaginable even a few years ago, most of them highly exciting, adventurous and rewarding. Consider a few of the career potentials. Each year top candidates among the graduating midshipmen are selected for the Nuclear Power Program. After an intensive course at the Nuclear Power School at Bainbridge, Maryland, they are ready to begin careers in one of the most intriguing and promising branches of the service. Another hundred have the opportunity to begin conventional submarine training at New London, Connecticut. To these groups is accorded the chance to equal and surpass the fabulous exploits of the heroes of modern submarine development: the polar passages of the *Nautilus*, the *Skate* and the *Sargo*; the submerged circumnavigation of the world by the *Triton*; and the defensive patrols of the Polaris submarines.

There will be ever-increasing opportunities in the vast new dimensions of space. No Navy man will ever forget that the first American into space on 5 May 1961 was Commander Alan B. Shepard, Jr., USN, of the Class of 1944.

From each class, candidates are selected for the Advanced Science and Engineering Program, called the Burke Program, in order that the Navy may be supplied with its own scientists and technological experts of the highest caliber and training. These men pursue courses of advanced study leading usually to the doctoral degree.

The complex nature of modern naval and military requirements and the wide variety of careers open to young officers may be indicated by the following table of duty assignments for the Class of 1962.

Number of New Officers Assigned	*Type of Duty*
194	Surface Ships
	9 to Large Combatants
	7 to Amphibious Types
	170 to Destroyers
	8 to Mine Sweepers
202	Aviation Training
100	Submarine School
79	Nuclear Power School
5	Advanced Science and Engineering Program
9	Civil Engineer Corps
33	Supply Corps
1	EDO (Engineering Duty Only)
59	United States Marine Corps
85	United States Air Force
12	United States Army

These statistics indicate, in a very significant way, the essence of the modern Naval Academy. Some of these types of duty are as old as American military service itself; others are as new as tomorrow. In similar fashion, the Naval Academy combines tradition with progress, pride in the past with confidence in the future. It builds and grows, though its purpose is unchanging. From the solid foundation of a century of service rendered, it develops a structure of even greater service to come. This is Annapolis Today.

The Annapolis Log

Highlights in the History of the
United States Naval Academy,
In Chronological Order

1608: The first white man of record to see the land now occupied by the United States Naval Academy was Capt.
John Smith, who explored the mouth of the Severn.

1649: Ten families of Puritans, driven out of Virginia, bought
some land near the mouth of the Severn River in Maryland and settled a town to which they gave the name of
Providence.

1670: The name of the town of Providence, after becoming
Town of Proctor's and later Town of Severn, was
changed to Anne Arundel Town.

1694: Anne Arundel Town was selected to be the capital of
the Colony, which had formerly been at St. Mary's.

1696: The name of Anne Arundel Town was changed to Annapolis, in honor of Princess Anne, second daughter of
James II, later to become Queen Anne of England.

1708: The town of Annapolis was incorporated as a city.

1760: A stone windmill was built on the easternmost extremity
of Annapolis, giving the place the name of "Windmill
Point."

1763: Gov. William Paca of Maryland, one of the signers of
the Declaration of Independence, built the mansion
which since 1899 has been known as Carvel Hall.

1794: The United States Navy was created by an Act of Congress—by a slim margin of just two votes.

1794: The President was authorized by Congress to appoint 48
midshipmen.

1800: The first suggestion for a naval school was made by John Adams, second President of the United States, in a recommendation to Congress.

1803: Lieut. David Porter, an American prisoner of war, conducted a school for imprisoned American midshipmen in Tripoli.

1808: The War Department purchased from the Dulany family the land on which the stone windmill stood, comprising 9¾ acres.

1808: The War Department built a circular rampart on Windmill Point, on the site of the stone mill.

1816: Representative Burwell Bassett introduced a resolution requesting the Secretary of the Navy to report a plan for a naval academy.

1817: The first "practice cruise" for the training of midshipmen was made, at the suggestion of Commodore William Bainbridge, in the U. S. brig *Prometheus*; summer.

1819: The first examination ever held for promotion in the U. S. Navy was held in New York, when 39 midshipmen out of 89 passed.

1821: A naval school was informally established on board the U. S. frigate *Guerrière* at New York.

1821: A second naval school was informally established on board the U. S. frigate *Java* at Norfolk, Va.

1822: Secretary of the Navy Thompson proposed a school for the instruction of young naval officers, but the House of Representatives did not respond.

1827: The grade of "passed midshipmen" was established (to prevail until 1862).

1833: A third naval school was started informally at the Boston Navy Yard.

1836: A memorial urging the establishment of a naval school was drawn up by 55 officers of the *Constitution* and by 16 officers of the *Vandalia* and forwarded to Congress.

1839: The Philadelphia Naval School was established at the Naval Home, Philadelphia, with a one-year course.

1839: Congress made the first appropriation for building steam vessels, thus emphasizing the need of technical training of naval officers.

*Ordnance study, 1890.
Midshipmen are measuring the
velocity of a shell
from a field howitzer.*

*F*ootballers of 1894, with the captain
wearing the first helmet ever worn in a football game.

1841: Lieut. M. F. Maury, sometimes called "The Father of the Naval Academy," contributed articles to the *Southern Literary Messenger* called "Scraps from a Lucky Bag" that exposed the paralyzing effects of political corruption on the Navy.

1841: Two midshipmen were dismissed for fighting a duel with pistols at Bladensburg.

1841: To establish the authority of rank over midshipmen, the instructors at the Philadelphia Naval School were made commissioned officers.

1842: Prof. William Chauvenet became head of the Philadelphia Naval School; April.

1842: Acting Midshipman Philip Spencer, son of the Secretary of War, was hanged for mutiny on board the *Somers;* Dec. 1.

1843: Prof. William Chauvenet drew up a program of a 2-year course of study at the Philadelphia Naval School; it was approved by the Secretary of the Navy, but revoked by his successor.

1845: George Bancroft became Secretary of the Navy; Mar. 11.

1845: The practically deserted army post of Fort Severn, between the harbor of Annapolis and the Severn River, was urged as the site of a naval school by Capt. Isaac Mayo.

1845: The War Department transferred the Fort Severn reservation to the Navy Department; Aug. 15.

1845: The Philadelphia Naval School was transferred from Philadelphia to Annapolis.

1845: Commander Franklin Buchanan was appointed the first commanding officer of the Naval School at Annapolis; Aug. 14.

1845: The Naval School at Annapolis was formally opened; Oct. 10.

1845: The entrance age for the Naval School was fixed at a minimum of 13 and a maximum of 16 years.

1845: The first entrance examinations were held for midshipmen; Oct. 16.

1846: Congress made the first appropriation, $28,200, for "repairs, improvements and instruction at Fort Severn, Annapolis, Md."

1846: Of the 47 graduates of the Naval School during 1846–7–8 (date of 1840), Richmond Aulick ranked 1st, thereby becoming the first official graduate, and William N. Jeffers 4th.

1846: The first June Week dress parade was held in honor of the Board of Examiners; June 27.

1846: The midshipmen of the '40 date presented Bulwer's "Lady of Lyons," initiating the custom of giving theatrical performances; fall.

1846: The first naval ball—the forerunner of the hops—was held in the new mess hall; Jan. 15.

1847: Congress appropriated $28,200 and authorized the purchase of 7 additional acres for use by the Naval School.

1847: Of the 136 graduates of the Naval School during 1847–8–9–50 (date of 1841), John Wilkes, Jr., ranked 1st, John H. Upshur 17th, Samuel R. Franklin 20th, Edward Y. McCauley 29th, Francis A. Roe 32nd, Oscar C. Badger 46th, John L. Davis 49th, James E. Jouett 99th, John H. Russell 115th, Stephen B. Luce 126th, and Walter W. Queen 136th.

1847: Commander George P. Upshur became Superintendent of the Naval School; Mar. 15.

1848: During the years 1848–9 (date of 1842), the Naval School graduated 7 midshipmen.

1850: The Naval School at Annapolis was officially designated as "The United States Naval Academy"; July 1.

1850: Commander Cornelius K. Stribling became Superintendent of the Naval Academy; July 1.

1850: The Board of Visitors was created.

1850: The system of marking on the scale of 4 was established; July 30.

1850: The course at the Naval Academy was established at 4 years.

1850: A special uniform was devised for use by the acting midshipmen.

1851: The yacht *America* first won the famous international trophy.

1851: During the years 1851–2 (date of 1845), the Naval Academy graduated 3 midshipmen, of whom Ralph Chandler ranked 2d.

1851: The course at the Naval Academy was set at 4 consecutive years, with an annual summer practice cruise of 3 months; Nov. 15.

1852: The sloop-of-war *Preble* made its first foreign summer practice cruise.

1852: During the years 1852–3 (date of 1846), the Naval Academy graduated 16 midshipmen, of whom Lewis A. Kimberly ranked 7th and Bancroft Gherardi 15th.

1853: During the years 1853–4 (date of 1847), the Naval Academy graduated 47 midshipmen, of whom George E. Belknap ranked 11th, Andrew E. K. Benham 21st, and Joseph P. Fyffe 37th.

1853: The enlisted band of the Naval Academy was organized.

1853: Commander Louis M. Goldsborough became Superintendent of the Naval Academy; Nov. 1.

1854: The Naval Academy graduated 6 midshipmen (date of 1851—three-year course), of whom Thomas O. Selfridge ranked 1st, and initiated the first June graduation ceremonies.

1854: The first death in the Naval Academy was that of Acting Midshipman Weisman.

1855: During the years 1855–6 (date of 1849), the Naval Academy graduated 21 midshipmen.

1855: The Naval Academy graduated 12 acting midshipmen (date of 1951), of whom Montgomery Sicard ranked 8th; June.

1856: The Naval Academy graduated 21 midshipmen (date of 1850), of whom John G. Walker ranked 1st, Francis M. Ramsay 3d and Richard W. Meade 5th; June.

1856: The Naval Academy graduated 19 acting midshipmen (date of 1852), of whom Robert L. Phythian ranked 3d; June.

1857: The Naval Academy graduated 15 acting midshipmen, of whom Frederick V. McNair ranked 12th; June.

1857: Capt. George S. Blake became Superintendent of the Naval Academy; Sept. 15.

1858: The Naval Academy graduated 15 acting midshipmen, of whom George Dewey ranked 5th and Albert Kautz 15th; June.

1859: The Japanese Bell was received; Jan. 12.

1859: The Naval Academy graduated 20 acting midshipmen, of whom Alfred T. Mahan ranked 2d and Norman V. H. Farquhar 6th; June.

1860: The Tripolitan monument, which for 52 years had stood in Washington, was brought to Annapolis.

1860: The Herndon monument arrived at Annapolis; June 14.

1860: The Naval Academy graduated 25 acting midshipmen, of whom Winfield S. Schley ranked 18th; June.

1860: The U. S. frigate *Constitution*, in command of Capt. David D. Porter, arrived at Annapolis for duty as a school ship; Aug.

1861: Midshipman W. E. Yancey of Alabama was the first Southerner to resign from the Academy as the result of the controversy between the North and South; Jan. 15.

1861: The *Constitution* sailed from Annapolis with the midshipmen aboard to find safety at Fort Adams, near Newport, R. I.; Apr. 25.

1861: The studies of the midshipmen were resumed at Fort Adams, near Newport; May 13.

1861: The Naval Academy graduated 27 acting midshipmen, of whom William T. Sampson ranked 1st; no graduation exercises. Ordered into active service: April 24 and soon after May 10.

1861: The Naval Academy graduated 32 acting midshipmen (date of 1858), thirteen months ahead of schedule, and ordered them into active service; of this class, Louis Kempff ranked 9th; May.

1861: The Naval Academy graduated 55 acting midshipmen (date of 1859) one year and eleven months ahead of schedule, and ordered them into active service; May.

1862: The epoch-making book *Seamanship*, written for the instruction of midshipmen by Rear Admiral Stephen B. Luce, was first published.

1862: The Naval Academy was placed under the supervision of the Bureau of Navigation of the Navy Department; July.

1862: The status of students was changed from "acting midshipmen on probation" to "midshipmen"; July 16.

1862: The pay of the midshipman was raised from $350 to $500 a year.

1862: The *Santee* reached Newport, R. I., and became an additional school ship for the Naval Academy; Oct.

1863: The Naval Academy graduated 21 midshipmen (date of 1860) thirteen months ahead of schedule, with Henry Glass ranking 1st, Philip H. Cooper 5th, James H. Sands 20th, and Yates Stirling 21st; May.

1863: The Naval Academy graduated 29 midshipmen (date of 1860) nine months ahead of schedule, with William C. Wise ranking 1st, Purnell F. Harrington 3d, Robley D. Evans 12th, Colby M. Chester 15th, Charles V. Gridley 19th and Charles D. Sigsbee 21st; Sept.

1864: The Naval Academy graduated 31 midshipmen (date of 1861) nine months ahead of schedule, with Caspar F. Goodrich ranking 1st, Bowman H. McCalla 4th, French E. Chadwick 5th, and Charles J. Train 24th; Nov.

1865: The Naval Academy returned to Annapolis from Fort Adams, R. I., following the Civil War; Sept. 11.

1865: Rear Admiral David D. Porter became Superintendent of the Naval Academy; Sept. 9.

1865: The Naval Academy graduated 54 midshipmen (date of 1861), with George A. Converse ranking 1st, Royal B. Bradford 3d, George W. DeLong 10th, Joseph E. Craig 17th, Charles M. Thomas 21st, Albert S. Snow 23d, George C. Reiter 24th, Willard H. Brownson 28th, William W. Mead 31st, Edwin S. Houston 37th, Edwin Longnecker 42d, Thomas Perry 49th, and Charles H. Stockton 50th; Oct.

1866: The old official mansion of the governors of Maryland, together with 4 acres of ground, were added to the Naval Academy's grounds.

1866: The Naval Academy graduated 73 midshipmen, with Henry W. Lyon ranking 5th, Asa Walker 7th, Charles S. Sperry 10th, William M. Little 19th, Chapman C. Todd 44th, and William T. Swinburne 57th; June.

1866: The battalion of midshipmen was reorganized into four divisions of 6 gun crews each, and the mess crews were discarded as units.

1867: The Naval Academy grounds were enlarged by the purchase of 10 acres of land bought from St. John's College; Nov. 5.

1867: Serious athletic work was begun at the Naval Academy with the formation of class baseball clubs.

1867: The Navy Department assumed direct care of the Naval Academy, assigning to the Bureau of Navigation merely administrative routine; Mar.

1867: The first publication by midshipmen made its appearance under the name of *Shakings*.

1867: The class of 1867 was the first to designate itself officially by its graduating year ('67) and to adopt a class badge and class colors.

1867: The Naval Academy graduated 87 midshipmen, with Benjamin F. Tilley ranking 1st, John P. Merrell 12th, Joseph G. Eaton 13th, Eugene H. Leutze 22d, Park Benjamin 24th, and John E. Pillsbury 79th; June.

1868: By the "Strawberry Hill" and "Prospect Hill" purchases, the Naval Academy grounds were increased by 65 acres, comprising the cemetery, the U. S. Naval Hospital, the old golf course and the Superintendent's garden; July 15.

1868: The class of 1868 graduated 81 midshipmen, with Royal R. Ingersoll ranking 2d, Robert M. Thompson 10th, Raymond P. Rodgers 11th, Seaton Schroeder 15th, Charles W. Chipp 22d, Nicholas L. Roosevelt 39th, Richard Wainwright 49th, and John A. Rodgers 62d; June.

1868: The Naval Academy graduated 16 acting third assistant engineers (date of 1866), and 2 cadet engineers (date of 1867); June.

1869: The midshipmen's dirk was again prescribed as part of the uniform, replacing the sword when on boat duty.

1869: Beginning with the class of 1873, the course was extended to 4 years at the Naval Academy and 2 years at sea.

1869: Class rings were introduced.

1869: The class of 1869 graduated 74 midshipmen, with William W. Kimball ranking 7th, Giles B. Harber 9th, William P. Potter 11th, Newton E. Mason 22d, Uriah R. Harris 24th, Herbert Winslow 25th, Kossuth Niles 27th, Nathaniel J. K. Patch 30th, William P. Day 37th, George P. Colvocoresses 42d, Arthur P. Nazro 45th, Edward B. Barry 48th, Samuel P. Comly 52d, Daniel D. V. Stuart 53d, Thomas S. Phelps 65th, and Albert G. Berry 70th; June.

1869: Commodore John L. Worden became Superintendent of the Naval Academy; Dec. 1.

1870: The class of 1870 graduated 68 midshipmen, with John Hubbard ranking 5th, Joseph B. Murdock 9th, and Hugo Osterhaus 45th; June.

1870: Congress enacted a law that deprived midshipmen of their rank and graded them as "cadet midshipmen"; July 15.

1871: Hazing at the Naval Academy made its first serious appearance; fall.

1871: The frigate *Constellation* was assigned to the Naval Academy as a practice ship; May 25.

1871: The class of 1871 graduated 49 cadet midshipmen, of whom Sidney A. Staunton ranked 1st, Chauncey Thomas 3d, Aaron Ward 5th, and William A. Marshall 34th; June.

1872: The class of 1872 graduated 25 cadet midshipmen, of whom John C. Frémont ranked 12th; June.

1873: The yacht *America*, which won the famous international cup race in 1851 and for many years belonged to the Naval Academy, was sold by George M. Robeson, Secretary of the Navy.

1873: The class of 1873 graduated 29 cadet midshipmen, of whom Walter C. Cowles ranked 5th, Austin M. Knight 6th, Charles J. Badger 8th, Albert A. Michelson 9th and Jiunzo Matsumura 28th; June.

1873: The Naval Academy graduated 5 cadet engineers (date of 1871), of whom John K. Barton ranked 4th; June.

1873: The course of instruction was changed by law from 4

years to 6 years, 2 of which were to be at sea; Mar. 3.

1874: Congress increased the course of instruction for cadet engineers at the Naval Academy from 2 years to 4 years; Feb. 24.

1874: The entire Third Class was deprived of its summer vacation as a punishment for hazing; May.

1874: Congress passed a law requiring the Superintendent of the Naval Academy to order a court-martial in hazing cases and to dismiss offenders; June 23.

1874: The class of 1874 graduated 30 cadet midshipmen, of whom Bradley A. Fiske ranked 2d and John M. Bowyer 26th; June.

1874: The grounds of the Naval Academy were increased by the purchase of several acres known as "Lockwoodville," the approximate site of Isherwood, Griffin and Melville Halls.

1874: The Naval Academy graduated 10 cadet engineers (date of 1872), of whom George B. Ransom ranked 2d, Abram V. Zane 6th, John R. Edwards 7th and Albert B. Willits 9th; June.

1874: Rear Admiral Christopher R. P. Rodgers became Superintendent of the Naval Academy; Sept. 22.

1875: The class of 1875 graduated 32 cadet midshipmen, of whom Cameron McR. Winslow ranked 3d, James M. Helm 4th, Nathaniel R. Usher 12th, Frank F. Fletcher 14th, and William B. Caperton 31st; June.

1875: The Naval Academy graduated 16 cadet engineers (date of 1873), of whom Walter F. Worthington ranked 5th; June.

1876: The class of 1876 graduated 42 cadet midshipmen, of whom Stimson J. Brown ranked 1st, Walter McLean 13th, Henry T. Mayo 14th, Charles F. Pond 19th, and DeWitt Coffman 32d; June.

1876: The Naval Academy graduated 3 cadet engineers (date of 1873); June.

1877: The pay of a midshipman was fixed at $950 a year.

1877: The entire battalion of midshipmen behaved so gallantly in fighting a big fire in Annapolis that the Superintendent rewarded them by restoring the privilege of smoking.

1877: The class of 1877 graduated 45 cadet midshipmen, of whom William F. Fullam ranked 1st, Albert G. Winterhalter 5th, Augustus F. Fechteler 12th, Albert Gleaves 18th, Albert W. Grant 26th, Herbert O. Dunn 29th, William S. Benson 36th, Koroku Katsu 44th and Jiro Kunitomo 45th; June.

1878: Commodore Foxhall A. Parker became Superintendent of the Naval Academy; June 13.

1878: The class of 1878 graduated 36 cadet midshipmen, with Thomas S. Rodgers ranking 2d, James H. Glennon 5th, Harry S. Knapp 6th, Wm. L. Rodgers 9th, Harry McL. P. Huse 11th, and George R. Clark 26th; June.

1878: The Naval Academy graduated 14 cadet engineers, with Robert S. Griffin ranking 5th, Frank W. Bartlett 8th, John L. Gow 12th, and George E. Burd 14th; June.

1879: The Naval Academy received a certificate from the Paris Exposition of 1878 for "the best system of education in the United States"; spring.

1879: Superintendent Foxhall A. Parker died during the graduation exercises; June.

1879: The class of 1879 graduated 41 cadet midshipmen, with John Hood ranking 2d, Edward E. Hayden 4th, and Thomas Snowden 22d; June.

1879: The Naval Academy graduated 23 cadet engineers, with Francis T. Bowles ranking 3d and Harold P. Norton 11th; June.

1880: The class of 1880 graduated 62 midshipmen, with Philip R. Alger ranking 1st, Albert P. Niblack 11th, William C. P. Muir 21st, Edward Simpson, Jr., 27th, William S. Sims 33d, and Hugh Rodman 61st; June.

1880: The Naval Academy graduated 17 cadet engineers, with Thomas W. Kinkaid ranking 14th; June.

1880: The Naval Academy football team invented and first used the tightly laced canvas jackets, made from sail cloth; autumn.

1881: The class of 1881 graduated 72 cadet midshipmen, with John A. Hoogewerff ranking 4th, Tasuka Serata 14th, Charles A. Doyen 19th, Henry B. Wilson 21st, Sotokichi Uriu 26th, George Barnett 29th, J. W. Weeks 39th, and Yenouke Enouye 72d; June.

1881:   The Naval Academy graduated 24 cadet engineers; June.

1881:   The entire Third Class was quartered on the *Santee* and required to recite on the *Constellation*, in an effort to break up hazing; Oct. 4.

1881:   Commander Francis M. Ramsay became Superintendent of the Naval Academy; Nov. 14.

1882:   The class of 1882 graduated 60 cadet midshipmen, with Lewis Nixon ranking 1st, Spencer S. Wood 2d, Joseph L. Jayne 12th, and Edwin A. Anderson 19th; June.

1882:   The Naval Academy graduated 23 cadet engineers; June.

1882:   Congress enacted a law that classified the students of the Naval Academy as "naval cadets," and honorably discharged graduates when no vacancies were available; Aug. 5.

1882:   Congress passed a law that abolished the distinction between line officers and engineers during the academic probationary period; Aug. 15.

1882:   The Naval Academy football team played its first game, winning from the Clifton Football Club 8 to 0; Nov. 30.

1883:   A spontaneous outbreak of midshipmen, as a protest against the dismissal of one for giving out advance information about an examination, resulted in the dismissal of three midshipmen and wholesale confinement of the rest of the class; Feb. 1.

1883:   The class of 1883 graduated 54 naval cadets, with George W. Littlehales ranking 8th, Charles W. Dyson 9th, Alexander S. Halstead 18th, and Cyrus Townsend Brady 30th; June.

1884:   The class of 1884 graduated 46 naval cadets, with Washington L. Capps ranking 3d, Clarence S. Williams 5th, Roger Welles Jr. 9th, John D. McDonald 15th, Hilary P. Jones 17th, William R. Shoemaker 23d, Charles P. Plunkett 24th, Robert L. Werntz 27th and Josiah S. McKean 29th; June.

1885:   The class of 1885 graduated 36 naval cadets, with David W. Taylor ranking 1st, John G. Tawresey 3d, George W. Kline 9th, Joseph Strauss 14th, Edward W. Eberle 21st, and Robert E. Coontz 28th; June.

1886: The class of 1886 graduated 25 naval cadets, with William H. G. Bullard ranking 3d, Joseph W. Oman 5th, and Philip Andrews 8th; June.

1886: The Graduates' Association was founded; June.

1886: Commander William T. Sampson became Superintendent of the Naval Academy; Sept. 9.

1887: The class of 1887 graduated 44 naval cadets, with Robert Stocker ranking 1st, Elliot Snow 3d, Mark L. Bristol 5th, Newton A. McCully Jr. 7th, Andrew T. Long 18th, Thomas Washington 21st, Archibald H. Scales 22d, Victor Blue 29th, Guy H. Burrage 32d, and Richard H. Jackson 36th; June.

1888: The class of 1888 graduated 35 naval cadets, with Curtis D. Wilbur ranking 3d, Ashley H. Robertson 4th, John A. Lejeune 13th, Samuel S. Robison 14th, Charles F. Hughes 20th, Eli K. Cole 24th, Herman O. Stickney 29th, and Henry A. Wiley 34th; June.

1889: The Naval Academy grounds were increased by 15 acres adjoining College Creek.

1889: All Navy personnel was placed under the jurisdiction of the Bureau of Navigation, thereby restoring control of the Naval Academy to that Bureau.

1889: The Academic Board was authorized by law to divide the 1st class, when entering upon its final year, into candidates for the Line, Marine Corps and Engineering Corps.

1889: The class of 1889 graduated 35 naval cadets, with Richmond P. Hobson ranking 1st, George H. Rock 2d, Nathan C. Twining 4th, Benjamin F. Hutchison 5th, William V. Pratt 6th, Sumner E. Kittelle 7th, George R. Marvell 8th, Louis McC. Nulton 9th, William D. MacDougall 14th, Thomas P. Magruder 16th, Louis R. de Steiguer 18th, William C. Cole 23d, and Ben H. Fuller 25th; June.

1889: By act of Congress, the age limit of cadets was raised from 14 to 15 years minimum and from 18 to 20 years maximum.

1890: The Navy Athletic Association was formed, under the

stimulus of Col. Robert M. Thompson, of the class of 1868.

1890 Capt. Robert L. Phythian became Superintendent of the Naval Academy; June 13.

1890: The class of 1890 graduated 34 naval cadets, with Frank H. Schofield ranking 4th, Jehu V. Chase 5th, Henry J. Ziegemeier 7th, Montgomery M. Taylor 13th, George W. Williams 15th, Charles B. McVay 18th, Carl T. Vogelgesang 19th, John H. Dayton 26th, Lucius A. Bostwick 27th, William A. Moffett 31st, and Julius L. Latimer 32d; June.

1890: Worden Field was opened.

1890: The monument to the dead of the *Jeannette* Expedition was unveiled in the cemetery; Oct. 30.

1890: The first football game between West Point and Annapolis was won by the midshipmen, 20 to 0; Nov. 29.

1891: The class of 1891 graduated 46 naval cadets, with Richard M. Watt ranking 3d, Reginald R. Belknap 5th, Arthur L. Willard 12th, Harley H. Christy 13th, Henry H. Hough 16th, Noble E. Irwin 17th, Thomas J. Senn 25th, Richard H. Leigh 34th, and George W. Laws 43d; June.

1891: The Naval Academy Athletic Association was founded by Commander Colby M. Chester; Dec. 15.

1892: The colors of the Naval Academy were changed from red and white to blue and gold; Mar. 6.

1892: The class of 1892 graduated 40 naval cadets, with John D. Bueret ranking 1st, Homer L. Ferguson 3d, Luke McNamee 5th, John R. Y. Blakely 8th, Joel R. P. Pringle 26th, and John H. Russell Jr. 34th; June.

1893: The smoking of cigarettes by midshipmen was officially banned; Feb. 28.

1893: Physical training was established at the Naval Academy by Dr. Berger.

1893: The class of 1893 graduated 44 naval cadets, with Frank H. Clark Jr., ranking 5th, Walter S. Crosley 10th, Edward H. Campbell 13th, and Frank B. Upham 31st; June.

1894: The class of 1894 graduated 47 naval cadets, with David F. Sellers ranking 5th, Ridley McLean 9th, Winston Churchill 13th, Joseph M. Reeves 38th, and Hutch I. Cone 42d; June.

1894: Capt. Philip H. Cooper became Superintendent of the Naval Academy.

1895: The class of 1895 graduated 41 naval cadets, with Frank H. Brumby ranking 4th, Harris Laning 8th, Henry V. Butler Jr. 13th, William H. Standley 22d, Walter R. Gherardi 23d, and Worth Bagley 29th; June.

1896: The class of 1896 graduated 38 naval cadets, with Thomas T. Craven ranking 4th, Ralph Earle 6th, Wat T. Cluverius Jr. 15th, Leigh C. Palmer 18th, Albert W. Marshall 19th, and Dudley W. Knox 23d; June.

1897: The class of 1897 graduated 47 naval cadets, with William G. DuBose ranking 1st, Joseph W. Powell 3d, Harry E. Yarnell 4th, Arthur J. Hepburn 6th, Thomas C. Hart 13th, Orin G. Murfin 14th, Walton R. Sexton 23d, William D. Leahy 35th, and Clarence S. Kempff 46th; June.

1897: The entire 4th class was confined to the *Santee* for a week because of unwillingness to reveal the identity of two classmates who fired off explosives on the vessel July 5.

1897: The Naval Academy Alumni Association of New York was founded.

1898: The official coat-of-arms of the Naval Academy, designed by Park Benjamin of the class of 1868, was adopted by the Navy Department.

1898: The class of 1898 graduated 39 naval cadets two months ahead of schedule, with John Halligan Jr., ranking 1st, William C. Watts 3d, William T. Tarrant 23d, Yancy S. Williams 27th, and George T. Pettengill 30th. They were handed their diplomas informally at a brief ceremony and were ordered to the fleet at the outbreak of the Spanish War; Apr. 2.

1898: Admiral Cervera and officers of the Spanish Navy were quartered in houses on Buchanan Row as prisoners of war; summer.

1898: Rear Admiral Frederick V. McNair became Superintendent of the Naval Academy; July 15.

1899: Work was begun on the construction of the present Naval Academy buildings in accordance with the plans of architect Ernest Flagg; Mar. 28.

1899: The class of 1899 graduated 53 naval cadets five months ahead of schedule, with Edward B. Fenner ranking 4th, Claude C. Bloch 14th, Henry E. Lackey 16th, Joseph K. Taussig 17th, Edward C. Kalbfus 18th, Clark H. Woodward 19th, Cyrus W. Cole 21st, John W. Greenslade 27th, Adolphus E. Watson 28th, Harry L. Brinser 34th, Charles E. Courtney 38th, Frederick J. Horne 41st, and Alfred W. Johnson 42d; Jan.

1899: The line and engineer corps of the Navy were united in one body and graduates of the Naval Academy were assigned to the Line, Engineer and Marine Corps.

1900: Commander Richard Wainwright became Superintendent of the Naval Academy; Mar. 15.

1900: The class of 1900 graduated 61 naval cadets, with Charles P. Snyder ranking 4th, Joseph R. Defrees 6th, Samuel W. Bryant 9th, John D. Wainwright 23d, Sinclair Gannon 24th, George W. Steele Jr. 25th, J. F. Hellwig 26th, Charles S. Freeman 33d, Hayne Ellis 40th, Charles R. Train 55th, H. W. Osterhaus 57th, and Hiroaki Tamura 61st; June.

1901: The class of 1901 graduated 67 naval cadets, with Ernest J. King 4th, Adolphus Andrews 18th, Holden C. Richardson 21st, Manley H. Simons 29th, Ivan E. Bass 31st, William S. Pye 32d, Arthur P. Fairfield 36th, Walter N. Vernou 44th, George F. Neal 51st, and John Downes Jr. 55th; June.

1901: Construction work was begun on Bancroft Hall—the world's largest dormitory.

1902: The Naval Academy grounds were increased by the purchase of 12 additional acres.

1902: The class of 1902 graduated 59 naval cadets, with James O. Richardson ranking 5th, Emory S. Land 6th, George J. Meyers 16th, Edward J. Marquart 17th, Gilbert J. Rowcliff 26th, Louis B. Porterfield 27th, J. C. Townsend 43d, and Wilson Brown 44th; June.

1902: Congress passed a law that abolished the title of "naval cadet" and restored the name of "midshipman"; July 1.

1902: Capt. Willard H. Brownson became Superintendent of the Naval Academy; Nov. 6.

1903: Dahlgren Hall, the new armory, and Macdonough Hall, the new gymnasium, were first occupied; Mar. 7.

1903: The class of 1903 graduated 50 midshipmen, with Walter S. Anderson 6th, H. D. Cooke 9th, Samuel M. Robinson 11th, Ralston S. Holmes 15th, Chas. A. Blakely 27th, Howard R. Stark 30th, Frank H. Sadler 42d; June.

1903: The military organization of midshipmen was expanded from four companies to eight companies; Sept. 1.

1903: The battalion of midshipmen made its first appearance as a brigade; Oct. 26.

1904: The cornerstone of the Chapel at the Naval Academy was laid by Admiral Dewey; June 3.

1904: The class of 1904 graduated 62 midshipmen, with David M. LeBreton ranking 1st, Andrew C. Pickens 2d, John E. Otterson 7th, Husband E. Kimmel 13th, Forde A. Todd 35th, Wm. F. Halsey Jr. 43d, A. B. Reed 50th, David W. Bagley 57th; June.

1905: The *Santee* was declared unsanitary and its use as a station ship at Annapolis was discontinued.

1905: Isherwood Hall and the Officers' Club were built.

1905: The class of 1905 graduated 114 midshipmen, with Ormand L. Cox ranking 3d, Royal E. Ingersoll 4th, Herbert F. Leary 5th, Chester W. Nimitz 7th, Albert T. Church 12th, Wm. R. Furlong 31st, Arthur B. Cook 36th, Harold G. Bowen 43d, Stanford C. Hooper 55th, John H. Newton Jr. 76th, John M. Smeallie 107th, H. R. Greenlee 109th, and Benjamin Dutton 111th; June.

1905: Rear Admiral James H. Sands became Superintendent of the Naval Academy; July 1.

1905: *Reef Points* made its initial appearance; Oct. 24.

1906: Bancroft Hall and Superintendent's house completed.

1906: The class of 1906 graduated 116 midshipmen, with Robert L. Ghormley ranking 12th, Wm. L. Calhoun 13th, Russell Willson 14th, Wm. A. Glassford Jr. 21st, Frank J. Fletcher 26th, Arthur LeR. Bristol Jr. 27th, and Milo F. Draemel 34th; June.

1906: Forward pass first used in Army-Navy football game.

1906: Sleeve insignia to distinguish the four classes were adopted; Aug. 21.

1906: The Naval Academy graduated 86 midshipmen of the class of 1907 (first section) nine months ahead of schedule; Sept.

1906: The Naval Academy song "Anchors Aweigh" was sung for the first time at the Army-Navy football game; Nov.

1907: The Academy graduated 50 midshipmen of the class of 1907 (second section) four months ahead of schedule; Feb.

1907: New Administration Building officially occupied; Mar. 4.

1907: The gymnastic team made its début in intercollegiate athletics when it met University of Pennsylvania; Mar. 9.

1907: The Naval Academy Hospital was opened; Mar. 15.

1907: The Naval Academy graduated 73 midshipmen of the class of 1907 (third section); June.

1907: The Naval Academy made its first appearance in an intercollegiate rowing regatta, Poughkeepsie; June 26.

1907: Mahan, Sampson and Maury Halls were completed.

1907: Capt. Charles J. Badger became Superintendent of the Naval Academy; July 15.

1908: The Naval Academy Chapel was completed at a cost of $374,194 and was opened for divine service; May 24.

1908: The class of 1908 graduated 201 midshipmen, with L. C. Stark ranking 123d; June.

1909: Old Fort Severn was demolished to make way for the modern structures of the Naval Academy; June 17.

1909: The class of 1909 graduated 174 midshipmen; June.

1909: The School of Marine Engineering was established, with a 2-year post-graduate course; June 9.

1909: Capt. John M. Bowyer became Superintendent of the Naval Academy; June 10.

1910: The class of 1910 graduated 131 midshipmen; June.

1911: Capt. John H. Gibbons became Superintendent of the Naval Academy; May 15.

1911: The class of 1911 graduated 193 midshipmen; June.

*S*team Engineering Building,
United States Naval Academy, 1869.

*M*idshipmen participating in a howitzer drill in 1869, and the Class of 1903 embarking for a sham battle.

*M*idshipmen enjoying an
afternoon with their drags, 1903.

1912: The *Santee*, after 50 years of consecutive duty with the Naval Academy, sank; Apr. 2.

1912: The class of 1912 graduated 136 midshipmen, with Richard E. Byrd ranking 63d; June.

1912: The figurehead of Tecumseh was removed from the Seamanship Building and placed in front of Bancroft Hall; Sept. 5.

1912: The captured Spanish cruiser *Reina Mercedes* arrived at Annapolis for service as a station ship; Oct. 1.

1913: The body of John Paul Jones was placed in the crypt below the Chapel; Jan. 26.

1913: The Post-Graduate School was opened; Feb. 1.

1913: The foremast of the USS *Maine* was set up in the yard; May 5.

1913: The class of 1913 graduated 139 midshipmen; June.

1913: *The Log* made its first appearance; Oct. 31.

1914: Capt. William F. Fullam became Superintendent of the Naval Academy; Feb. 7.

1914: The Midshipman's Drum and Bugle Corps made its first public appearance at a baseball game with St. John's College; May 20.

1914: The class of 1914 graduated 154 midshipmen; June.

1914: The midshipmen were organized into a regiment of four battalions, with three companies to each battalion; Sept. 24.

1915: The class of 1915 graduated 179 midshipmen; June.

1915: Capt. Edward W. Eberle became Superintendent of the Naval Academy; Sept. 20.

1916: The present system of appointing midshipmen to the Naval Academy was approved by Congress; Feb. 15.

1916: The class of 1916 graduated 177 midshipmen; June.

1917: The class of 1917 graduated 183 midshipmen in March, owing to the exigencies of the World War, and the class of 1918 graduated 203 midshipmen; June 28.

1918: Griffin Hall was built.

1918: The class of 1919 graduated 199 midshipmen one year ahead of schedule, for service in the World War; June.

1919: Capt. Archibald H. Scales became Superintendent of the Naval Academy; Feb. 12.

1919: The USS *Cumberland* arrived for duty as a training ship for colored employees; May 17.

1919: The class of 1920 graduated 460 midshipmen one year ahead of schedule; June.

1920: An outbreak of hazing led to an extended Congressional investigation.

1920: The class of 1921 graduated 285 of its midshipmen one year ahead of schedule; June.

1920: Luce Hall was built.

1921: The class of 1921 graduated the balance of its class, 260 midshipmen; June.

1921: Rear Admiral Henry B. Wilson became Superintendent of the Naval Academy; July 5.

1921: The famous racing yacht *America* was formally received at the Naval Academy; Oct. 1.

1922: The new bandstand was built.

1922: The class of 1922 graduated 539 midshipmen; June.

1923: The Department of Physical Training was established.

1923: Lawrence Field was formally dedicated; Apr. 11.

1923: The class of 1923 graduated 412 midshipmen; June.

1924: The Natatorium was dedicated; Apr. 10.

1924: The class of 1924 graduated 522 midshipmen; June.

1924: The first issue of the *Trident* was published; Oct. 27.

1925: The class of 1925 graduated 448 midshipmen; June.

1925: Rear Admiral Louis M. Nulton became Supt.; Feb. 23.

1925: Summer aviation training for 2d Classmen began; June.

1926: The alma mater hymn "Navy Blue and Gold" was first sung in public; Apr. 24.

1926: The class of 1926 graduated 456 midshipmen; June.

1926: The 3-year rule for intercollegiate athletics was adopted.

1927: Hubbard Hall, the crew house, was built.

1927: The gateway at the No. 3 Gate was erected as a memorial to the class of 1907; June.

1927: The class of 1927 graduated 579 midshipmen; June.

1928: The class of 1928 graduated 173 midshipmen; June.

1928: Rear Admiral Samuel S. Robison became Supt.; June 16.

1929: The class of 1929 graduated 240 midshipmen; June.

1930: The original wooden statue of Tecumseh was removed and a bronze replica erected.

1930: The class of 1930 graduated 402 midshipmen; June.
1930: The Naval Academy was accredited by the Association of American Universities; Oct. 25.
1931: Thompson Stadium was dedicated; May 31.
1931: Rear Admiral Thos. C. Hart became Superintendent; May 1.
1931: The class of 1931 graduated 441 midshipmen; June.
1932: The class of 1932 graduated 421 midshipmen; June.
1933: The Departments of Seamanship and of Navigation were combined in a single department.
1933: The class of 1933 graduated 432 midshipmen, who were the first to receive their commissions as ensigns together with their B.S. degrees; June.
1934: The class of 1934 graduated 464 midshipmen; June.
1934: Rear Admiral David F. Sellers became Supt.; June 18.
1935: The class of 1935 graduated 442 midshipmen; June.
1936: The class of 1936 graduated 263 midshipmen; June.
1937: Melville Hall was completed.
1937: The class of 1937 graduated 323 midshipmen; June.
1938: Rear Admiral Wilson Brown became Superintendent; Feb. 1.
1938: The class of 1938 graduated 436 midshipmen; June.
1939: The first unit of the Naval Academy Museum was built.
1939: The class of 1939 graduated 581 midshipmen; June.
1940: The class of 1940 graduated 456 midshipmen; June.
1941: Rear Admiral Russell Willson became Superintendent; Feb. 1.
1941: The class of 1941 graduated 399 midshipmen; Feb. 7.
1941: Twenty-two acres were added to the Academy grounds at the foot of the slope in front of the Naval Hospital by pumping silt from the Severn River into a steel-bulk-headed area along the shore. Seven and a half more acres (now known as Holland Field) behind Thompson Stadium were also added. The yard now comprises some 245 acres.
1941: The cornerstone of Ward Hall, new ordnance building, was laid; May 19.
1941: The class of 1942 graduated 563 midshipmen; Dec.
1942: Rear Admiral John R. Beardall became Supt.; Feb. 1.

1942: The class of 1943 graduated 615 midshipmen; June.

1942: Ensign W. E. Maxon was first graduate to marry following removal of ban requiring two years of service; June.

1942: King Peter II of Yugoslavia, King George II of Greece, and Prince Olav and Princess Martha of Norway, with their children, visited the Academy.

1942: Two battalions of midshipmen, wearing distinguishing white caps, impersonated West Point cadets to form the Army cheering section at the Army-Navy football game. Because of wartime travel difficulties, no West Pointers attended the game, played in Annapolis to limit attendance. (In the 1943 game at West Point, the cadets were all too successful in returning the compliment—the West Point "midshipmen" cheered (?) Navy to a 13–0 victory!)

1943: The class of 1944 graduated 765 midshipmen; June.

1944: The class of 1945 graduated 915 midshipmen; June.

1945: The Naval Academy celebrated its Centennial. Three special platoons of midshipmen paraded in uniforms of 1845, 1870 and 1900. A memorial Chapel service on Sunday, Oct. 7, honored the 729 graduates who died in line of duty in the Academy's first hundred years of existence; Oct. 10.

1945: The class of 1946 graduated 1046 midshipmen, the largest class ever to graduate from the Naval Academy; June.

1945: Vice Admiral Aubrey W. Fitch became Superintendent; Aug. 16.

1945: Return to the regular four-year course (from the wartime three-year course) was authorized by the President.

1946: The class of 1947 graduated 820 midshipmen; June.

1947: Rear Admiral James L. Holloway, Jr. became Superintendent; Jan. 15.

1947: The class of 1948A graduated 500 midshipmen; June.

1948: The class of 1948B graduated 410 midshipmen; June.

1949: The class of 1949 graduated 790 midshipmen; June.

1950: Vice Admiral Harry W. Hill became Superintendent; April 28.

1950: The class of 1950 graduated 691 midshipmen; June.

1950: His Imperial Majesty Mohammad Reza Shah Pahlavi, Shahinshah of Iran, visited the Academy; Nov. 17.

1951: The President of France, Vincent Auriol, visited the Academy, the first French Chief of State to do so; March 30.

1951: The bell of the USS *Enterprise* (CV6), erected at the right of the entrance to Bancroft Hall, was dedicated as "a modern symbol of the fleet's fighting spirit" and companion piece to the old bell brought back from Japan by M. C. Perry; May 19.

1951: The class of 1951 graduated 722 midshipmen; June.

1951: The Naval Postgraduate School moved to Monterey, California, upon the completion of the fall term; Nov. 21.

1952: The class of 1952 graduated 783 midshipmen; June.

1952: The Naval Academy varsity crew won the 1952 Olympic Rowing Championship at Helsinki, Finland; July 23.

1952: Vice Admiral C. T. Joy became Superintendent; Aug. 4.

1952: A new wing was added to the Mess Hall, which can now accommodate 4,000 at one sitting.

1953: The class of 1953 graduated 924 midshipmen; June.

1954: The class of 1954 graduated 852 midshipmen; June.

1954: Rear Admiral W. F. Boone became Superintendent; Aug. 12.

1954: Her Majesty Queen Elizabeth of England, the Queen Mother, visited the Academy and reviewed the Brigade Dress Parade; Nov. 8.

1955: The class of 1955 graduated 740 midshipmen; June.

1956: Rear Admiral William R. Smedberg III became Superintendent; March 15.

1956: Dr. Sukarno, first President of the United States of Indonesia, visited the Academy; May 22.

1956: The class of 1956 graduated 681 midshipmen. The civilian faculty appeared in academic garb in procession at graduation exercises for the first time; June.

1957: King Saud of Saudi Arabia visited the Academy; Feb. 2.

1957: The new Field House was dedicated; June 5.

1957: The class of 1957 graduated 848 midshipmen; June.

1957: The *Reina Mercedes*, a Spanish cruiser taken at Santiago in the Spanish-American War and the Naval Academy station ship since 1912, was decommissioned and towed away for scrap: Nov. 6.

1958: The class of 1958 graduated 899 midshipmen; June.

1958: Rear Admiral Charles L. Melson became Superintendent; June 27.

1959: The class of 1959 graduated 793 midshipmen; June.

1959: A new academic program was instituted enabling midshipmen to extend the range of their studies by advanced placement and an electives program.

1959: The Naval Academy's new 28,135-seat Navy-Marine Corps Memorial Stadium was dedicated; Sept. 26.

1960: Approximately 54.5 acres of land were added to the Academy grounds by filling in areas of the Severn River and Spa Creek to create Dewey Field and the new Farragut Field.

1960: The class of 1960 graduated 797 midshipmen; June.

1960: Rear Admiral John F. Davidson became Superintendent; June 22.

1961: The class of 1961 graduated 785 midshipmen; June.

1961: The new additions to Bancroft Hall, including the 7th and 8th wings, the Brigade Library, the Assembly Hall and the Reflecting Pool, were completed.

1962: The class of 1962 graduated 780 midshipmen; June.

1962: Midshipman Edwin Linz scaled the greased Herndon Monument in the "No More Plebes" ceremony in a record-breaking three minutes flat; June 6.

1962: Rear Admiral Charles C. Kirkpatrick became Superintendent; Aug. 18.

1962: The Naval Academy Museum opened its new addition, which doubled its display space and made possible the exhibition of valued collections hitherto inaccessible; Aug. 23.

1962: Lieutenant Commander James A. Lovell, Jr., USN, and Captain Thomas P. Stafford, USAF, both of the Class of 1952, were selected as members of the new team of astronauts; Sept. 17.

1962: Astronaut Walter M. Shirra, Jr., of the Class of 1945, circled the globe three times in the most successful space flight thus far; Oct. 3.

Appendix II

Midshipman Lingo

ANCHOR, *n*. The last in a group; the unit rated lowest.

ANCHOR MAN, *n*. The midshipman who stands at the bottom of his class in academic rating.

BATT, *n*. Battalion.

BEAR A HAND, *v*. Sailor slang for "shake a leg."

BELAY THAT, *v*. Stop that; quit what you're doing.

BILGE, *v*. To flunk out; to be dropped from the Naval Academy.

BILGER, *n*. A midshipman who has been dropped.

BILL, *n*. The perennial name of the Navy goat.

BIRD DOG, *v*. To set one's sights on somebody else's drag; to play the traditional role of the wolf in ship's clothing; also used loosely to refer to any kind of alert, determined and purposeful pursuit.

BLACK "N," *n*. An imaginary award to the recipient of the stiff punishment that goes with a Class "A" offense (the most serious kind).

BLIND DRAG, *n*. A girl invited by a midshipman to a hop "sight unseen"—usually at the behest of a third party.

BLOU, *n*. Short for the one-syllable word "blouse."

Bow-Wow, *n*. The Battalion Officer of the Watch (BOOW).

BRACE, *v*. To assume the rigid military posture.

BREEZE, To SHOOT THE, *v*. To argue or discuss; particularly applied to the refighting of the Civil War in bull sessions.

BRICK, *n*. "The girl with the thick glasses."

BRICK, *v*. To provide a midshipman host to such a girl.

BULKHEAD, *n*. A wall.

BULL, *n*. Any course in the English, History and Government Department.

BULL SESSION, *n*. A talk fest.

BUST, *v*. To make a mistake, to fail.

BLUE TRAMPOLINE, *n.* A midshipmen's bed.

BUCKET, *n.* One who dangles at the bottom of the academic well.

BUSH, *n.* Weekly list of those who live dangerously: almost, but not quite, unsat; between 2.5 and 2.7.

CARRY ON, *v.* To continue about one's duties in a normal manner.

CHARLIE NOBLE, *n.* The smokestack in the galley.

CHIT, *n.* Any form, requisition, note, bill, etc.

CHOP, *v.* Double time.

CHOW HOUND, *n.* A man who loves his vittles.

CLUTCH, *v.* To get buck fever; to choke up at the crucial moment.

CRAB, *n.* A girl who lives in Crabtown—meaning Annapolis.

CRABTOWN, *n.* Annapolis, "a fishing village on the banks of the Naval Academy."

CRACK, *v.* To open; commonly used in reference to ports, the windows on a ship.

CUT, *n.* A "slash," one who studies too much, gets too high grades, etc.

DAGO, *n.* The impolite term applied to any foreign language.

DEMO, *n.* A demerit.

DOPE, *n.* Information.

DRAG, *n.* A young woman guest of a midshipman; a lady escort.

E.D., *n.* Extra duty, assigned for disciplinary reasons.

EXEC, *n.* The Executive Officer.

EYES IN THE BOAT, *v.* The naval command to keep one's "head and eyes to the front."

FIN OUT, *v.* To straighten out one's fingers.

FIRST CLASS ALLEY, *n.* Privileged area in the mess hall between tables and bulkhead.

FLYING SQUADRON, *n.* The last ten midshipmen to report back to quarters after escorting their drags home from a hop. "They run all the way across town and get in late anyway."

FRAP, *v.* To put on the conduct report.

FRIED, *v.* To get fried is to be put on the daily report of conduct.

FRUIT, *n.* Anything easy.

GOUGE, *n.* Any written information accepted as usefully definitive; the "answer."

GRAVY, *n.* Excess over the 2.5 required for passing.

GRAVY TRAIN, *n.* The midshipman's friend in town who has a heart and feeds the brute.

GREASE, *n.* Influence or pull.

GREASEBALL, *n.* A midshipman who applies a bit of oil to the wheels of his own progress.

GREASE MARK, *n.* A midshipman's mark in that vital rating, "Aptitude for Service."

GUARD, *n.* The duty or watch; "He's got the guard today."

GYRENE, *n.* A marine.

HAPPY HOUR, *n.* A study hour with nothing to study; any interval of leisure devoted to impromptu fun.

HEAD, *n.* The toilet room, or what serves as such aboard a ship.

HELL CATS, *n.* The members of the Midshipman Drum and Bugle Corps.

HOP, *n.* A dance, formal or informal.

IRISH PENNANT, *n.* Any loose end indicative of untidiness.

JIMMYLEGS, *n.* A uniformed guard or watchman on duty in the Yard.

JOE GISH, *n.* The traditional name applied to all midshipmen; Midshipman "John Doe."

JUICE, *n.* The course in Electrical Engineering.

KAYDET, *n.* The midshipman's brother-in-arms; a cadet of the United States Military Academy.

KNOCK OFF, *v.* To stop work—or whatever one happens to be doing.

LADDER, *n.* A stairway.

MAN OVERBOARD, *interj.* "Your spoon is in your cup"; the term used in the mess hall to call a midshipman's attention to his social error.

MIDDY, *n.* The name of a blouse worn by girls and never a term of reference to a midshipman.

MISERY HALL, *n.* The quarters in Macdonough Hall where the minor injuries of athletes get fixed up.

MONTHLY INSULT, *n.* The allowance in actual cash allotted to each midshipman out of his salary.

NAV, *n.* A contraction of "Navigation" for the use of tired talkers.

NAVY JUNIOR, *n.* Offspring of a naval officer; companion term to "Army Brat."

NON REG, *adj.* A contraction for "non-regulation."

O.A.O., *n.* The initials for "One-And-Only" (also for "On-And-Off" and "One-Among-Others").

O.D., *n.* Officer of the Watch.

PAP, *n.* The daily report of conduct, bearing the offenses of delinquents and the demerits awarded, posted on the bulletin board.

PIPE DOWN, *v.* To shut up; keep quiet.

PLEBE, *n.* The lowest living form of midshipman life; the Fourth classman.

PODUNK, *n.* The midshipman's home town.

POLLYWOG, *n.* A midshipman (or anyone else, for that matter) who has never crossed "the line," as the Equator is called.

PORT, *n.* A window on a boat.

P-RADE, *n.* The dress parade of the midshipmen.

P-WORK, *n.* Practical exercise, or test.

RACK, *n.* Where a midshipman would like to be longer and oftener—his bed.

RADIATOR SQUAD, *n.* A non-existent organization whose members lead sedentary lives and do not participate in athletics.

RATE, *n.* A privilege by virtue of rank.

RATE, *v.* To merit or be entitled to something.

RATEY, *n.* One who makes use of the ratings of others.

RED EYE, *n.* The ketchup in the mess hall.

R.H.I.P. Initials of the phrase "Rank hath its privileges."

R.H.I.R. The reverse of the coin; "Rank hath its responsibilities."

RIVER, *n.* Midshipman slang for an examination.

ROBBERS' ROW, *n.* The merchants whose stores extend along Maryland Avenue and who trade with the midshipmen.

SANDBLOWER, *n.* A midshipman who towers about 5'6".

SAT, *adj.* Abbreviation for "satisfactory," indicating passing marks of 2.5 or better in studies.

SAVVY, *adj.* Wise, academically high-standing.

SCUTTLEBUT, *n.* (1) A drinking fountain. (2) A rumor or

dubious origin.

SEA GULL, *n*. A bird of any kind that is served in the mess hall under the general classification of "chicken."

SEAMO, *n*. Work in Seamanship.

SECURE, *v*. To knock off work.

SEGUNDO, *n*. A Second classman.

SKINNY, *n*. The course in Chemistry and Physics.

SHELLBACK, *n*. A person who has crossed "the line," meaning the Equator.

SHOVE OFF, *v*. To go away, depart; to beat it.

SICK BAY, *n*. The headquarters of the medical officers where midshipmen explain their ailments to sophisticated doctors.

SKIVVIES, *n*. Underclothes.

SLASH, *n*. and *v*. A grind; to be ostentatiously diligent over the books.

SLIP STICK, *n*. A slide rule; sometimes referred to as a "guess rod," "answer master," or "divining rod."

SPOON, *n*. and *v*. An upperclassman who has made himself the personal friend of a plebe by shaking his hand; to "knock off rates" by this act.

STAR, *n*. A bright boy who gets this stuff easily and maintains an academic average of 3.4 or better, so called from the star he is entitled to wear on the collar of his dress uniform.

STEAM, *n*. The course in Marine Engineering.

STEERAGE, *n*. The midshipmen's soda fountain.

STEP OUT, *v*. To bear a hand.

ST. JOHNNY, *n*. A student (also known less elegantly as an "inmate") of St. John's College, in Annapolis; also "Johnny."

STRIPER, *n*. A midshipman officer, designated by the stripes of braid on his sleeve.

SWABO, *n*. Zero.

TEA FIGHT, *n*. A tea dance.

TREE, *n*. The lists of academic delinquents (or "unsats ') that are posted every week, and term.

TROU, *n*. Trousers; another contraction for tired talkers.

TWO-BLOCK, *v*. To raise anything as high as it will go; a flag is two-blocked when it has reached the top of its halyard;

also used figuratively, as in the command, "Two-block your tie!"

Uncover, *v.* Remove headgear.

Unsat, *adj.* Unsatisfactory; applied especially to midshipmen who do not attain the passing mark of 2.5.

W. T. Door, *n.* Joe Gish's roommate.

Wife, *n.* A roommate.

Wooden, *adj.* A bit slow on the mental pick-up; academically low-standing.

Yard, *n.* Naval Academy grounds.

Yard Engine, *n.* A young lady who lives in the Yard.

Youngster, *n.* A midshipman of the Third Class.

Zip, *n.* Zero.

Appendix **III**

How to
Become a Midshipman*

Each candidate for admission to the Naval Academy must:
1. Meet general eligibility requirements.
2. Obtain a nomination.
3. Qualify scholastically (academically).
4. Qualify physically.

GENERAL ELIGIBILITY REQUIREMENTS

CITIZENSHIP

All candidates for admission to the United States Naval Academy must be male citizens of the United States, except as provided by law for limited numbers of citizens of other American Republics, and the Philippine Republic. An alien can be admitted as a midshipman only by an Act of Congress.

AGE

Age limits are established by law. Candidates must be between 17 and 22 years of age. Each candidate must have reached his 17th birthday but not have passed his 22d birthday on or before 1 July of the year in which admission is desired to be eligible for admission.

CHARACTER

Candidates must be of good moral character. This prerequisite is usually passed upon by the Member of Congress making the nomination. The Secretary of the Navy may, however, decline to accept the nomination of any candidate in the event conclusive evidence of unsuitable character is submitted. For other sources of appointments, investigation of character qualifications rests jointly with those authorized by law to sponsor such nominations and the Navy Department.

* Reprinted from *United States Naval Academy, Annapolis, Maryland, Catalogue of Information, 1962–1963.* By permission.

MARITAL STATUS

No person who is married, or who has been married, is eligible for admission to the Naval Academy, regardless of his other qualifications. Midshipmen may not marry, and any midshipman found to be or have been married will be discharged.

OBTAINING A NOMINATION

There are several ways of obtaining a nomination for admission to the Naval Academy. The variety of types of nominations is intended to make it possible for young men from all over the United States to compete for appointments as midshipmen. In the following paragraphs, prospective candidates may learn what appointments they may be eligible for, and how to apply for a nomination for each. In some cases, candidates will find that they are eligible for more than one type of nomination. In such cases, it will usually be to their advantage to apply for more than one nomination.

Candidacy must be established in time to participate in the March administration of College Entrance Examination Board Tests. The Naval Academy will also consider for academic qualification results obtained on the immediately preceding December or January tests of the College Board. Early application and participation in the entrance tests is encouraged. Only the Chief of Naval Personnel may issue authority to take the necessary College Board tests as a formally designated candidate for appointment to the Naval Academy.

PRESIDENTIAL APPOINTMENTS

Presidential appointments are available to sons of officers and enlisted personnel of the regular Army, Navy, Marine Corps, Air Force, and Coast Guard. To make application for appointment from this source, the candidate or his parent should address a letter to the Chief of Naval Personnel, Navy Department, Washington 25, D. C., clearly indicating the Service connection of the parent and giving the son's full name and date of birth. The letter of application should also designate the year in which admission to the Naval Academy is desired. Letters of application should be forwarded any time after July 1 of the year preceding that in which admission is desired, but not later than February 1 of the admission year.

Seventy-five candidates may be appointed annually from this

source. In the event of vacancies in the annual quotas of appointments authorized from the Navy and Marine Corps and the Naval and Marine Corps Reserves, qualified Presidential nominess in excess of the normal Presidential quota may be admitted to fill such vacancies.

CONGRESSIONAL APPOINTMENTS

The Vice President of the United States, each United States Senator, each Representative in Congress, and the Resident Commissioner of Puerto Rico may have five appointees at the Naval Academy at any one time. The Vice President makes his nominations from the United States at large. The United States Senators must make their nominations from among residents of their respective States, and the Members of the House of Representatives must make their nominations from among residents of the Congressional districts which they represent.

Members of Congress are authorized to nominate a maximum of six candidates for each vacancy. The Candidates so nominated are usually designated as the principal and the first, second, third, fourth, and fifth alternates. Members of Congress may designate their nominees as competitive alternates and leave to the Academic Board at the Naval Academy the designation of the principal and the arrangement of the alternates based upon order of merit.

Application for nomination should be made directly to the Vice President Senator or Representative. It is in order for a candidate to include in his letter of application for a nomination such items as favorable endorsements by school officials and others. Application should be made at least a full year in advance of the year in which the candidate hopes to enter as a midshipman, because some Members of Congress require candidates to compete for nominations by taking a special examination for that purpose. Such examinations are usually held in July or November, and they are not to be confused with, or considered a substitute for, the College Entrance Examination Board tests required by the Naval Academy.

APPOINTMENTS FROM THE REGULAR NAVY OR
REGULAR MARINE CORPS

One hundred and sixty appointments annually are available to enlisted men on active duty in the regular Navy or Marine

Corps. Enlisted men desiring to become career commissioned officers should apply to their commanding officers for permission to take a preliminary screening examination which will be given throughout the Naval Establishment early in July of the calendar year preceding that in which admission to the Naval Academy is sought. Those who successfully pass the initial screening measures will be assigned to the preparatory school which the Navy maintains to aid enlisted candidates in their preparations for the formal entrance tests and for the Naval Academy program. The entrance tests consist of the College Entrance Examination Board Scholastic Aptitude Test and achievement tests in English and mathematics. The competitive rating of the successful candidates will be determined by the Naval Academy Academic Board, and will be predicated upon a "whole man" evaluation, including test scores; school records; extracurricular activities, both athletic and non-athletic; and upon the assembled evidences of motivation and good character. Qualified candidates in excess of this quota may be appointed to fill vacancies in the quotas of the President and the Naval and Marine Corps Reserves.

APPOINTMENTS FROM THE NAVAL RESERVE OR
MARINE CORPS RESERVE

One hundred and sixty appointments annually are available to enlisted men of the Naval and Marine Corps Reserves, whether on active or inactive duty. Applicants must have had at least 1 year in the Reserve by July 1 of the year of admission to the Naval Academy. They must have attended a minimum of 26 drills between July 1 and March 15, and must have had 14 days of active duty for training between April 1, 1962, and March 15, 1963. Active service may be accepted in lieu of drills, 1 full day of active service being the equivalent of one drill.

Those who are successful in obtaining authority to compete for appointment from this source will be authorized to appear for the formal entrance tests, which consist of the College Entrance Examination Board Scholastic Aptitude test and the one-hour achievement tests in mathematics and English. The competitive rating of the successful candidates will be determined by the Naval Academy Academic Board, and will be predicated

*T*he Brigade Commander is obviously very
impressive to the young man with his hands on
his hips. Perhaps, someday. . . .

upon a "whole man" evaluation, including test scores; school records; extra-curricular activities, both athletic and non-athletic; and upon the assembled evidences of motivation and good character. Qualified candidates in excess of this quota may be appointed to fill vacancies in the quotas of the President and of the Regular Navy and Marine Corps.

Naval and Marine Corps reservists who are on regular (not training) active duty at the time of formal nomination for appointment may also apply for assignment to the preparatory school which the Navy maintains to aid enlisted candidates in their preparations for the entrance tests, and for the Naval Academy program.

APPOINTMENTS FROM HONOR MILITARY AND NAVAL SCHOOLS

An honor graduate or a prospective honor graduate of a designated honor military or naval school should apply to the principal of his school for nomination as a candidate for admission to the Naval Academy. Each designated honor military or naval school may nominate 3 honor graduates or prospective honor graduates each year to compete among themselves for 10 vacancies for midshipmen. The details of submitting nominations are handled by the school concerned and the Chief of Naval Personnel, Navy Department, Washington 25, D. C.

APPOINTMENT FROM NROTC UNITS

Only contract students in the Naval Reserve Officers Training Corps units at the various colleges and universities are eligible to apply for appointments from this source. Contract students should apply to the professor of naval science at the college or university, who will turn forward his recommendations to the president of the college. Not more than 3 candidates may be nominated each year by each of the educational institutions in which an NROTC unit is in operation to compete among themselves for 10 vacancies to the Naval Academy.

OTHER SOURCES OF APPOINTMENTS

Those applying for nominations under the laws providing for the sons of deceased veterans and the sons of holders of the Medal of Honor should write to the Chief of Naval Personnel, Navy Department, Washington 25, D. C. Such applicants should give the full name, rank or rating, and organization of the deceased veteran or the holder of the Medal of Honor, the full name of the candidate for appointment as midshipman, his date of birth, and such other pertinent information as will assist in the positive identification of both the parent and the candidate. Residents of the District of Columbia should apply directly to the Commissioners of the District of Columbia for full details at least 1 year in advance of the year in which the candidate hopes to enter as a midshipman.

Application for appointment from the Canal Zone must be addressed to the Governor of the Canal Zone, and application for the appointment of a native of Puerto Rico must be addressed to the Governor of Puerto Rico.

ADDITIONAL APPOINTMENTS FROM AMONG QUALIFIED ALTERNATE NOMINEES AND COMPETITIVE CANDIDATES

The Secretary of the Navy is authorized to appoint additional midshipmen from qualified alternates and qualified competitive quota candidates in order to bring the Brigade of Midshipmen to authorized strength. When the number of additional admissions is determined, the Academic Board will review the records of all scholastically qualified candidates within each nomination source. Application by the individual is not necessary or desired since all qualified candidates are considered by the Academic Board. Selections will be made from those whose records are outstanding in scholarship, whose character and personality are established as decidedly superior in statements of recommendations from school and other officials, and in whose cases there is marked evidence of leadership potential as indicated by class offices held, participation in extracurricular and community activities, and other achievements of note. At least two-thirds of those so appointed must be from qualified congressional alternates.

QUALIFYING ACADEMICALLY

SCHOLASTIC PREPARATION

The scholastic requirements for admission to the Naval Academy and the arrangement of the first year course of instruction anticipate a 4-year high school course as the minimum of preparation. The ideal arrangement of preparatory studies is one which includes 4 years of English; at least 3 years, but preferably 4 years of mathematics including algebra, geometry, and trigonometry; chemistry; physics, U. S. history; at least 2 years of a foreign language; and mechanical drawing. The remaining courses necessary to round out the full high school schedule should be chosen from courses such as biology, the foreign languages, philosophy, astronomy, economics, government, physical geography, or from among other subjects in the social or physical sciences. At least 15 units of credit should be presented. Graduation from an accredited 4-year high or preparatory school (or its equivalent) is mandatory, and the record of work done must be acceptable to the Naval Academy Academic Board in terms of subject matter and level of achievement. Preparation should be thorough, because at the Naval Academy the pace is rapid and midshipmen are required to participate in other areas of instruction looking toward the development of suitable military character.

The courses in the desirable subjects that are offered in the high and preparatory schools throughout the country that are accredited by the recognized accrediting agencies are adequate in content and scope to fulfill Naval Academy requirements and in the preparation for the essential College Entrance Examination Board tests.

METHOD OF QUALIFYING

There are two methods by which a candidate may qualify academically for admission to the Naval Academy:

1. College Board tests and secondary school record.
2. Secondary school and college certificates.

Candidates holding noncompetitive congressional nominations and the sons of holders of the Medal of Honor are permitted to utilize either of the two methods, and in these instances it is the candidate's responsibility to determine which method offers him the greater possibility of success. All other candidates must take the necessary College Entrance Examination Board tests in December, January, or March of the school year preceding admission.

In the following brief description of the two methods, only the essential features are covered. Candidates, prospective candidates, and school officials are invited to correspond with the Admissions Officer, U. S. Naval Academy, Annapolis, Md., regarding any point in the admission requirements on which further information is desired.

All candidates for admission must have an accredited high school certificate. It is important that each candidate insure that his complete high school record and the record of any college work which he may have completed be furnished the Naval Academy.

COLLEGE BOARD TESTS AND SECONDARY SCHOOL RECORD METHOD

The basic method of qualifying is by presenting an acceptable secondary school record and taking the College Entrance Examination Board tests, as follows: The Scholastic Aptitude Test (verbal and mathematics sections), the English Achievement Test, and either the Intermediate or the Advanced Mathematics Achievement Test.

All candidates for appointment from the various competitive sources and all other candidates not qualifying by the College Certificate Method must take this series of tests.

Each duly nominated candidate must register with the College Entrance Examination Board for the December, January, or March series of tests as promptly as possible after receiving the necessary instructions from the Bureau of Naval Personnel, Navy Department, Washington 25, D. C. These instructions will provide for payment by the Navy of fees for tests.

Information on the tests, including dates of administration, location of testing centers, dates by which candidates must register, method of application, etc., is published in a booklet entitled *Bulletin of Information.* A copy may be obtained without charge by writing to the College Entrance Examination Board, Post Office Box 592, Princeton, N. J., or Post Office Box 27896, Los Angeles 27, Calif.

Satisfactory scores on the College Entrance Examination Board Tests will be determined by the Academic Board of the Naval Academy. No candidate will be admitted to the Naval Academy unless in the opinion of the Academic Board he shows the requisite mental qualifications.

A high school certificate is required for eligibility and school records will be a consideration in determining whether or not a candidate is to be accepted. A good secondary school record is one which reports grades of good quality for a desirable arrangement of preparatory courses chosen from those listed above under the heading of "Scholastic Preparation," and a breadth of school interests and extracurricular activities indicative of a well-rounded student.

COLLEGE CERTIFICATE

This method of fulfilling the educational requirements for admission is available only to candidates holding noncompetitive congressional nomination and to sons of holders of the Medal of Honor.

To qualify by the college certificate method, a candidate must, in addition to satisfying the requirements in a secondary school certificate, present a certificate from an accredited junior college, technological school of college grade, college, or university, attesting the completion of 1 year of college work with grades acceptable to the Naval Academy. The college certificate must include at least 6 semester hours of mathematics selected from college algebra, trigonometry, calculus, etc., 6 of college English and/or history, and sufficient other subjects acceptable to the Naval Academy to establish a total of at least 24 semester hours of credit for the year's work. College credits which have been used to offset deficiencies in a high school certificate will not be counted toward meeting the requirements for an acceptable college certificate.

Any candidate who is at all uncertain as to his ability to qualify by the college certificate method is strongly advised to take the entrance examination. However, failure to score acceptably on the entrance examination will disqualify the candidate for entry in that year.

QUALIFYING PHYSICALLY

The Chief of Naval Personnel, Navy Department, Washington 25, D. C., will send to each duly nominated candidate an authorization designating time and place of physical examination. Physical examinations are conducted at specified naval hospitals, and other specified naval activities in various parts of the United States. Candidates are required to be physically fit, well-formed, and of sound constitution. The physical requirements are exacting. The best interests of the Government, the Navy, and the individual demand that they be so.

Detailed information concerning the physical requirements and the list of places at which examinations are given is contained in the pamphlet "Regulations Governing the Admission of Candidates into the United States Naval Academy as Midshipmen," which may be obtained from the Chief of Naval Personnel or from the Naval Academy.

General Information

Pay and Allowances

The pay of a Midshipman is $111.15 a month ($1,333.80 a year), commencing at the date of his admission. The purpose of this pay is to cover expenses associated with training at the Naval Academy, including the following items:

a. Prescribed uniforms and required clothing.
b. Textbooks and equipment.
c. Sundries (for cleanliness, health, and relaxation).
d. Services (laundry, tailor, cobbler, and barber).
e. Moderate allowance for extracurricular activities (to broaden professional background and competence).
f. Leave money (provided a sufficient balance is maintained in the account).
g. Moderate allowance to maintain outfit.
h. Funds to purchase necessary uniforms and equipment for graduation outfit so that the graduate will be in all respects ready to assume duties as a commissioned officer.

In addition, there is a ration allowance at the rate of $1.35 per day intended to provide board. It is used entirely for that purpose.

Midshipmen are expected to live frugally and within the limits of their pay. Maintenance allowances are designed to meet normal demands. Through wise use of pay, it is possible to have funds available to meet expenses during annual leave periods.

Medical, dental, and hospital services are furnished without cost to all midshipmen in a fashion similar to services furnished to other personnel of the Navy on active duty.

Entrance Deposits

In order to defray part of the initial outfitting, candidates upon admission to the Naval Academy must deposit the sum of $300 (exceptions are made in cases of extreme hardship down to $100 minimum). In addition, the Government advances $600 for the purpose of outfitting, such advance constituting an obligation against the individual account until sufficient credit has accumulated to liquidate the advance. The advance is systematically liquidated at a rate of $20 a month, commencing with October of the second year in the Naval Academy.

Index

19254

J. M. HODGE LIBRARY
WHARTON COUNTY JUNIOR COLLEGE
WHARTON, TEXAS